THE FILMS OF DENYS ARCAND

Global Film Directors

Edited by Homer B. Pettey, Professor of Film and Comparative Literature at University of Arizona, and R. Barton Palmer, Calhoun Lemon Professor Emeritus of English at Clemson University

Volumes in the Global Film Directors series explore cinematic innovations by prominent and emerging directors in major European, American, Asian, and African film movements. Each volume addresses the history of a director's oeuvre and its influence upon defining new cinematic genres, narratives, and techniques. Contributing scholars take a context-oriented approach to evaluating how these directors produced an identifiable style, paying due attention to those forces within the industry and national cultures that led to global recognition of these directors. These volumes address how directors functioned within national and global marketplaces, contributed to and expanded film movements, and transformed world cinema. By focusing on representative films that defined the directors' signatures, these volumes provide new critical focus upon international directors, who are just emerging to prominence or whose work has been largely ignored in standard historical accounts. The series opens the field of *new auteurism* studies beyond film biographies by exploring directorial style as influencing global cinema aesthetics, theory, and economics.

Recent titles in the Global Film Directors series:

Nam Lee, *The Films of Bong Joon-ho*
Jim Leach, *The Films of Denys Arcand*

THE FILMS OF DENYS ARCAND

JIM LEACH

RUTGERS UNIVERSITY PRESS
New Brunswick, Camden, and Newark, New Jersey, and London

Library of Congress Cataloging-in-Publication Data

Names: Leach, Jim, author.
Title: The films of Denys Arcand / Jim Leach.
Description: New Brunswick : Rutgers University Press, [2020] | Series: Global film directors series | Includes bibliographical references and index.
Identifiers: LCCN 2019040029 | ISBN 9780813598864 (paperback) | ISBN 9780813598871 (hardback) | ISBN 9780813598888 (epub) | ISBN 9780813598895 (mobi) | ISBN 9780813598901 (pdf)
Subjects: LCSH: Arcand, Denys, 1941 June 25—Criticism and interpretation.
Classification: LCC PN2308.A68 L43 2020 | DDC 791.4302/33092—dc23
LC record available at https://lccn.loc.gov/2019040029

A British Cataloging-in-Publication record for this book is available from the British Library.

∞ The paper used in this publication meets the requirements of the American National Standard for Information Sciences—Permanence of Paper for Printed Library Materials, ANSI Z39.48-1992.

www.rutgersuniversitypress.org

Manufactured in the United States of America

As always, this book is dedicated to Jenny.

CONTENTS

PREFACE

As I outline in my opening chapter, Denys Arcand is one of the most important—but also one of the most controversial—Quebec filmmakers. What I will argue in this book is that his films and their reception have been shaped by the many tensions and contradictions that have emerged in Quebec society and culture over the past sixty years. Although my main focus will be on the films themselves, I will also be concerned with the critical and cultural discourses that have surrounded them. As an English Canadian, my perspective on this dialogue between a filmmaker and his environment is inevitably that of an interested outsider, even if the films are technically products of a bilingual national cinema. Although Arcand has worked in English, Quebec remains the immediate cultural context for all his films, but I will also try to show how they speak to broader social and cultural developments that make them relevant to viewers elsewhere.

I have organized the book (with one exception) chronologically in order to discuss the films in relation to historical developments during Arcand's career, but it is not intended as a biography. As will be apparent, I have relied heavily on the biographical work of Réal La Rochelle, who writes from the perspective of a friend of the filmmaker and offers an invaluable inside account of his life and work. However, I have deliberately chosen instead to work at "arm's length," although my basically sympathetic approach to his films will no doubt annoy the filmmaker's many detractors in Quebec. Indeed, one of my concerns will be to examine why the films have generated so much hostile criticism there, based very often on apparently personal antagonism rather than close critical analysis.

Films are, of course, never simply expressions of the personal vision of an individual artist. As we shall see, Arcand has often presented himself as an artist (or auteur), but he would be the first to agree that a film is a collective product, and many others have contributed to making the films what they are. For the most part, I have not dwelt on their input, but they have clearly helped create the vision that these films put forward. As industrial and cultural products, Arcand's films have also been shaped by the circumstances in which they were produced, which have made certain possibilities available while foreclosing on others. In other words, they are products of the time and place in which they were made, and the contradictions that the filmmaker sees as an essential aspect of his film style are also very much present in the world around him.

In what follows, all translations from the French are my own unless otherwise stated. I have used the French titles of the films throughout, but the English release titles or literal translations are included when I first mention them and in the filmography at the end of the book. Production budgets are in Canadian dollars, while international box-office amounts are in U.S. dollars.

THE FILMS OF DENYS ARCAND

INTRODUCTION
Denys of Quebec

> I make films for Ingmar Bergman, and he will no doubt never see them.
> —Denys Arcand

Denys Arcand is best known outside Canada for three films that were nominated for the Academy Award for Best Foreign-Language Film: *Le déclin de l'empire américain* (*The Decline of the American Empire*; 1986), *Jésus de Montréal* (*Jesus of Montreal*; 1989), and *Les invasions barbares* (*The Barbarian Invasions*; 2003), the last of which won the award. Yet Arcand has been making films since the early 1960s, when Canadian cinema was developing a new approach to fiction filmmaking grounded in the documentary tradition associated with the National Film Board (NFB). Since that time, Quebec filmmakers (more successfully than their English Canadian counterparts) have produced a varied but distinctive body of work that deserves to be much better known. Although its film industry has had to contend with the dominance of the Hollywood studios and the vagaries of government film policy, Quebec regularly produces commercially successful popular films, appealing mainly to audiences within the province, as well as celebrated "art films" that have earned critical praise at international film festivals.

Arcand has been called one of "the emblematic figures of Quebec cinema" who has created "a characteristic style made up of a generous dosage of corrosive humor, impertinence and dialectical rigor" (Bachand 2006, 91). He was certainly, thanks to his Oscar-nominated films, the most internationally successful Quebec filmmaker until a new generation—including Denis Villeneuve, Jean-Marc Vallée, Philippe Falardeau, and Xavier Dolan—emerged in the new millennium. While all these younger directors have recently been making films in Hollywood, Arcand has remained in Quebec, but his films have generated a great deal of controversy there. He has also been called "the most famous enfant terrible of the Québécois postwar generation of filmmakers" (La Rochelle 2005, 10): his early films made at the National Film Board were subject to censorship, he has been the target of hostile and sometimes venomous criticism, and some of his later films have suffered from producer-imposed cuts and poor distribution.

Outside Quebec, Arcand's work has been associated with art cinema (a term whose implications I will discuss later in this chapter), but local critics have often accused him of being too concerned with the box office; the truth is his work straddles the two kinds of filmmaking in a precarious but fascinating way. His career has spanned the entire history of modern Quebec cinema, and he has worked in a wide range of production circumstances. He has made feature-length documentaries, genre films, and art films. Yet his films have rarely fitted comfortably into the critical discourses that seek to define these categories. With their unsettling blend of irreverent humor and a bleak view of the future of Quebec and of Western civilization generally, Arcand's films explore questions of identity that are endemic to Quebec culture but also increasingly relevant to many nations in the modern world.

One of my main concerns in this book will be to chart the contours of Arcand's career—that have allowed him to appear as both "emblematic" and "enfant terrible." I will return to this topic later in this introduction, and the rest of the book will consist of close readings of the films in the contexts of their production and reception. However, as a Quebec filmmaker, he has had to negotiate the difficult terrain of Canadian cinema, which is, as Geoff Pevere has put it, "something much more sensitive, complex, and problematic than just another national cinema" (2002, 103). Accordingly, I will first look briefly at the major developments in the Canadian film industry that have affected Arcand's films and the critical response to them before examining, in rather more detail, the social and cultural developments in Quebec from the end of World War II to the present.

SCREENING CANADA

One immediate problem in approaching Canadian cinema is the question of whether we are dealing with a single national cinema or "*two* cinemas: the 'Canadian' and the 'Québécois,' whose interests are divergent" (Marsolais 1968, 104)—a question that could be applied to many aspects of Canadian life. However, because Quebec is not an independent nation, even if many of its citizens wish it were, its filmmakers must deal with a system in which the primary source of funding comes from the Canadian government. Since Canada is officially a bilingual country, it produces films in both English and French, and since relatively few Canadians are comfortable in both languages, the effect is to fragment

Denys Arcand as the judge in *Jésus de Montréal.*

an already relatively small domestic market. These films also have to compete with Hollywood productions, which are as popular in Canada as in most of the rest of the world.

The Hollywood studios have always regarded Canada as part of the North American domestic market, and they have largely controlled film distribution and exhibition throughout Canada, with the result that the country cannot maintain a film industry of its own without government support. Historically, the federal government, under pressure from Hollywood, has always been unwilling to enact a quota system to ensure that a reasonable proportion of Canadian films are shown in Canadian cinemas, and the only alternative measure has been government subsidies to film producers (see Leach 2011, 2–3). Unfortunately, film policy, at both the federal and provincial levels, has proved unpredictable and has resulted in a precarious and volatile situation for filmmakers.

The first important government initiative to support filmmaking in Canada came with the creation of the National Film Board in 1939. Although some Catholic priests in Quebec had produced documentaries in the 1930s in support of the Church's project of preserving cultural traditions by promoting settlements in remote rural areas, it was the NFB—under the leadership of John Grierson, who had earlier created documentary film units in Britain—that established Canada as a major producer of documentaries. The Board's mandate, as later defined in the Film Act of 1950, was to "interpret Canada to Canadians and to other nations" (quoted in Morris 1984, 283). Its promotion of modernization and an inclusive pan-Canadian national identity was directly opposed to the conservative traditions in Quebec, which were supported, during the postwar period, by the Church and the Union Nationale government led by Maurice Duplessis. Indeed, Duplessis did his best to prevent the distribution of NFB films in Quebec.

To counter the "modern" ideas promoted, in different ways, by the NFB, Hollywood, and postwar French cinema, the Church lent its moral support to a short-lived attempt to create two commercial film studios in Quebec. Between 1944 and 1953, these studios produced a cycle of highly popular films in support of an "ideology of conservation," which, as described by Christiane Tremblay-Daviault, stressed the importance of rural life as "the only guarantee of the perpetuation of the Catholic faith and French culture, the city being a place of perdition and factories, an invention of the devil" (Tremblay-Daviault 1981, 55). However, the two films that proved most popular, both set in rural Quebec in the past—*Un homme et son péché* (*A Man and His Sin*; Paul Gury, 1948), in which a miser abuses his young wife until she dies, and *La petite Aurore l'enfant martyre* (*Little Aurore's Tragedy*; Jean-Yves Bigras, 1951), about a young girl tortured and beaten to death by her stepmother—hardly depicted the ideology in a very positive light. For Arcand, these "films from the era of darkness are tableaux of sexual aberration, each more disturbing than the last" (quoted in La Rochelle 2005, 307), but the fact that both were remade in the first decade of the twenty-first century suggests that these stories still have resonance for filmmakers and audiences.[1]

The production of these studio-bound melodramas came to an end in the 1950s with the introduction of television in Quebec, and the new medium became a major factor in sowing doubts about traditional values. For the NFB, however, television provided a new outlet for its documentaries. During the 1950s, young filmmakers at the NFB turned away from the authoritative and omniscient voice-of-God style of documentary favored by Grierson to a more informal, investigative style that became known variously as *cinéma vérité* or *direct cinema* (in Quebec, *le direct*).[2] Although the Board was originally located in Ottawa, where it worked mainly in English, its headquarters moved to Montreal in 1956, and francophone filmmakers were heavily involved in the development of the new approach. Many Canadian filmmakers who went on to direct fiction films, including Arcand, got their starts making documentaries at the NFB, with the result that critics have often viewed the national cinema (in both languages) as essentially a realist cinema grounded in documentary traditions and, as such, have tended to reject or ignore the many films that do not correspond to this definition.

Inspired by the NFB's direct cinema documentaries, as well as by the low-budget films of the French New Wave, several young filmmakers created fiction films that used lightweight cameras and sound equipment to develop a style that emphasized improvisation and location shooting. Films such as Claude Jutra's *À tout prendre* (*Take It All*; 1963), Gilles Groulx's *Le chat dans le sac* (*The Cat in the Bag*; 1964), and in English Canada, Don Owen's *Nobody Waved Good-Bye* (1964) helped pave the way for a new approach to narrative cinema. All these filmmakers had worked at the NFB, and the latter two films were made there using budgets intended for short documentaries, but an important precursor to this movement was a student production made at the Université de Montréal in 1962. As we shall see in chapter 1, Arcand was one of the codirectors of *Seul ou avec d'autres* (*Alone or with Others*; 1962), although he later dismissed the film as, in his words, a painful attempt "to liberate ourselves through sophomoric humour" (quoted in La Rochelle 2005, 311).

These films were successful enough to suggest that feature-film production might be possible in Canada, and in 1968, the federal government responded by creating the Canadian Film Development Corporation (CFDC). Its mandate was to invest in feature films produced in the private sector with the aim of building a Canadian film industry. However, from the beginning, the CFDC was hamstrung by the difficulty of getting the films shown in cinemas owned by, or with close ties to, the Hollywood studios. There was also a lack of clarity about whether it should support films that, like the direct cinema films, addressed Canadian cultural concerns or popular genre films that would supposedly be more commercial (Leach 2011, 29). In 1978, the government decisively opted for the commercial option by passing the Capital Cost Allowance Act (CCA), which offered a 100 percent tax deduction on investments in Canadian films. The result was a short-lived production boom that produced a few commercial successes but mainly benefited the lawyers who put together funding packages for films that usually starred minor Hollywood actors and were set in anonymous North American locations. Direct cinema filmmakers were frozen out during this period, and the act was especially resented in Quebec because it encouraged the production of English-language films that would appeal to the large U.S. market (but rarely did). Like many Quebec filmmakers, Arcand was unable to find support for his personal projects and was forced to find work in television or as a director for hire (see chapter 4).

The commercial failure of most of the films made under the CCA led the government to change its film policy yet again. In 1984, the CFDC was rebranded as Telefilm Canada with a mandate to assist television as well as film production.

Since few Canadian films received a theatrical release, the new agency would invest mainly in medium-budget films that could at least be shown on the emerging specialty television networks (which had to comply with government regulations that required a fixed amount of Canadian content). This new policy did result in a revival of Canadian cinema, and Quebec filmmakers also benefited from the Société Générale du Cinéma du Québec (later the Société de développement des enterprises culturelles), which the provincial government had created the year before. It was thanks to investment from these new agencies that Arcand was able to restart his career in spectacular fashion with *Le déclin*, although this project was initiated at the NFB (see chapter 4).

Despite the proliferation of funding agencies at the federal, provincial, and even municipal levels, the frequent shifts in Canadian film policy have tended to hamper the growth of a national cinema and have provided an unstable context for Arcand's career. The effects have been felt in English Canada as well as in Quebec, but especially in the last two decades, the Quebec film industry has been far more successful in overcoming these obstacles than its anglophone counterpart. Although the films are modestly budgeted by Hollywood standards, they are usually able to provide the production values that audiences have often felt that Canadian cinema lacked, and as we have seen, several young Québécois filmmakers have recently made the transition to working in Hollywood. Quebec also has a thriving television industry, and actors move freely between small and large screens, creating a sort of star system that allows audiences to become familiar with the performers and the personas they have developed.

As this account suggests, Quebec film production is often seen as divided between popular films aimed at the domestic market and art films that gather prestige at international festivals, with critics often denouncing the former to defend the latter. However, interest in Quebec cinema of both kinds is large enough currently to sustain three lively film magazines—*Séquences* (founded in 1955), *24 Images* (founded in 1979), and *Ciné-bulles* (founded in 1981)—that provide coverage of international cinema but with a strong emphasis on local filmmakers.[3] In comparison, in English Canada, the two magazines that were most interested in Canadian films, *Cinema Canada* (1967–1989) and *Take One* (1966–2006), have not survived, and the only real equivalent to the Quebec magazines is *Cinema Scope* (1999–), which provides excellent coverage of the international film scene and includes discussion of Canadian films and filmmakers (often from Quebec) on an occasional basis.[4]

The quality of film criticism in Quebec is very high, and the critics, far more than those in the rest of Canada, really care about the work of domestic filmmakers. As a result, the debates about what kinds of films are needed to sustain what is seen as vulnerable "national" cinema mean feelings often run high.

Film magazines and other media outlets have closely followed Arcand's career, even if not always sympathetically; he has attracted more than his fair share of abuse over the years. He has also frequently been interviewed about his work, and since the success of *Le déclin,* he has given numerous interviews in English. I have made liberal use of these interviews, but it should be noted that the director has often contradicted himself in describing his attitudes and motivations during his long career. These contradictions may be attributed to lapses of memory, his reaction to a particular interviewer, or the kind of provocation that also characterizes his filmmaking (in which contradictions often serve to unsettle the viewer). In any case, this means that while his comments often provide a valuable context for approaching the films, this interview material must be used with care.

QUEBEC: DUPLESSIS AND AFTER

Born in 1941 in the village of Deschambault on the north shore of the Saint Lawrence River, where his father worked as a marine pilot, Arcand was immersed in Quebec's predominantly Catholic cultural environment during his childhood and adolescence: he served as an altar boy and was educated at a Jesuit college. Although he later professed a certain nostalgia for the traditional values that sustained him at this time, he also recognized that he grew up in "a sleepy village in Quebec, a village where nothing was ever said, a village crushed under the weight of a Catholic silence" (quoted in Bergeron 2012, 111). This was during the period that later became known as the Great Darkness, when the influence of the Church was reinforced by the Union Nationale government that held power in Quebec from 1936 to 1960 (apart from a brief period during World War II). It was to preserve Quebec's French and Catholic heritage that the political and religious establishment encouraged the ideology of conservation, which stressed the need to defend the province against outside influences and celebrated the values of the rural way of life (Rioux 1969, 84).

These traditional values were suddenly swept away in a movement that became known as the Quiet Revolution, usually seen as beginning in earnest with the Liberal Party's victory in the 1960 provincial election. In a sense, Arcand's entire career as a filmmaker can be seen as a running commentary on the impact of these social changes, and he was among those in the 1960s and 1970s who called for more radical measures, including the separation of Quebec from the rest of Canada, but from the 1980s on, he has distanced himself from political movements and focused mainly on the problems of individuals trying to come to terms with the bureaucratic and technocratic society that emerged in the wake of the Quiet Revolution. While many Western societies have struggled

Maurice Duplessis calls an election in archive footage from Arcand's *Québec: Duplessis et après....*

with similar problems, the effects were felt more strongly in Quebec than elsewhere because of the suddenness of the break with the past, which had provided a strong sense of distinct cultural identity.

The Church, assisted by Duplessis, had tried to protect that identity by keeping Quebec apart from the rest of North America, treating it as a separate nation in all but name. When the Liberals won the 1960 provincial election, their slogan was *Maîtres chez nous* (Masters in our own house), but their agenda was very different from that of the Union Nationale. The new government set about modernizing Quebec and encouraging new confidence in dealings with the outside world. There was a desire for greater autonomy but no intention of separating from the rest of Canada. However, many Québécois believed that the francophone majority in Quebec could never achieve real control over its future within a predominantly English-speaking state. Their desire for independence was encouraged by a controversial speech given by French president Charles de Gaulle on a state visit to Quebec in 1967, when he proclaimed, "Vive le Québec libre!" (Long live free Quebec!). Already, a group calling itself the Front de Libération du Québec (FLQ) had begun a bombing campaign with the aim of forcing the federal and provincial governments to recognize the need for independence. When, in October 1970, the FLQ kidnapped a British diplomat and murdered a Quebec cabinet minister, Canadian prime minister Pierre Trudeau responded by invoking the War Measures Act. Intended for use only in wartime, this act declared a state of emergency and gave special powers to the army and police, with the result that almost five hundred people were arrested, most of whom were released without any charges.[5]

Although most people in Quebec did not agree with the methods of the FLQ, many supported the goal of autonomy, an aspiration that the scars left by the federal government's draconian response only reinforced. A more peaceful expression of this desire was the creation in 1968 of the Parti Québécois (PQ), which, under the leadership of René Lévesque, went on to win the 1976 provincial election. Although the Trudeau government had tried to defuse tensions in 1969 with the Official Languages Act, which affirmed that Canada was an officially bilingual nation, this initiative was opposed by many in Quebec who feared that pressures on French Canadians to become bilingual would eventually lead to their assimilation. Accordingly, in 1977, the new PQ government enacted Bill 101, which made French the official language in Quebec and restricted the use of English on signs and in the workplace.[6]

In accordance with its main electoral promise, the PQ held a referendum in 1980 on the question of separation from the rest of Canada. The victory of the No side in this divisive campaign was greeted with dismay by many intellectuals and artists (including filmmakers), but the issue was not settled, and a second referendum in 1995 produced the same result, although by a much narrower margin. After this second defeat, the diagnosis made by Quebec premier Jacques Parizeau on the night of the referendum, when he blamed the outcome on "money and the ethnic vote," stole most of the headlines. Parizeau's ill-considered remark cost him his job, but it did highlight the shift in the demographic makeup of the population of Quebec in the late twentieth century, with the growth of diasporic communities of recent immigrants who had little stake in the Québécois project of an independent francophone state. Although Parizeau later admitted that the word *ethnic* was badly chosen and that he had only meant to draw attention to the heavy No vote by "the non-francophones" (quoted in Haque 2012, 4), his outburst indicated the concern of the separatists that the traditional nationalist argument, based on Quebec's French linguistic and cultural roots, was even less likely to win majority support in the future.

After the Quiet Revolution, the people of Quebec had begun to refer to themselves as "Québécois" rather than "French-Canadians," now seen as designating a weak hyphenated form of identity, but it remains unclear exactly how the new term relates to the traditional definitions of Quebec culture. Does *Québécois* designate "francophones or the inhabitants of a territory?" (Dumont 1997, 80). That language and culture are still inextricably intertwined in public discourses in Quebec became even more clear in 2013 when Pauline Marois, leader of a minority PQ government, proposed the controversial Charter of Values. It was designed to restrict the religious practices of minority groups and pave the way for a new referendum in which, she hoped, Québécois voters could be rallied in support of their traditional cultural values. However, when Marois called an election in order to secure a majority that would allow her to implement her policies, she suffered a resounding defeat. Nevertheless, the concerns that led to the proposed charter have not disappeared, and the surprise victory of a new party, Coalition Avenir Québec, in the 2018 provincial election has once again brought them to the fore. The first act of the new premier was to announce that he would ban the wearing of the hijab and religious insignia by public servants, ostensibly because they conflicted with the secularization of post–Quiet Revolution Quebec.

Immigration has become a highly charged political issue in many Western countries in the twenty-first century, including the rest of Canada, but the impact in Quebec has affected the sense of cultural identity almost as much as the Quiet Revolution. According to Arcand, "Now the most common name at the Montreal School Board is no longer Tremblay but Nguyen" (quoted in La Rochelle 2005, 244), and this situation has encouraged attempts to make the case for independence more inclusive. However, the debate incited by the proposed charter tended to undercut these initiatives, and it does seem clear that some significant political change will be necessary to create the conditions for winning any future referendum on separation. In the twenty-first century, Arcand's most recent films, which I will discuss in the final chapter, have been concerned with the impact of the changing demographics in Quebec and of the emerging global media environment, both of which have placed great pressure on definitions of personal and cultural identity in Quebec, as in many other places. As Arcand is very much aware, however, these tensions, as far as Quebec is concerned, have their roots in Canada's colonial past.

"A GLOOMY VIEW OF HISTORY"

As in many other countries in the modern world, the past plays an active, if contested, role in Quebec culture. The visibility of the past in the present is nowhere more apparent than in the province's official motto, *Je me souviens* (I remember), which was originally adopted in the nineteenth century and has appeared on all vehicle license plates in the province since 1978. Another example is the Montreal hockey team, Les Canadiens, the name used by the settlers in New France in the territory that later became known as Quebec. The team's nickname, the Habs, similarly alludes to the original "habitants" who came from France and established farms, often in very harsh conditions. Anyone traveling through Quebec today will also be struck by the number of towns named after saints, a reminder of the dominant role that the Catholic Church played in Quebec society before the Quiet Revolution.

When he arrived at the Université de Montréal in 1960, at the beginning of the drive to modernize Quebec, Arcand decided to study history, but he explained, "What pushed me towards history was the desire to better understand contemporary events" (quoted in Tadros 1972a, 19). For him, "history is the study of the past with the aim of illuminating the present" (quoted in Jean 1989b, 47), and although he has admitted that he is not really a qualified historian, he acknowledges, "When I examine a question, I have a tendency to do so from a historical angle: was it worse before? Better?" (quoted in Coulombe 1993, 50). Although his background as a history student was instrumental in gaining him a position at the NFB (as we shall see in chapter 1) and most of his documentaries deal with Quebec history in some way, his commitment to the "historical angle" did not push him toward making historical fiction films (except for the time when he was unable to work on his own personal projects) because he felt that the past was ultimately unrecoverable, with the result that "all historical reconstruction is a fraud" (quoted in La Rochelle 2005, 282).

As he has explained, "I was taught at the University to take a very gloomy view of French Canadian history . . . that considers conquest the most important thing" (quoted in Wright and Magidson 1974, 22). From this point of view, the key event in Quebec history was the battle fought in 1759 on the Plains of Abraham just outside Quebec City, which resulted in what the Québécois refer to simply as "the Conquest." It occurred when, during the Seven Years' War (1756–1763) in Europe, the British were trying to weaken France by attacking its colonies; accordingly, an army was sent to attack New France, which occupied territory along the banks of the Saint Lawrence River. After a lengthy siege and a bloody battle, the British emerged victorious, and in the treaty of 1763 that ended the war, New France was ceded to the British. The French settlers felt that the mother country had abandoned them, and this sense of loss was exacerbated after the 1789 revolution that made France into a largely secular nation, while the former colony remained staunchly Catholic.

The francophone inhabitants of what became known as the Province of Canada (roughly present-day Ontario and Quebec) now found themselves under the rule of English-speaking authorities appointed by the British government in London. As Heinz Weinmann puts it, "Paradoxically, the Canadiens began to call themselves 'French,' but only because the Other, the conqueror, parasitically, took over their Canadian identity" (1987, 21). Not surprisingly, this situation led to much discontent and unrest during the following century, but Quebec duly became a province in the Dominion of Canada after the Act of Confederation in 1867. Originally, there were four provinces: Ontario and Quebec were joined by Nova Scotia and New Brunswick (the latter with a large French-speaking community). Other provinces were gradually added so that when Newfoundland became part of Canada in 1949, Quebec was one of ten mainly English-speaking provinces in a nation whose official language was English. The act essentially established the present-day political structure of the country, with powers being shared among federal and provincial governments, leading to many jurisdictional disputes. In Quebec, as we have seen, many among the French-speaking majority came to feel that the province lacked the power to protect its language and culture from the influence of the anglophone cultures that surrounded it.

This fear of assimilation was fueled by a report on the situation in the Canadian colony commissioned by the British government following an abortive uprising in 1837. Published in 1839, the report was written by John Lambton, first Earl of Durham, and became known simply as *Lord Durham's Report*. Durham's findings proved highly controversial, especially in Lower Canada (formerly New France). In particular, his characterization of the settlers there as "a people with no history" (quoted in Craig 1963, 150) has long rankled with those who identify with Quebec's francophone heritage. At the beginning of his report, Durham stated that he came to Canada expecting to find "a contest between a government and a people" but found instead "two nations warring in the bosom of a single state" (22–23). According to Arcand, this was an accurate assessment of the situation, and as we shall see in chapter 2, Lord Durham (played by English Canadian filmmaker Robin Spry) turns up in Arcand's documentary *Québec: Duplessis et après . . .* (*Quebec: Duplessis and After*; 1972) reading extracts from the report to support Arcand's thesis that little had changed in Quebec politics even after the Quiet Revolution. However, the objections to the report had less to do with its account of the situation than with its recommendation that the only way to deal with it was to gradually assimilate French Canadians into the English-speaking British Empire.

Durham's conclusion was essentially the same as that of Maurice Séguin, the historian who inspired Arcand's "gloomy view" of Quebec history. Arcand explains in his tribute to the historian that although Séguin hardly saw this solution as a desirable one, he taught that "the French-Canadian nation was too small and too weak to ever be able to aspire to independence" and was thus "condemned to a perpetual mediocrity until the weight of demographics and the pressures of the American Empire relegate it finally to historical oblivion" (2005, 136–137). The other key members of what became known as the "Montreal school" were Guy Frégault and Michel Brunet, and it was they who publicized the group's basic historical thesis rather than Séguin, who was an inspiring teacher but published little. These three historians came to be known as "one who thought, one who wrote, and one who shouted" (Wade 1968, 1014), the last being Brunet, who was "a prolific pamphleteer" (Lapalme 1977, 65). Brunet has been described as being "far more affirmative" about the history of Quebec than Séguin (Harcourt 2006, 148), but Arcand saw him rather as a follower of the master, one who had "a great talent for simplifying, popularizing his theses and putting them into grandiose formulas in newspapers and on the radio" (quoted in Jutras, La Rochelle, and Véronneau 1987–1988, 5).

In *Le déclin,* most of the characters are history professors at the (unnamed) Université de Montréal, but they seem completely uninterested in Quebec's past or, indeed, its future. Although Arcand set out in this film to eliminate all specific references to Quebec (see chapter 4), there are two brief allusions to academic debates about Quebec history. Near the end of the film, the working-class lover of one of the women rather surprisingly gives her a book by Brunet in a scene that, as Arcand explained, was intended as a tribute to the man who taught his "first history course" (quoted in Jutras, La Rochelle, and Véronneau 1987–1988, 5) and who had died recently. The book consists mainly of conference papers forcefully arguing that Quebec's problems stem from its colonial status, but Arcand has made it quite clear that these ideas originated with Séguin. The other specific reference to Quebec history in the film is a joke made by a professor at the expense of, in his words, "one of our eminent colleagues at Laval University who has spent twenty years on the history of Canadian Catholicism." In the context of the film, this is a rather obscure allusion, but it draws on the rivalry between the Montreal school and historians at Laval (in Quebec City).

Whereas Séguin had argued that Quebec had suffered from "the paralyzing hold of occupation" since the Conquest (1977, 80)—that French Canada would have developed into an independent nation but for the Conquest—the Laval historians objected that "the Conquest was not the source of a trauma that can explain all the difficulties French-Canadian society would have to endure afterwards" (Ouellet 1977, 174). For them, as for Durham, most of the blame lay with the French, who had exploited their colony without allowing it to develop its own resources and economy, with the result that the inhabitants could not compete with the entrepreneurial energies of the English settlers. Both groups of historians recognized that there were many problems caused by the dominance of the English majority in Canada, but whereas Séguin's thesis saw independence as the only but extremely unlikely solution, the Laval historians' account was compatible with the vision of a bilingual and multicultural Canada put forward by Pierre Trudeau after he led the Liberal Party to victory in the 1968 federal election. Trudeau came from Quebec but was a staunch federalist and had been "one of the fiercest opponents of the Montreal school in the 1950s," refusing "to view the Conquest as a trauma sufficiently powerful to deaden the will and consciousness of Quebec francophones" (Maclure 2003, 91–92).

As might be expected, Arcand was contemptuous of Trudeau, whom he saw as a devious politician who could be "Duplessis's twin brother" (quoted in La

Rochelle 2005, 118) even though Trudeau had been one of the founders, in 1950, of *Cité libre*, a journal strongly opposed to Duplessis and instrumental in spreading many of the ideas that would lead to the Quiet Revolution. During the 1960s, Arcand contributed to *Parti pris*, a more radical rival journal that supported the separatist movement in its struggle to end what it saw as Quebec's colonial status. His involvement with this journal suggests that at this time, Arcand was not totally committed to Séguin's pessimistic thesis and believed that political action might lead to the establishment of an independent state. The events of October 1970, coupled with his own experience of censorship at the NFB (see chapter 2), must have reinforced his identification with the Montreal school, and they certainly intensified his hatred of Trudeau.

Although Arcand briefly took out a Parti Québécois membership card at this time (Jean 1989b, 47), the pessimistic view of Quebec history he had adopted as a student left him unconvinced that the party could significantly change the situation. In 1974, he explained that he had "not found any political ideology which applies to an industrial country like Quebec" (quoted in Wright and Magidson 1974, 26), and after the No vote in the 1980 referendum organized by the PQ, he announced that he had lost interest in politics (La Rochelle 2005, 40). Even though his earlier films had often been criticized for lacking a clear political agenda, they were at least seen as engaged critiques of the state of Quebec after the Quiet Revolution, but now the dark vision that derived from his endorsement of the Montreal school ensured that he came under frequent attack from those who supported more activist approaches. In keeping with Séguin's teachings, Arcand insisted that history is not a moral discipline but rather "an account of the facts that have been produced up to now," and he claimed that his films "should be seen more as 'statements': they are as neutral as possible" (quoted in Patry 2011a, 12). A close reading of the films will reveal that they are rather more invested in moral (and political) issues than the director cares to admit, but they are underpinned by an approach to history that has alienated many of his critics.

In a very suggestive article, Éric Bédard has compared Arcand's interpretation of Séguin's teaching with that of Pierre Falardeau, a fellow Québécois director who was "a fervent militant for Quebec independence" (2006, 170). In all his films, and most explicitly in his two historical films—*Octobre* (*October*; 1994) and *15 février 1839* (*February 15, 1839*; 2000), dealing respectively with the October 1970 crisis and the earlier uprising against British colonial authorities that instigated the Durham Report—Falardeau shares Arcand's sense of Quebec's colonial status, but he insists on the need to fight to overcome it. There was certainly no love lost between these two filmmakers: obviously thinking of Falardeau, Arcand dismissed those "superficial minds [who] have wanted to give Maurice Séguin a reputation as a nationalist historian in the militant or political sense of the term" (2005, 136), while Falardeau, in what Réal La Rochelle calls "a violent and hateful" attack, accused Arcand of making "cynical, bourgeois cinema, colonized cinema" (2005, 207, 142).

It is worth extending this comparison to include another important Quebec filmmaker. Bernard Émond, who has a background in anthropology rather than history, depicts contemporary Quebec in as negative a light as Arcand and Falardeau. His great trilogy on the three canonical virtues (faith, hope, and charity)—*La neuvaine* (*The Novena*; 2005), *Contre toute esperance* (*Against All Hope*; 2007), and *La donation* (*The Gift*; 2009)—bears witness to the director's difficult position as an atheist and leftist intellectual who feels "nostalgia" for the Catholic past, not so much for the ideology of conservation in itself but for the "social solidarity and an existence full of meaning" that he thinks it provided (quoted in Coulombe 2001, 7). Émond rejects what he calls "postmodern logic," which, he claims, is "a logic of minorities . . . where anything goes, where one doesn't make judgments" (Galiero and Émond 2009, 139), thus undermining the traditional idea of a collectivity whose values are rooted in a common heritage. Arcand has also admitted to being "nostalgic" for his own childhood, "when religion provided a soothing answer to the most insolvable problems, while remaining quite aware of how much obscurantism and demagogy these false solutions contained," and he claims, "All my films exude this loss of faith" (quoted in La Rochelle 2005, 44). This sense of loss is much less explicit than in Émond's films, although, as we shall see, it features in the background in many of Arcand's later films.

Critics have been much less disturbed by Émond's pessimism, perhaps because his films can be situated comfortably within the domain of art cinema—comparisons with Ingmar Bergman are frequent and pertinent—in which dark and disturbing visions are to be expected. Similarly, Falardeau's historical films may depict the failure of attempts to bring about change, but they can be situated in the cinema of social protest. As we shall see, even though Arcand identified Bergman as his ideal (but unattainable) viewer, his films occupy a much less clearly defined territory: they may often be consumed as art cinema, but in many ways, they push against this category; they are often satiric and critical of the status quo, but unlike Falardeau's films, they do not promote a specific ideological agenda.

A CYNICAL AND PESSIMISTIC FILMMAKER?

Arcand's view of Quebec's history did not sit well with those who were still pursuing independence or political change. However, he has denied that he is really a pessimist, insisting that he is "simply lucid" in recognizing that "we [the Québécois] live in a small society on the margins of the American empire" (quoted in Coulombe 1993, 120), and he characterizes his vision as being, like Séguin's, "tragic" (quoted in La Rochelle 2014, 75). He has also called himself a "realist," adding that "people who call themselves realists are accused of pessimism by the optimists" (quoted in Bédard 2006, 175n). Although, when he was writing for *Parti pris*, he seemed to support the independence movement; by 1993, he was claiming, "I never made a militant film for or against the independence of Quebec, because I do not even know if I am for or against independence" (quoted in Loiselle 1995, 149). Throughout his career, he has maintained his commitment to Séguin's historical account, and he has recently explained, "I have always said that, under certain conditions, the independence of Quebec was certainly desirable, but that it remained improbable" (quoted in Bergeron 2012, 113).

Despite his disclaimers, Arcand has come under attack from a number of outspoken critics, mainly in Quebec, whose criticisms often seem driven by personal animosity. As we shall see, the filmmaker has experienced major critical and commercial successes in his career, punctuated by low points in which his films have failed to excite a great deal of critical or audience interest. His detractors often seem to rejoice at the failures and accuse the successes of selling out to the demands of either popular or international audiences—or both. Since there are many testimonies to Arcand's personal affability, the roots of this phenomenon seem to lie in the cynicism that these critics attribute to his abandonment of the cause of Quebec independence. In an essay published in the late 1980s, Pierre Véronneau observed that the filmmaker had already been "described as a cynic for at least fifteen years" (1987–1988, 24), and this view of Arcand may have originated in his association with Les Cyniques, a popular comedy troupe whose members were his fellow students at the Université de Montréal and whose first performance is featured in *Seul ou avec d'autres* (see chapter 1).

Certainly, the accusations of cynicism recur over and over again in critical discussions of Arcand's work, and Carl Bergeron has discussed the implications of this phenomenon in a book on the filmmaker that he called *Un cynique chez les lyriques*, which might be translated as "A cynic among the lyrics." The last part of this title refers to the work of François Ricard, who has characterized the Québécois born near the end of World War II and just after as the "lyric generation." This was the first generation to feel the full effects of the Quiet Revolution, with the result that they felt they were faced, according to Ricard, with "a world so shifting, prey to such profound and widespread transformations, which had broken so quickly with the past that it seemed suddenly weightless and evanescent" (1994, 115). For this generation, which came of age in the 1960s, the possibilities of social change seemed immense, and even though Arcand was born a few years before the period that Ricard specifies, he does seem to have been caught up in these hopes in his youth. However, they came into conflict with the sense of the weight and slow movement of history as taught by the Montreal school.

According to Bergeron, "Arcand is very much a cynic, but not in the sense that his critics intend" (2012, 12). These critics rarely define the sense in which they are using the term, but the common modern definition of a *cynic* is "someone who is self-serving and misanthropic." In the Quebec context, however, it is more likely to mean someone who has given up on the idea of Quebec as an independent nation. As we have seen, such a definition has some pertinence in relation to Arcand, but the filmmaker himself, in a commentary he contributed to Bergeron's book, traces the roots of his thinking back to classical philosophers such as Diogenes, Epicurus, and Lucretius (2012, 111). The humor of the comedy troupe Les Cyniques, and presumably their name, has also been likened to the "subversive and jubilatory philosophy" of Diogenes (Lafortune 2013, 414). Diogenes, and the other Greek cynics, "believed that philosophy was obliged to challenge the conventional values, beliefs, and customs of the community" (Mazella 2007, 14), motivated by what Arcand calls their "extraordinary love of lucidity" (quoted in Dorland 1986, 21). It is in this sense that Arcand's films set out to make people think about things they have taken for granted. Although he has claimed to be hurt by the venomous critical attacks on him and his work and to not understand the reasons behind them, Arcand has constructed a persona based on his reputation for cynicism in order to stir things up in the manner of the Greek cynics.

Another dimension to Arcand's cynical persona derives from the "political realism" of the sixteenth-century political theorist Niccolò Machiavelli (Bergeron 2012, 83). Machiavelli himself makes an anachronistic appearance, played by an actor, in Arcand's documentary on the 1980 referendum, *Le confort et l'indifférence* (*Comfort and Indifference*; 1981), commenting cynically on the motives of the politicians involved in the campaign. His contributions invite questions about just how much the director identifies with the Machiavellian viewpoint (see chapter 2), but according to Arcand, it is his "desire to pin down reality" that has made him enemies "on both sides of the barricades" (quoted in Bergeron 2012, 113).

He has claimed that his critics reproach him for "showing what Quebec is like" and that they "want Quebec to be like a speech by René Lévesque" (quoted in Bergeron 2012, 13n). The implication is that Lévesque, as the founder and leader of a party that advocated for an independent Quebec, appealed to the "lyric generation" and downplayed the problems and contradictions that stood in the way of his political agenda. In his documentary on the 1980 referendum, Arcand suggests that the optimism of the Yes campaign came up against the cynics—in the modern sense of the term, Trudeau and the No campaigners—who, he suggests, manipulated people into supporting the status quo. Arcand does not employ such unscrupulous tactics himself but rather seeks to expose the political reality that enabled these tactics to work so effectively. Although some critics have dismissed his later films as "reactionary" (usually providing little or no evidence), his pessimistic viewpoint is less a sign of a cynical lack of interest in political change than a rejection of what the Frankfurt school theorists called the "affirmative" character of "mass culture," which distracts attention away from the need for such change (a position that I will explore more fully in chapter 2). The complexity of his political outlook is well captured by Carl Bergeron's characterization of Arcand as a "non-leftist Marxist" (2012, 60).

One other recurring (and related) criticism is that his films show a gradual shift away from concerns with the collectivity to an emphasis on individual experience. To the extent that this is true, it reflects the rapid changes that occurred in Quebec during the Quiet Revolution and that were often seen as a consequence of exposure to American popular culture, which supposedly promotes individualism. The result of the 1980 referendum led to a period of "political disillusionment" in Quebec, in which, according to Denise Pérusse, "collective movements challenging the established order vanished, and were replaced by the cult of the individual and an egocentric ideology" (1995, 87n). While it is true that the relations between the collective and the individual in Arcand's films have changed, as is inevitable in such a long and varied career, these films are very much rooted in the specific concerns of Quebec society after the Quiet Revolution, its problematic relations to its past, and the prospects for its future.

In the films of Denys Arcand, as Pierre Barrette has suggested, the individual and the collective always "come together, reflect each other, [and] interpenetrate" (2003, 4), and his most recent film, *La chute de l'empire américain* (*The Fall of the American Empire*; 2018), has been seen as a critique of "the cult of the individual and the death of collective values" (Yakabuski 2018). Indeed, if there is a unifying thread that runs through all of Arcand's diverse output, it is the critique of a society in which the drive toward individual success (usually defined in monetary terms) has eroded any sense of public service or the common good, with the result that the rights of less "successful" individuals have been swept away in a bureaucratic system steeped in managerial jargon. This concern emerges most fully and bitterly in *L'âge des ténèbres* (*Days of Darkness*; 2007), set in a dystopian near future in which an elaborate machinery of government departments regulates the lives of individuals but can do nothing to solve the problems they face.

Although these issues are developed in ways that will have special resonance for Québécois audiences, the pressures of modernity and globalization that have confronted Quebec in the past sixty years have been increasingly felt in other Western societies, and the films have often resonated with international audiences. If Arcand's films before *Le déclin* seemed to be steeped in the particular debates and the cultural icons of their immediate time and place, historical developments have enabled audiences to connect with some of his later films in ways that transcend national boundaries. In the media-saturated world of the twenty-first century, with little sense of history and an increasing gulf between rich and poor, the traditional domain of politics becomes prey to irrational and unpredictable forces that seem beyond human control. From this perspective, Arcand's "cynicism" does look more and more like a "realistic" response to a global environment defined by a much more ruthlessly cynical order of things.

"SPASMODIC STORYTELLING"

Anticipating Bergeron's argument about Arcand's relation to the "lyric generation," Bart Testa has argued that his films "seem to stand in contrast to the lyricism" that the critic finds in the work of most Canadian filmmakers. According to Testa, Arcand's "formal choices consistently refuse the lyrical," and his cinema "looks for the gaps, hypocrisies and contradictions of Quebec society" (1987, 213). Rather than being cynical in the sense of being misanthropic, this attitude enables his films to function as dystopias that slightly exaggerate the present state of things to provoke thought about the historical processes that have caused these situations.[7] In this respect, they function much like the work of Jean Baudrillard, who has been called a "hyperbolic writer" who sets out to "displace received notions of truth and falsity in an age where reality is mediated as never before" (Bewes 1997, 21). I am not interested here in whether Arcand should be seen as a postmodernist (or whether Baudrillard should, for that matter), although I will discuss the arguments of critics who see him this way (see chapter 4). Since Arcand is even less a philosopher than he is a historian, his vision is conveyed not through reasoned argument but through the cinematic strategies he adopts to raise awkward questions about prevailing ideological assumptions that discourage any awareness of alternatives to the present state of affairs.

These films have been aptly described as sites of a "cohabitation of contradictions," revealing an openness to different points of view that "a very large majority of Quebec intellectuals considered . . . antagonistic, unbearable, deserving of anathema" (La Rochelle 1987–1988, 14). As Arcand himself puts it, "I perceive reality as ambiguous, relative . . . thanks to which I am accused of not having a point of view" (quoted in Jutras, La Rochelle, and Véronneau 1987–1988, 9). As a result, it is difficult to find a comfortable position from which to read his films; they demand an active response from their viewers and provoke a wide range of different and contradictory interpretations.

Arcand's critics, especially in Quebec, have resisted seeing his work in this way, so that, while he remains "moored to Quebec, both to its reality and the myth it represents, he has never felt integrated either in Quebec or a Canadian cinema" (La Rochelle 2005, 271). One of the reasons for this discomfort is his typically ambivalent attitude to the documentary tradition. Although, like many Quebec filmmakers, he began his career making documentaries at the NFB, these films already incorporated an implied critique of the documentary ideology of objectivity and authenticity.[8] When he left the NFB and started to make fiction films in the 1970s, he regretted not being able to continue his documentary exploration of the state of Quebec society, but he also welcomed the freedom that allowed him to "do many things you cannot do in documentary" (quoted in Tadros 1972b, 27). His frustration partly stemmed from the experience of censorship at the government institution (see chapters 1 and 2), but he also argued that documentary involves "a sort of dishonesty that comes from the fact it is ultimately your own vision of the world that appears whatever it is that the people express in your film" (quoted in Tadros 1972b, 28).

Unlike other documentary filmmakers who turned to fiction in the 1960s, Arcand argued that documentary and fiction were "two completely different things" and should not be mixed (quoted in Tadros 1973, 20). However, throughout his career, his films have depended, in many different ways, on a tension between a commitment to social criticism (usually associated with documentary) and a refusal "to take himself too seriously" (La Rochelle 2005, 271), and it is his wry sense of humor that seems to have most disturbed many critics in Quebec. Arcand has responded to their criticism by insisting, "Militants are always extremely serious people," and "unfortunately for me, I like to laugh" (quoted in Jutras, La Rochelle, and Véronneau 1987–1988, 9). In this respect, he is once again following the example of the Greek cynics, whose philosophy relied on "satiric or farcical language and gestures to communicate its serious philosophic message" (Mazella 2007, 23).

The tension between being serious and having fun cannot simply be mapped onto that between the documentary and fictional approaches. As we shall see, Arcand's documentaries are often satiric and include what he calls "fun" moments (quoted in Tadros 1972a, 21), while his fiction films continue the uncompromising analysis of Quebec society begun in his early documentaries. His experience in documentary is apparent in his fiction films in the way psychology is "subordinate to social conditions and historical facts" (Jean 1987–1988, 27). But whereas direct cinema filmmakers, such as Gilles Groulx and Michel Brault, sought to fuse documentary techniques and fictional narratives, Arcand plays on these tensions between the two modes.

The documentary influence is most visible in Arcand's first three fiction films (see chapter 3), in which the characters are viewed from a distance in an observational and dispassionate manner that leaves viewers to infer what is going on in their minds; they become involved in events whose implacable unfolding serves to illustrate the director's dark view of history. In the later films, from *Le déclin* onward, the viewers are confronted with characters whose positions in the narrative seem to invite the kind of identification conventionally expected of fiction films but who, despite being sympathetic in many ways, are deeply flawed. Their contradictions enable them to embody both the attractiveness of an individual living for the present moment and an awareness of the impossibility of arresting the forces of history that threaten the collectivity of which they are a part. The extent to which they are aware of this duality varies from film to film, but the effect is to challenge viewers to draw out the implications of the characters' actions and behavior without the assured psychological understandings that fiction films normally provide. The one major exception to this rule is probably Daniel in *Jésus de Montréal,* whose saintliness and apparent lack of sexual desire transcend Arcand's usual view of human nature. However, even this film is an example of what Arcand calls "the kind of ensemble film I do," whose narrative structure depends less on linear development with a central protagonist than on the juxtaposition of different groups and individuals, much like his feature-length documentaries (see chapter 2).[9]

As well as occupying an uncertain terrain between documentary and fiction, the films also undercut established distinctions between popular and art cinema. When Arcand turned to fiction filmmaking in the 1970s, he made three crime films that transplanted formulas familiar from Hollywood B movies into the context of modern Quebec society (see chapter 3), but because television had eaten into the market for such cheaply made genre films, these were distributed as art films. Later, although *Le déclin* became the highest-grossing film ever in Quebec at the time of its release, it was marketed internationally as an art film (and ended up earning around $30 million!). As a result, "his work is sometimes taken as that of a visionary, sometimes as that of an opportunist" (Jean 1989a, 39).

The most significant tension in Arcand's films, however, is that between the "tragic" vision, which results from his pessimistic outlook on history and the human condition, and the comic elements that derive from his refusal to take himself too seriously. This is perhaps most fully embodied in *Le déclin,* in which the lighthearted banter among a group of friends in the first part gradually gives way to a recognition of the emptiness and contradictions in their lives; however, it is present, in various degrees and combinations, in all the films. As I have argued, his double-edged tragicomic structures have left the filmmaker open to charges of cynicism, which may be true, but only if the term is used in its classical sense: a playful demonstration of the absurdity of a social order that people tend to take for granted. In what follows in this book, whenever I refer to Arcand's cynicism, it will be in this sense.

I will be exploring the impact of these tensions on the characteristic strategies that Arcand adopts in his films, and it will be useful to offer a preliminary outline of what he himself calls his "spasmodic storytelling" (quoted in La Rochelle 2005, 273). His critics often maintain that his films are fairly conventional, or even downright incompetent, in their use of cinematic language, and Arcand himself claims to "love styles that don't call attention to themselves" (quoted in La Rochelle 2014, 11). He suggests that this explains his admiration for the films of Luis Buñuel, but the choice of Buñuel as an exemplary director makes clear that he is not thinking of the conventional storytelling of classical Hollywood cinema. As he puts it, Buñuel made "films that are like exterminating angels [in that] they attack without warning" (quoted in La Rochelle 2005, 75), the implication being that his films are deceptively simple for the purpose of jolting audiences out of their complacency.[10] Similarly, Arcand's films are full of unexpected juxtapositions in which the editing can hardly be said to be concealing itself, and much the same is true of the elaborate camera movements found in many of the later films.

In both his documentaries and fiction films, Arcand creates what André Loiselle and Brian McIlroy have called "dialogic structures through the juxtaposition of contradictory and irreconcilable elements at every level of a film's diegesis" (1995, 2). This approach disturbs the spectator's relations to the film: unlike in conventional narrative cinema, it is rarely easy to identify completely with the central characters in Arcand's films. Even sympathetic characters often do or say things that demand a critical response, and many of the critical misunderstandings that the films have engendered stem from this effect of simultaneously drawing us in and pushing us away. The narrative structures depend less on a linear progression that aligns the viewer with one character's project and more on montage effects that bring different viewpoints into collision. Thus Arcand argues that the presence of an actor playing the role of Machiavelli in *Le confort et l'indifférence* is "a fundamentally historical procedure, which very simply illuminates the meaning of the . . . referendum," and he compares it to the "fundamentally cinematic procedure" of "montage as defined by Sergei Eisenstein" (quoted in Jean 1989b, 47).

However, his films, unlike those of the Soviet director, do not aim to provoke spectators into coming to a specific conclusion as a result of the collision of the elements that the montage brings together. As Peter Wilkins has suggested, "It is no wonder these films cause the critics such problems when they are always taking the ground of judgment out from under the audience's feet" (1995, 130). Indeed, Arcand's films are designed to unsettle critics and spectators alike, creating an ambiguity that parallels, and at the same time exposes, the contradictions and uncertainty of modern social reality.

1 • ALONE OR WITH OTHERS

Arcand and the Quiet Revolution

> We had a long way to go and we haven't made much progress.
>
> —Denys Arcand

As we have seen, the beginning of the Quiet Revolution is usually dated to the 1960 provincial election in which the Liberal Party under Jean Lesage finally ousted the conservative Union Nationale government, with a mandate to modernize a province that had been largely sheltered from outside influences for many years. From being a socially and politically conservative province, dominated by the Catholic Church, Quebec was suddenly exposed to modern influences and the social changes that were affecting other countries in the Western world. Arcand was nineteen years old in 1960 and just beginning his studies at the Université de Montréal. His films can be described as an ongoing reflection on, and engagement with, the consequences of the rapid changes that took place in Quebec at this time.

His first experience as a filmmaker—apart from *À l'est d'Eaton* (East of Eaton's; 1959), a short amateur effort made with his friend Stéphane Venne, which has not survived—came as a member of a collective at the university. As we saw in the introduction, *Seul ou avec d'autres* (1962) is a fiction film made using the techniques developed by young filmmakers at the NFB to make direct cinema documentaries, and several of these filmmakers were on hand to assist the students in their efforts. Arcand's involvement in this project would lead to his recruitment by the NFB, where he made three short documentaries that deal with aspects of Quebec's history, but his iconoclastic approach ensured that they addressed the present as much as they did the past. In this chapter, I will discuss Arcand's ambivalent response to the Quiet Revolution from his perspective as a history student and as manifested in these early films.

THE QUIET REVOLUTION AND AFTER . . .

Although 1960 is a convenient date for marking the beginning of the Quiet Revolution, the signs of change were already becoming apparent in the years immediately after World War II, when many soldiers returned to Quebec having been exposed to new ideas abroad. The arrival of television in the early 1950s, including cross-border transmissions from the United States, also introduced viewers to ideas that challenged the traditional teachings of the Church. In 1959, Cardinal Léger, the archbishop of Montreal, expressed his concern about the impact of television in spreading "new so-called modern values, such as freedom of speech, individualism and professionalization" (quoted in De Koninck 1995, 143). Although many saw these values as endemic to popular American television programs, the NFB documentaries broadcast on Canadian television also explored the new cultural environment in ways that were equally disturbing to the upholders of the status quo. Made without the preplanning and authoritative voice-of-God commentary of earlier NFB documentaries, these films encouraged the questioning of authority that characterized the emerging youth culture, felt throughout the Western world but with even greater intensity in the context of the Quiet Revolution in Quebec.

However, the direct cinema documentaries also reflected uncertainty about what should replace the old values and the cultural identity they supported, a problem that became even more apparent in the fiction films that emerged from the direct cinema movement in the early 1960s. At the beginning of Gilles Groulx's *Le chat dans le sac* (1964), Claude (Claude Godbout), the young protagonist, speaking to the camera, declares, "I am French Canadian; therefore, I am searching for myself." His words illustrate a cultural situation in which there was a strong sense of a distinct French Canadian identity but also an increasing difficulty in describing exactly what it was without falling back on the old traditions that were being swept away. Because there was a strong concern that the French language and culture were vulnerable in the context of the new social and political order emerging in the 1960s, it was not easy to find terms to describe what distinguished the new outlook in Quebec from what was happening elsewhere. Although Groulx's protagonist wants to contribute to change by becoming a journalist, he finds his way blocked by editors who think his ideas imprecise. At the end of the film, his relationship with Barbara (Barbara Ulrich), an anglophone Jewish woman, breaks down, and he retires to the countryside, where he reads about the FLQ bombings and watches a young woman skating in a winter landscape, finding himself caught between destructive political activism and an idealized image of sexual purity. Another character called Claude, played by the director himself, comes to a similar impasse in Claude Jutra's *À tout prendre* (1963).

Ironically, it was Alexis Tremblay, an old man living in an isolated rural area, who became an icon of the separatist movement after his appearance in the NFB documentary *Pour la suite du monde* (*For Those Who Will Follow*; Pierre Perrault and Michel Brault, 1963).[1] As Perrault put it in his epilogue to René Lévesque's book *An Option for Quebec*, the independence movement found inspiration in the term "*acharnation*—our 'stubbornation,' that staggering word invented by Alexis Tremblay" (Lévesque 1968, 128). There is no voice-of-God commentary, and the language spoken by Alexis and the other islanders in interviews and voice-overs provided evidence of a distinctive French culture with its roots in a past that was rapidly disappearing. The film depicts the revival of the traditional practice of trapping beluga whales, under the guidance of Alexis, who describes the beliefs and values of the "ancestors" in order to, as the film's title suggests, pass them on to the younger generation. Yet for many young people, as for Groulx's and Jutra's protagonists, it was not easy to adapt these traditional values to the needs of a modern urban society. The new "Québécois" identity, which replaced the hyphenated "French Canadian" one, was seen as more dynamic and self-assured, but the changes could also be experienced as an "identity crisis" (Beauchemin 2002, 132).

Historians generally agree that "in the space of little more than fifty years, between the end of the Second World War and the close of the twentieth century . . . Quebec went from being one of the most socially traditional, politically conservative, and religiously devout regions of the developed world to one of the least" (Christiano 2007, 21). There remains, however, considerable disagreement about the long-term effects of this rapid change. For Arcand, the Quiet Revolution did not really "bring us into the modern world"; there was just "a small acceleration" (quoted in Jutras, La Rochelle, and Véronneau 1987–1988, 6). He dismissed it as "an epiphenomenon," which failed to deliver the radical social changes that its proponents had promised, and he felt that the major change in Quebec society was "the disappearance of religion" (quoted in La Rochelle 2014, 104). Yet the sudden decline of the Catholic Church in Quebec was itself the most obvious outcome of the Quiet Revolution, leaving a cultural vacuum that led to widespread uncertainty about how to respond to the new situation.

Looking back on the rapid changes in Quebec culture, Arcand, along with many others, felt that the hopes of the Quiet Revolution had been betrayed because of the overreliance by successive governments on the state apparatus to replace the Church, which had largely controlled such vital social services as health and education. He argued that new ways of thinking had not emerged because "mentalities change much more slowly than governments and social structures" and that Catholic dominance had been replaced by "a strong and directive state . . . which tried to control almost everything, leading to today's disastrous consequences in hospitals and the system of education" (quoted in La Rochelle 2005, 274). Of course, similar complaints have been made in most Western nations (as in the rest of Canada), but Arcand's diagnosis points to his complete disillusionment with the results of the Quiet Revolution. While Duplessis had favored the Church and private enterprise, the Lesage government embarked on an extensive program of laicization and nationalization with the objective of creating a progressive modern state. However, the strategy adopted by the new regime to accomplish this goal was to take control of Quebec's institutions and resources and to manage them, under the influence of so-called technocrats, in the belief that technological progress would lead to social change. Ironically, the long-term effect is that the private sector has flourished and the public domain has struggled, as Arcand has shown in many of his films.

Nevertheless, for many years, the dominant story about the Quiet Revolution depicted it through the metaphor of a movement from darkness into light. According to this account, it swept away "la grande noirceur," the Great Darkness, of a past in which the development of Quebec was held back by the Church and a government that resisted progress. Accompanying this metaphor was another in which the Quiet Revolution was a movement from childhood into adulthood, "the veritable coming-of-age of a people in its belated encounter with modernity" (Christiano 2007, 22). However, as with the euphoria generated by the youth culture and the various liberation movements in the 1960s, the changes in Quebec were also seen as the triumph of individualism over the collective values that the Church had fostered in Quebec.

The desire to reaffirm or rediscover collective values was a driving force behind the movements supporting independence that emerged in Quebec in the 1960s, and the perceived opposition between individualism and the collective was at the root of the nationalists' antipathy toward Pierre Trudeau, whose election as Canadian prime minister in 1968—on a wave of "Trudeaumania"—was identified with the movements that supposedly promoted individualism. From Trudeau's perspective, "nationalism is rooted in the state, in the collectivity; while liberalism is rooted in the person, in the individual" (1998, 95). Although he approved of the progressive measures carried out by the provincial Liberals after 1960, Trudeau felt that their election slogan, *Maîtres chez nous*, smacked of "the return of *nationalism* under a new guise" (105). The violence of the FLQ campaign in the late 1960s was to prove him a prophet, but his response in imposing the War Measures Act in October 1970 tended to discredit Trudeau's concern for individual freedoms.

As Ronald Rudin has pointed out, "Many of the sorts of problems that Quebec has experienced over the past twenty years have been evident throughout the West" (1997, 204), but the disintegration of the hopes of the Quiet Revolution led many in Quebec to place the blame on the rapid sweeping away of those values that had defined a distinctive cultural identity. One of the key thinkers who reflected on the impact of the Quiet Revolution was the sociologist Fernand Dumont, whose assessment was, in some ways, close to Arcand's. Dumont felt that after 1960, modernization had been based on "the principles of technocratic rationality," while the "desire for social justice," which had inspired the Quiet Revolution, had been forgotten (1997, 24). Whereas "in the past, we never doubted the specificity of our culture . . . now, some people claim that apart from language nothing distinctive remains to us" (81–82). For Dumont, the main problem was the "denial of the past" in order to take control of the future, with the result that the Québécois people had become what Lord Durham said the French Canadians were in his notorious report: "a people without history" (106–107).

As we have seen, Arcand regarded Lord Durham as a serious commentator on the situation of Quebec after the Conquest, and he shared Dumont's concern with the crippling effect of living without a sense of the past. There is no question of reviving the past in Arcand's films, in which history operates as a force shaping the present, however much it may have been forgotten. Despite his reservations about the impact of the movement, Arcand has been accurately portrayed as "very much a child of the Quiet Revolution," but one who, like many other members of his generation, proved "reluctant to embrace explicitly political points of view founded on positivity rather than critique" (Marshall 2001, 148). His early films thus came under attack both from diehards who resented the social changes of the 1960s and from those who advocated more sweeping reforms along socialist and/or nationalist lines.

THE INITIATION OF DENYS ARCAND

Although it was very much an amateur effort, *Seul ou avec d'autres* represented an important moment in Quebec film history, since "the last previous commercial full-length fiction film produced in Quebec was in 1953" (Daudelin 1980, 95n3). The opening credits indicate that three students—Denis Héroux, Denys Arcand, and Stéphane Venne—directed the film, with "technical assistance" from Michel Brault and Gilles Groulx, both NFB filmmakers experienced in the new style of documentary. Others from the NFB, including Marcel Carrière, Bernard Gosselin, and Claude Jutra, participated in the production without credit. Arcand would later suggest that the number of people involved in making the film resulted in a certain "incoherence" rather than the personal vision of a single filmmaker that an art film required (quoted in Houle, Leduc, and Hamelin

1971, 12). However, although their approaches may have clashed on this film, all the filmmakers involved in this group effort went on to become important figures in Quebec cinema in the following years.

Héroux was the driving force behind the project: he was, in effect, the producer, persuading the university's student council to support the production of a film about life on campus rather than the usual annual theatrical review. Like Arcand, he was studying history, but what he learned from Séguin was the crucial importance of the economy in the cultural field. This idea influenced his development as a director and as a producer who wanted to make commercial films that would reach a large audience. He certainly achieved his goal when he made *Valérie* (1968), in which a frustrated young woman leaves her convent school and becomes a high-class prostitute. This film initiated a subgenre that *Variety* dubbed "Maple Syrup Porno"; made on a budget of $99,000, the film grossed more than $1.5 million and was credited with establishing "the commercial viability of the Quebec film industry" (Morris 1984, 305, 191). As a result, Héroux would become "a millionaire and a genuine Canadian film mogul" (Dorland 1983, 14), but his dubious reputation in Quebec film culture was summed up by Robert Daudelin, who wrote that after *Seul ou avec d'autres,* Arcand went on to become "a first rate director," while Héroux proved himself as "a capable businessman" (Daudelin 1980, 95n2).

It was, presumably, Héroux who chose the basic narrative for the student film, in which, as Arcand pointed out, the depiction of a female student's first days in college anticipated Héroux's follow-up to *Valérie, L'initiation* (*The Initiation*; 1969), albeit without the nudity and overt sexuality (Houle, Leduc, and Hamelin 1971, 12). Arcand collaborated with Venne on the initial scenario, but Venne's main contribution was the musical score. He went on to become a popular songwriter and composer, with several film scores to his credit. Apparently, the original idea was to make a more conventional fiction film, and according to Arcand, the first draft of the scenario was "all dialogue," but it "was thrown into the wastebasket by its authors; the second draft was just a rough sketch for directing the actors' improvisations" (quoted in La Rochelle 2005, 73). Since Arcand was a member of the university's dramatic society and had experience in improvisational theater, he took charge of directing the actors (Jean 1989b, 46).

Brault, who had recently returned from France—where he had collaborated on Jean Rouch's landmark cinéma-vérité film *Chronique d'un été* (*Chronicle of a Summer*; 1961)—was the principal cinematographer, and he claimed that it was he who, after reading the initial scenario, said, "Let's improvise," so that "while keeping to the outline of the scenario, [they] improvised" (quoted in Bonneville 1972, 10).[2] However, Brault gave the students credit for "putting the characters in contradictory situations (by giving them conflicting directions!)" (quoted in Marsolais 2011, 102) about what was going on in their scenes, a piece of mischief that sounds like something Arcand would have dreamed up. The other key figure in giving the film its final shape was Groulx, who edited the film, drawing on his experience of making key direct cinema documentaries, such as *Golden Gloves* (1961) and *Les raquetteurs* (*The Snowshoers*; 1958), on the latter of which he was credited as codirector with Brault. Both of these young, but experienced, NFB filmmakers would go on to make major contributions to Quebec cinema in the following years: after making his directorial debut with *Le chat dans le sac*, Groulx created a series of militant films that blend fiction and documentary in innovative ways, and Brault worked as a cinematographer on many important films and was also active as a director, beginning with *Entre la mer et l'eau douce* (*Drifting Upstream*; 1967), from a screenplay by Arcand, and *Les ordres* (*Orders*; 1974), dealing with the impact on people's lives of the War Measures Act in October 1970.

Seul ou avec d'autres begins with the arrival of Nicole (Nicole Braün) on her first day at the university. She meets Pierre (Pierre Létourneau), who shows her around and tells her that she can miss classes with impunity. Later, she meets Marie-José (Marie-José Raymond), who has had an unhappy affair with a law student and warns her about the behavior of male students. Nicole goes for a drive into the city with Carl (Carl Mailhot), another student, whom she decides she does not like, while Pierre meets Michelle (Michelle Boulizon) and invites her to a jazz concert. The next day, Nicole attends a philosophy class, and Pierre learns that Michelle is leaving shortly to spend a year or two in Paris. Nicole goes to a performance by Les Cyniques, just beginning their very successful career (see the introduction), whose "irreverent and iconoclastic satire" (Aird 2013, 11) was a symptom of—and a major contribution to—the changing cultural climate in Quebec culture at this time. After attending a drunken initiation party, Nicole eventually goes back to Pierre, and the final sequence takes place at the annual dance marking the beginning of classes, where the couple embrace and seem ready for a relationship that will last for at least the coming year.

Although the narrative focuses on Nicole's personal experience, a broader viewpoint is provided by brief extracts from an interview with Guy Rocher, a sociology professor, who makes the case for a more modern and less rigid education system, claiming that, while universities should approach the universal from a local perspective, in Quebec, "the local eats the universal." The soundtrack also carries two voice-overs commenting on what we witness: one represents Nicole's rather naive thoughts about what she has experienced, and the other is a more cynical male voice (provided by Arcand himself), which questions her conclusions. Thus when Nicole says she does not know why she decided to go to university, Arcand suggests it was perhaps to meet young men. In both cases, it is as if the speakers are watching a screening of footage from the film, a device often used by Rouch in his documentaries, including *Chronique d'un été*. As the above plot summary makes clear, all the characters have the same first names as the (non)actors who play them, as was the case in other fiction films derived from direct cinema documentary, including *À tout prendre* and *Le chat dans le sac*, as well as *Nobody Waved Good-Bye*, the English Canadian counterpart to the Quebec films.

As Héroux admitted, the story was "nothing special" (quoted in Bonneville 1973, 5), and whatever merits the film has come from the way it was filmed. The use of improvisation, by the film crew as well as the actors, gives the film something of the feeling of a direct cinema documentary, and it has even been described as "a 'staged' documentary" (Morris 1984, 267). Yet creating this effect proved difficult for technical reasons. As Brault explained, he had to use a 35-millimeter Arriflex camera, which was designed for silent filmmaking, and because it made a noise, he had to film from "far away, using the zoom and telephoto lens" (quoted in Bonneville 1972, 10).

This problem was only an issue in those sequences that used sync sound, which for Brault was the "defining characteristic" of direct cinema (Loiselle 2007, 40). In other sequences, the camera could move closer to the actors, and the film begins with close-ups of a pair of hands putting on gloves and Nicole with a bus ticket in her mouth. Despite these shots, her perspective is primarily established not by close-ups and subjective camera angles but by her voice-over commentary, which begins as she walks into the campus wearing sunglasses, introducing herself, establishing that the year is 1961 and that she is seventeen. More typically, the camera observes her and the other characters either from a distance or in close-ups made possible by the zoom lens. When she first meets Pierre, they walk past parked mopeds and cars, and the camera follows beside and above them while we hear their conversation as if they are much closer. The meeting between Nicole and Marie-José is filmed from a distance through the fence of a tennis court, but the camera zooms in, and there is an extreme close-up of Marie-José in distress as she describes the end of her affair. In another sequence, the camera is placed behind Pierre and Michelle as they sit on steps on the campus, and when she walks away after telling him she is leaving for Paris, he whistles sadly and stands, revealing a microphone cord dangling from his jacket.

Similar technical issues had confronted Brault on *Les raquetteurs*, in which a sense of immediacy is created with very few shots using sync sound. According to André Loiselle, he solved the problem in that film in such a way that it oscillates "between observation and participation, distance and proximity, identification and detachment" so that it becomes "an ethnographic document that looks at a culture simultaneously up close and from afar" (2007, 49). Much the same could be said of *Seul ou avec d'autres*, but the critical consensus was that the application of direct cinema techniques to a fiction film in this case offered only a "jumbled" anticipation of more successful later examples (Daudelin 1980, 96).

One of the characteristics of direct cinema, as inspired by Rouch, was that the filmmakers should not conceal their intervention in the reality before the camera, since the real subject of the film is their engagement with the people they are filming. In this spirit, in editing *Seul ou avec d'autres,* Groulx retained the exposure of the microphone cord and moments when focus is temporarily lost due to adjustments to the zoom lens, and he drew attention to the way the soundtrack had been constructed. He intercut the conversation between Nicole and Carl as they drive into the city with that between Pierre and Michelle on the steps, and the words of one couple are often heard over shots of the other, encouraging us to compare and contrast the two couples. At times, music drowns out the voices, and there is a cut to a black screen as Pierre and Michelle talk (presumably to cover a technical problem with the camera). In the journey through the city, Groulx also kept a shot in which Nicole, who is supposedly new to the city, pokes her tongue out at someone off-screen whom she seems to know.

When it was finished, the film caused quite a stir. Brault took it with him to the Congrès de Lyon in March 1963, where the delegates were discussing the development of a "synchronous 16mm camera" and were amazed that Brault had done what he did before the "new Éclair camera" came on the market (Marsolais 2011, 70). The film was also shown at the Cannes Film Festival, and Héroux was pleased that the film exposed French viewers to "the Québécois milieu" (quoted in Bonneville 1973, 5). It also received a warm reception from audiences in Montreal, where, as Arcand reports, Héroux rented a theater to show the film, and they "thought nobody would come, but the place was full for a month" (quoted in La Rochelle 2014, 93). According to Marcel Jean, thirty thousand people saw it there (Jean 2014, 383), and it was later shown on television (Bonneville 1973, 6).

Despite the film's unexpected popularity, it came under attack from critics opposed to the Quiet Revolution as well as from some of those who supported it. In *Séquences,* a film journal with close ties to the Catholic Church, Léo Bonneville, the editor, proclaimed loftily, "For us, the cinema is an art that deserves respect," insisting that it "demands . . . of those who serve it that they believe in their subject and treat it with sincerity." After complaining about the film's "detachment," he noted that it had made "a splash" in France and commented, "No need to say more" (1965, 13). From the opposite side of the ideological divide, Robert Daudelin dismissed it as "an impressionistic and improvised chronicle of the life and love affairs of a campus, where all social preoccupations and any idea of protest seems [*sic*] missing" (1980, 96). In his survey of films from this period, Yves Lever agreed that "except for a slightly iconoclastic tone or anticlerical moment, nothing in this film refers to the Quiet Revolution" (1991, 407).

Although the film did, in effect, present itself as a reportage on Quebec at the time of the Quiet Revolution, with traditional values and Catholic theology giving way to a new, more individualist lifestyle, there is certainly no explicit reference to political protest. According to Lever, the film ignores the "highly innovative ideas" that were emerging at the university and would "profoundly influence the course of things" (1991, 407), but in 1961, during the film's production, the writer Claude Jasmin complained of university students in general that they "do not partake of any revolutionary or even evolutionary movement" (quoted in Loiselle 2007, 59). Within a year, the political implications of the Quiet Revolution would emerge in full force, but here the filmmakers were content to "seize an atmosphere" (Jean 2014, 384), and the winds of change are apparent mainly in the lack of deference to the rules and ideas that had traditionally applied to university life.

When Nicole attends a philosophy class, the lecturer describes the ideals of Christian marriage and refers to Saint Thomas's insistence that sex is for "generation." There is an abrupt cut to couples lying on the grass in a churchyard, and then the camera moves around the class, paying special attention to the legs of the female students. Later, when she goes to see Les Cyniques, a stand-up comedian welcomes "rosary fans" to *Cult Night in Canada*, in a sketch that mocks the religious broadcasts that families tuned into in great numbers by translating their language into that of the equally popular broadcasts of all-in wrestling: a priest even delivers a plug for Red Cap Beer (an actual brand, but punning on the color of a Cardinal's hat). As in much of their later work, Les Cyniques here create a virtual montage effect, much like those Arcand would develop in his films, juxtaposing two apparently opposed phenomena to bring out the unexpected elements that link them. Their humor, much of which "would today be described as politically incorrect" (Aird 2013, 32), foreshadows the satiric provocations in Arcand's films, but the group, which disbanded in 1972, remained committed to the separatist cause, and their work never excited the kind of denunciations that have greeted much of the filmmaker's output.[3]

This was, in fact, the first show put on by the group, which would eventually settle down to a four-man team but that, on this occasion, had twelve members, including Arcand (who was also responsible for publicizing the event in the student newspaper; Aird 2013, 25, 491n9). Their irreverent attitude to Catholicism made them a major force in the Quiet Revolution and was calculated to outrage the old guard (and the critics at *Séquences*), as was the film's title, which is an ironic allusion to the formula used in the confessional when someone confesses to a sexual sin. The priest would then ask, "Alone or with others?"; however, in the context of the discourses around the Quiet Revolution, the title also draws attention to the challenge of the new individualism to the traditional emphasis on the collective. As Nicole rides on a bus during the credits sequence, the title appears with the word *SEUL* emphasized by capital letters and repetition, and the film shows her struggling to integrate herself into the rites of collective life on campus. In the final sequence, she overcomes her loneliness and settles for a romantic union (however temporary) with Pierre.

Despite the general indifference of critics at the time and the oblivion to which it was subsequently consigned, *Seul ou avec d'autres* is still of much more than historical interest. As Arcand admitted, it is somewhat incoherent due to a lack of resources and experience, as well as the different interests of the filmmakers involved, but its depiction of modern youth illustrates the impact of the Quiet Revolution on Quebec culture and some of the contradictions that it entailed. The adaptation of documentary techniques pointed forward to later films that were accepted as more successful examples of this strategy, but it should be noted that *À tout prendre* also came under attack from critics on both sides. In the radical film journal *Objectif*, Michel Patenaude objected that it tried out "all styles imaginable, without ever adopting its own" (1963, 43), while Bonneville, in his review in *Séquences*, complained that the only rebellion in the film takes place "at the level of the individual" (1965, 14).[4] While *Le chat dans le sac* was widely accepted as a more adequate response to the challenges of the Quiet Revolution, even it ended with its protagonist at an impasse. The ambiguities and contradictions of *Seul ou avec d'autres* were, to some extent, endemic to the culture within which it was made.

ICONOCLASTIC HISTORY

The success of *Seul ou avec d'autres* was impressive enough that the student council agreed to support a follow-up film. *Jusqu'au cou* (Up to the neck; 1964) dealt more explicitly with the political dimensions of the Quiet Revolution, depicting a philosophy student whose pursuit of a young woman, who is his father's mistress, involves him with a group of activists planning a bombing. Héroux was now credited as the sole director as well as the screenwriter, but the film was not well received and is now even harder to find than its predecessor. Arcand may have contributed to the screenplay, but by this time, he had graduated and found a job, which led to his decision to abandon graduate studies and become a filmmaker. He had applied for a summer job at the NFB, not knowing that some of the filmmakers who had assisted on *Seul ou avec d'autres* had told Fernand Dansereau, the head of French-language production, "If ever he asks for a job, give him one" (Arcand, quoted in Jean 1989b, 46). He was promptly hired and asked to write a report on the Board's existing films about Canadian history in order to prepare for a new series of historical films that had been commissioned for the centenary of the Canadian Confederation in 1967.

In his report, Arcand explained that what he called "modern historical science" was "moving away from the cult of the hero to focus exclusively on documents and social structures" (quoted in La Rochelle 2005, 297). He put forward his belief that history is important only for the light it sheds on the present: "History is not a series of dramatic or comical anecdotes, it is above all a knowledge of chains of events leading up to the present moment. The goal of this knowledge is to explain the present situation and, to some degree, shed light on future prospects opening up before us at the present time" (298). His recommendation was that the NFB should "produce a series of film documents that would . . . provide a synthesis of the history of Canada under the French regime" (297), and he made it clear that this series should adopt his view of history as opposed to the traditional accounts that glorified the great men who had founded Quebec.

After finishing his report, Arcand was asked to come up with "a sample scenario" (quoted in Houle, Leduc, and Hamelin 1971, 13), and he wrote one for a short documentary on Samuel de Champlain, the French explorer who founded Quebec City, before he returned to the university. However, since none of the contracted filmmakers at the NFB wanted to make a historical film, Dansereau decided to ask Arcand to direct it. Given the tenor of Arcand's report and his frequent contributions at the time to *Parti pris*, Dansereau must have known that he was taking a risk. He was confiding the task of making a film on Champlain, a revered figure in Quebec history, to an inexperienced young man with a political agenda. As we shall see, the result was the first of many of Arcand's films that embarrassed the Board, but he had now become a permanent employee there with job security.

At this early stage of his career, Arcand had evidently not developed his aversion to historical reconstruction, since of the thirteen ideas for historical subjects mentioned in his report, three are said to offer opportunities for "dramatization" (quoted in La Rochelle 2005, 299). However, the prospect of making a documentary on a historical topic presented a challenge in light of his insistence in the report that history was only of value for what it said about the present situation. Since documentaries are necessarily composed of visual material filmed in the present, depictions of the past could only take the form of images of monuments or dramatizations. The exception to this rule is the compilation film, but there were obviously no filmed records of the early history of Quebec. This problem was only heightened by the direct cinema approach, which depended on capturing reality as it unfolded before the camera. Arcand's *Champlain* (1964) and the two short films that followed it, *Les Montréalistes* (*Ville-Marie*; 1965) and *La route de l'Ouest* (*The Westward Road*; 1965), were definitely not in the tradition of direct cinema, but the budding filmmaker found cinematic ways of imposing his vision on the material.

Arcand acknowledged that it was Bernard Gosselin who "showed [him] how to make films." Gosselin, who had assisted Brault on *Seul ou avec d'autres*, was the cinematographer on *Champlain* and was involved in editing the film. Arcand says of the experience, "Since he wanted to show me everything and I wanted to learn everything, we put everything into *Champlain*" (quoted in Houle, Leduc, and Hamelin 1971, 13). The film was part of an NFB series called *Artisans de notre histoire* (Makers of our history) and, as such, was intended to celebrate the achievements of the seventeenth-century explorer who became known as "the father of New France." Although the voice-over commentary mentions this formula at the beginning, and the film recounts the history of Champlain's activities in North America from his arrival in 1603 to his death in 1635, the objective is less to celebrate the historical importance of a great man than to explore the social and economic factors that shaped the colonial enterprise. The commentary, spoken by a female voice—as opposed to the authoritative male voice-of-God in classic documentaries—describes the events in Champlain's life, while a male voice reads extracts from contemporary texts, including the reports published by Champlain on his frequent returns to France. Shots of the locations mentioned (obviously taken in the present) and stylized drawings by Frédéric Back illustrate the narration, avoiding the need for dramatization.

Two devices in particular broke with the expected approach to historical documentaries and led to a great deal of controversy. The frequent allusions in the commentary to events occurring in Europe at the time are the first example of Arcand's concern with "the interdependence of things" (Véronneau 1987–1988, 24) and serve, in this case, to contrast the privations of life in the new colony with the state of civilization in the Old World. Similarly, the buoyant brass music from the period on the soundtrack (played by Le Quintette de cuivres de Montréal) contrasts with the harsh conditions that confront Champlain in the New World (and with the drumming that accompanies his dealings with the native peoples). What proved even more disturbing was the inclusion of shots of present-day Quebec City, especially in the final sequence, which consists of a montage of shots of the modern city in which Champlain's name is used as a brand name for various businesses and attractions. The NFB responded to complaints about the film by producing a new version called *Québec 1603, Samuel de Champlain*, about half the length of the original, which eliminated all the present-day shots and all the references to events taking place elsewhere. It became a conventional chronicle of Champlain's exploits and a reinforcement of his status as the father of French Canada, which is now mentioned at the end rather than the beginning.

As Réal La Rochelle pointed out, *Champlain* is not the "vibrant homage" the NFB expected but "the revelation of a talented adventurer . . . in the service

"The Father of New France": Champlain's name is adopted by the tourist industry.

of the economic interests of French colonization" (1971, 3). Arcand's view of the explorer and his historical reputation accords with that of the American historian Mason Wade in his book *The French Canadians*, originally published in 1955, in which he argues that the principles that guided Champlain's actions were "first trade, then geographical curiosity, and finally missionary activity. This order is often reversed by French-Canadian historians, partly because history in French Canada has so largely been written by idealistic clerics" (1968, 11). Arcand's film pays due attention to Champlain's restless exploration in the vain search for a passage to the north or west that would offer a new route to China and to his interaction with the indigenous peoples, who were sometimes friendly but resistant to the missionaries who tried to convert them to Christianity. Yet it also makes clear that the prime motive for colonization was trade, especially the fur trade, and that the establishment of settlements was designed to ensure French control of the territory. The spirit of the Quiet Revolution is very apparent in this attempt to "destabilise the version of history that had been offered in Québec schools for generations" (MacKenzie 2004, 142). As Yves Lever suggests, the film is "one of the best indicators of the Quiet Revolution" in which Arcand "reveals an astonishing freedom of mind" (1991, 135).

If Arcand's original script had been accepted, the film would have been even more outspoken in its attack on the myth of Champlain. However, the NFB's historical advisers asked for changes, and he had to write a new version that met with their approval (Véronneau 1987–1988, 24). In the first version of the commentary, there was a long passage asking why the French even wanted a colony in this inhospitable area of North America: "What justification can be found for this artificial country built against the laws of history? Champlain? Missionaries? Their tombs are silent and our birth inexplicable" (quoted in Véronneau 1987–1988, 25). Once the film was finished, the NFB also forced Arcand to remove a sequence that suggested that Champlain was a pedophile (La Rochelle 2005, 86). However, during the shoot, the director, like other NFB filmmakers, had quietly reinstated some of the contentious passages from the first draft (Véronneau 1987–1988, 24).

Presumably, Arcand was not surprised to find that "the tone of the film did not please the anglophone director of production Mr. Grant MacLean" or that, when it was shown on television, "there were protests from several historico-political associations" (quoted in Houle, Leduc, and Hamelin 1971, 14). According to Lever, "The NFB thought it would be good to present it at the annual congress of the Association canadienne-française des éducateurs de langue française in 1965, thinking that this informed public would be receptive to the 'revolutionary' conception of this film and to its demystifying dimension. It was quite the reverse" (1991, 133). Nor was it unexpected that *Champlain* was not welcomed at *Séquences,* where Father Henri-Paul Sénécal dismissed it as "a film of a supercilious and detached style," which offered "a miserabilist portrait" of the great man (1964, 41). In particular, the critic objected to "the arbitrary linkage of Canadian history to universal history, which has the effect of significantly diminishing Champlain's historical stature," and of course he objected to the sequence depicting the "ridiculous exploitation of Champlain's name" in the modern city (41–42).

However, if the film offended the defenders of the faith, it also refused to adopt a clear political perspective such as might have been expected from a radical contributor to *Parti pris.* Thus Pierre Véronneau argues, "Even if it translates into a revised history, stamped by Marxist thought, *Champlain* stands apart from the nationalist awakening of the 1960s, which proclaimed the importance of the survival of the francophone people." Accordingly, he sees the film as the first expression of an outlook that permeates Arcand's later films and results in a cinema that "feeds on paradox rather than on certainty" (1995, 13).

Despite the reservations about the film, from both inside and outside the NFB, Arcand was allowed to make two more films in the series. In the case of *Les Montréalistes,* Arcand did not write the scenario, but the film deconstructs the official version of events as much as *Champlain* had done. It deals with the origins of Montreal, just as the earlier film was concerned with the settlement of Quebec City. It recounts the establishment of a religious community known as

"The times are changing": the Quiet Revolution in progress at the beginning of *Les Montréalistes*.

Ville-Marie in 1642, where a group of nuns could pursue their devotions away from what they perceived as the decadence of French society. They were also dedicated to converting the local "savages," but the community was forced to become a fort in order to protect itself from attacks by the Iroquois. Ironically, as the commentary points out, the colony would grow to become the "business center" of French Canada in complete contrast to the values of those who founded it.

As in *Champlain*, Arcand frames this story with sequences set in contemporary Montreal. The film opens with shots of the demolition of a church, in the ruins of which the camera picks out a newspaper with a headline proclaiming, "The times are changing," underlining the impact of the Quiet Revolution on the Catholic values on which the city was founded. At the end, there is a sudden cut to the neon lights of modern Montreal, where we see fashion models posing in a museum with wax figures that have been used earlier in the film to represent the historical personages who settled Ville-Marie. Once again, these modern sequences were calculated to unsettle the official story and to demonstrate that, since history is of value only for what it tells us about the present, it is important to question received notions of what really happened in the past.

Yet the real challenge of this film comes not from the present-day shots but from its account of the religious motivations of the city's founders. As Arcand describes his view of their behavior, they were "real believers," but their "faith was so excessive that it could border on sexual pathology" (quoted in Ramirez 2014, 153). The piety of the nuns, and their teachings, emphasized the need for "mortification," and we see a nun praying with a whip beside her. Arcand was, however, made to cut a shot in which the nun flagellated herself even though he insisted he could "document its historical accuracy" (MacKenzie 2004, 143). He was allowed to include a text written by a nun that refers to the flesh as an "enemy," and the commentary refers to the original settlement as a "folie à dieu."[5] As might be expected, then, *Séquences* was enraged by a film that was acidly, but correctly, identified as "an extrapolation of the past considered from the angle of the present" in which the filmmakers depicted "a page of religious history through the deforming prism of their anti-religious prejudices" (Sénécal 1966, 51). On the other hand, in *Le Devoir*, Jean Basile praised Arcand for "taking an objective and perceptive look at a 'people without history' in such a way that he ends up finding one and imposing it on us." He thought the film offered "a new spirit, a new vision of things" (quoted in Lever 1991, 323).

As MacKenzie describes it, "The film becomes a narrative of the Catholic history of Montreal, a history based on the celebration of repression and pain," which, he suggests, helps explain "the guilt-ridden narratives of the first cycle of French-Canadian features," such as *Un homme et son péché* and *La petite Aurore* (2004, 142). Yet while the iconoclastic vision of *Les Montréalistes*, like that of *Champlain* before it, can be seen as the product of Arcand's cynicism, what is most important for his future development is the emergence of a method of constructing films using "specifically cinematic means . . . that suggest more than they say" (Véronneau 1987–1988, 25–26). Thus in these short historical films, Arcand does not reject the traditional versions of history outright but exposes the contradictions and bad faith that have transformed history into myth. In other words, he depicts the legendary figures who explored and settled Quebec not as frauds and hypocrites but as human beings caught up in historical forces that they did not fully understand and whose reputations have been inflated to suit the ideological purposes of those who followed them. By juxtaposing past and present, and by creating a counterpoint between image and commentary, "he is able to support rather contradictory theses because the organization of his films does not correspond to a univocal discourse" (Véronneau 1987–1988, 26).

The final film in what became known as Arcand's historical trilogy is quite different from its predecessors.[6] Rather than being concerned with a specific period in Quebec history, *La route de l'Ouest* explores a much broader topic, the question of who first discovered Canada. Although Arcand himself has virtually disowned the film, claiming, "It was so bad that it was greeted with the most beneficent silence" (quoted in Houle, Leduc, and Hamelin 1971, 14), it does take his thought further in ways that anticipate his future work. The opening commentary refers to the gaps and mysteries in our knowledge of the past, accompanied by a montage of shots of rockets blasting off and controllers at NASA, suggesting a parallel between the explorers who sailed west from Europe in the distant past and the present-day exploration of space. After an allusion to the peoples who came to North America from the East, ancestors of the indigenous population encountered by later colonists, the film describes explorers from various parts of Europe who gradually reached different parts of the continent. A recurring image of a map represents the parts of Canada discovered by different explorers as if they were islands until the gaps are filled in by later discoveries. The last sequence returns to the space program, juxtaposed with Disneyland's representations of the past and future. A final caption quotes Nietzsche on the human need to keep moving west in search of the unknown.

Although La Rochelle objected that the film "depicts the past with romanticism and nostalgia" (1971, 3), its main concern is with how we can know the past. The commentary begins with a poetic invocation of humanity's place within the universe: "Uncertainty is the most familiar condition of human intelligence. Lost in a cosmos whose laws we do not know, confusion and anxiety accompany us every day. Because we know today that the sands are moving and that what we call knowledge is just a series of mirrors that reveal only new mysteries." As Marcel Jean points out, "This film announces the content of *Jésus de Montréal* 25 years in advance" (1989c, 63), and these opening words anticipate the sonorous commentary that accompanies the images of outer space in a documentary shown at the planetarium in the later film. In this sense, *La route de l'Ouest* establishes Arcand as "the filmmaker of uncertainty," whose refusal to believe in "a unique version" of truth would set him at odds with all those who claim to possess all the answers (Véronneau 1987–1988, 24).

The view of history underpinning all three of these short films is, as we have seen, derived from the work of Maurice Séguin, who saw human thought as being shaped by "the economy/politics/culture triad" (La Rochelle 2005, 88) rather than by the activities of great individuals somehow divorced from these forces. Such a perspective differentiates Arcand's films from those of Pierre Perrault, who, in *Pour la suite du monde*, initiated a body of work that calls for the recovery of the past to create a foundation for a future state that would be shaped by the French Canadian heritage. Without necessarily rejecting that heritage, Arcand's films call for a more complex engagement with history that would allow its implications to be examined critically in the light of the needs of the present.

2 · SUBJECTIVE DOCUMENTARIES

Arcand at the NFB

A good documentary is always improvised. The filmmaker follows his camera.

—Denys Arcand

Arcand's arrival at the National Film Board, as a result of connections made during the filming of *Seul ou avec d'autres,* was somewhat fortuitous, as was his engagement as a director because no one at the Board wanted to make historical documentaries. Nevertheless, his status as a civil servant ensured that he could continue to work there, even if his films often failed to satisfy his employers. After *La route de l'Ouest,* however, two other historical documentary projects were canceled, and Arcand had "nothing more to do" (quoted in Houle, Leduc, and Hamelin 1971, 14). He wrote the screenplay for Michel Brault's *Entre la mer et l'eau douce* (1967) and then left the NFB, along with Brault, Gilles Groulx, Bernard Gosselin, and Jean Dansereau, to form a company called Les Cinéastes associés. They worked on a project for the Quebec Pavilion of the Montreal Expo, which was to take place in 1970 to celebrate the centenary of the Canadian Federation, and Arcand directed a short film called *Montréal, un jour d'été* (*Montreal on a Summer's Day*; 1965), also intended for the expo. However, the company found it difficult to secure interesting commissions. Although Arcand no longer had job security at the NFB, he returned there and made two more shorts, *Volleyball* (1966) and *Parcs atlantiques* (*Atlantic Parks*; 1967), commissioned by the federal government; however, in 1968, he found himself reduced to making commercials for Coca-Cola.

He returned to his family home in Deschambault and contemplated becoming a history teacher. Instead, he decided that in the future, he would make only, as he put it, "films that pleased and interested me" (quoted in Bonneville 1979, 36), and he returned once again to the NFB on a freelance basis. He proposed the project that became *On est au coton* (We're fed up), and rather surprisingly, the proposal was accepted, perhaps because Jacques Godbout, a prominent novelist and filmmaker, was the director of French production at the time (but not for long; Evans 1991, 180). The resulting film was the first of three feature-length documentaries Arcand made for the NFB. *Québec: Duplessis et après . . .* (*Quebec: Duplessis and After*) followed quickly, but *Le confort et l'indifférence* (*Comfort and Indifference*) came only after Arcand had made the three crime films that will be subject of the next chapter. All three documentaries came under fire from critics inside and outside the Board, and although it means departing from the otherwise chronological organization of this book, I will treat them together in this chapter in order to explore the ways in which they push against the limits of the documentary mode as well as those of the NFB as an institution.

Arcand's attitude toward the NFB was highly ambivalent (like his attitude to most things). On the one hand, he welcomed the freedom it offered him during production, pointing out that *On est au coton* was "a colossal undertaking" that required employing six men for two years, which was "possible only at the NFB" (quoted in Houle, Leduc, and Hamelin 1971, 22). On the other hand, films were subject to censorship during preproduction and after they were made. All projects had to be approved by a committee that required a detailed scenario and could demand changes to remove undesirable elements, as Arcand had found on *Champlain* and *Les Montréalistes*. Given the lack of oversight during filming, it was fairly easy, as Arcand had already realized, to deviate from the approved scenario, but the finished product could be recut (as was the case with the alternative version of *Champlain*), censored, or even withheld from release. The latter rarely happened, but in the fraught political climate of the late 1960s, several Québécois filmmakers ran into trouble after making films that were seen to support the separatist option. In an essay published in *Parti pris* in 1964, Arcand described himself and his colleagues at the NFB as "colonized" filmmakers whose work had to reflect "the opinion of the Canadian government" (quoted in La Rochelle 2005, 305–306).

As noted in the previous chapter, Arcand's historical shorts did not adopt the direct cinema style favored by other young filmmakers at the Board. However, although Bill Marshall is right to say that Arcand was "less influenced by *le direct* than by a historicizing *longue durée* which in its use of often ironic counterpoint challenged the orthodoxies of the NFB's official discourse" (2001, 149), his subsequent feature-length documentaries do share certain characteristics with direct cinema. They eschew voice-over commentary, and during production, they were open to unexpected developments that could change the filmmaker's view of the subject matter. Thus in *On est au coton*, Arcand expected to find textile workers angry at their working conditions but instead found that they seemed quite fatalistic, and *Québec: Duplessis et après . . .* and *Le confort et l'indifférence* were, of course, filmed before the outcomes, respectively, of the 1970 provincial election and the 1980 referendum. However, with their constant use of comparison and contrast, largely created by organizing the filmed material during post-production, these films seem closer to the "essay film," a documentary form that calls into question the myth of objectivity: they "articulate a subjective, personal point of view" (Rascaroli 2009, 3) and "represent an attempt to work out some reasoned line of discourse on a problem" (Lopate 2017, 112).[1] Since the problems that Arcand's films address have to do with the situation in Quebec as he sees it, they offer a perfect illustration of the interdependence of the personal and collective in his work.

In both direct cinema and essay films, the presence of the filmmakers is openly acknowledged to varying degrees, challenging the conventional notion of documentary objectivity. The difference is that, in direct cinema, the aim is to engage with the film's subjects and allow them to express themselves (as in *Pour la suite du monde*), while in the essay film, what is important is the argument that represents the filmmaker's personal response to the reality depicted. Arcand does not appear before the camera in his films in the manner of Michael Moore (or Michael Rubbo in his NFB work), but he did call *On est au coton* his "first personal film" (quoted in Loiselle 1995, 140). Although he acknowledged the teamwork that went into making the films, he called "the idea of documentary-truth, so-called cinéma-vérité . . . complete humbug" and insisted, with respect to his documentaries, "I speak for nobody but myself." For Arcand, in documentary, "coherence is not created in the shooting but in the editing" (quoted in Bonneville 1979, 39).

The result was three films that "are among the most powerfully pessimistic documentaries Canada has produced" (Harkness 1989, 235). Arcand set out to make films that were far removed from the typical NFB documentaries, which were designed, he said, to prove that "all goes well in Canada" (quoted in Harkness 1989, 235), and it is hardly surprising that they put an even greater strain on his relationship with the Board than his historical shorts. As discussed in the introduction, his pessimistic outlook led to a reputation for cynicism, but it is better seen as akin to the "negative dialectics" practiced by the theorists of the Frankfurt school, such as Theodor Adorno and, especially, Herbert Marcuse, whom Arcand has acknowledged as an important influence on his thinking (Sklar 1986b, 48) and whom he quotes in *On est au coton*. From this perspective, it is vital to resist the "affirmative" ideology that supports the status quo by concealing contradictions and problems. The effect, in Arcand's films, is not simply a gloomy denunciation of the prevailing system (although this system is seen to be totally corrupt) but rather an iconoclastic demolition of anything that is taken for granted. As I have said elsewhere, his "tactics of negation and exaggeration discourage ready-made responses that provide comfort by ignoring the full complexity of the situation" (Leach 2003, 90).

"THAT'S THE WAY THE SYSTEM IS BUILT": *ON EST AU COTON*

The project that Arcand pitched to the NFB in 1968 did not concern the textile industry. At that time, it was called *Les informateurs*, which translates literally to "the informants" but here means something like "the advisers." It was intended to be "a three-part story of technocrats who are the backbone of the modern state" (Evans 1991, 180). Arcand wanted "to bring to light the limits of technological and managerial thought then prevalent in North America" (Véronneau 1995, 15), but as he was researching this topic, he soon decided that he needed a test case to confront the technocrats with a difficult challenge. The textile industry was a major pillar of the Quebec economy, but as in many other Western countries, it was struggling to compete with less expensive foreign imports and with the effects of the emergent global economy. Once the filmmakers became aware of the dire situation of the workers in the textile mills, the concern with technocracy slipped into the background (but as we shall see, it did not completely disappear).

Later events suggest that the film's denunciation of the working conditions of the mainly francophone employees and the business practices of the mainly anglophone employers took the NFB and the mill owners by surprise. Yet the title should have given them due warning. *On est au coton* obviously refers to "cotton" as one of the mainstays of the textile industry, but it is also a pun on a colloquial Québécois phrase that has been variously translated as "we're fed up," "we're angry," and "we're exhausted." It is likely that this play on words was lost on the English-speaking owners and on Sydney Newman, who had been appointed NFB commissioner in August 1970, but another warning sign might have been Arcand's choice of Gérald Godin as the main researcher on the project. Godin, who had established a reputation as a poet, was a founding member of *Parti pris*, the militant journal for which Arcand had written many articles. Shortly after his involvement in the film, he was one of the intellectuals arrested during the October Crisis, and he later became a Parti Québécois minister. Using a fright tactic familiar from the Duplessis years, the Canadian Textile Institute accused him of being "an avowed Marxist" (*La Presse* 1971, D9).

Filming took place from September 1968 to February 1970 (Jean 2014, 312), but the film only started to run into trouble after the huge amount of material the filmmakers had shot was edited into an almost three-hour feature that focused on working conditions in the industry and the impact of mill closures.

During the shoot, as Arcand acknowledged, "I had complete freedom to do what I wanted in extraordinary conditions," and in the process, he had found that the workers were "neither desperate nor angry," as he had first thought, but apparently resigned to their situation (quoted in Bonneville 1979, 37). In fact, the workers in the film do not seem so much resigned as "fed up," as the title suggests. While they are not activists, like the strikers of the past depicted in the historical sections of the film, the repression with which the Duplessis government put down past strikes, with the aid of the police and the clergy, had been replaced by a more insidious style of management in which companies felt no concern for the well-being of their employees, who received little support from politicians or even from the union, which past workers had fought so hard to get accepted. During past strikes, the owners had threatened to close the mills but, when *On est au coton* was shot, the mills were closing anyway, so strikes were no longer an effective option.

The film opens with the camera moving toward a man in an office. A caption identifies him as the deputy mayor of Coaticook, a town in southeast Quebec close to the U.S. border, where the local textile mill was scheduled for closure. Although he seems rather uncomfortable, he welcomes the off-screen filmmakers and confirms that they are federal employees from the National Film Board. This rather artificial introduction (since it is unlikely that this is really the film crew's first meeting with the official) is followed by a shot of a teletype machine loudly punching out a list of the film's collaborators printed on NFB letterhead.[2] The camera then penetrates into the mill and tracks past the machines and their operatives with the deafening noise of the machines on the soundtrack; when there is a sudden cut to the empty factory after it has closed, the visceral effect of the silence that follows underscores the oppressiveness of the workplace and the vacuum created by its closure.[3] The deputy mayor then explains that he was unable to argue with the company's decision after he had seen its books.

This opening sequence thus establishes the film crew as an active (if largely unseen) presence in the film while depicting both the weakness of politicians in dealings with private enterprise and the terrible alternative facing the workers: dreadful working conditions or unemployment. Although we do glimpse the filmmakers on-screen on a few later occasions, the only sequence in which attention is drawn to the director occurs when a policeman writes him a ticket for filming outside one of the mills without permission. As we have seen, Arcand insisted that the film reflects his own personal response to a situation that he had not known about before, but the presence of the filmmakers is felt less in terms of their interventions during the process of filming and more in the arrangement of the various elements during the editing process. As in the three historical shorts and in many of Arcand's later films, the viewer is confronted with what Véronneau calls a "discursive structure" that "alternates the past and

"Have you asked permission?": the director receives a ticket in *On est au coton*.

the present, and compares and cross-checks them" (1995, 23), ultimately leaving the viewer to make connections among the various elements of the film and draw conclusions from them.

Alongside shots taken inside and outside a number of mills, the organization of the film weaves together several different elements, or what Gilles Marsolais calls "threads" (pun presumably intended), to create its overall view of the textile industry (1992, 58): the present crisis in Coaticook, a historical account of workers' struggles in the past, and a political analysis of the larger system in which the textile industry operates. The first of these threads is conveyed in sequences depicting emergency meetings and individual interviews that illustrate the impact of the closing of the mill on its workers. We learn that even when the mill was open, many workers had to take a second job to make ends meet, and there is an interview with a retired worker who has contracted silicosis and received no pension, accompanied by shots of flakes of cotton adhering to the machinery in the mill. In several extracts from an interview with Carmen Bertrand, a young worker at the mill, she describes her first day on the job and talks about the things she plans to buy after the mill closes, which is when she will move to Montreal and, she hopes, make more money.

The present situation is placed in a historical context through sequences in which Madeleine Parent, a former activist, describes strikes in the industry from the 1930s to the 1950s, which were brutally put down by the Duplessis regime. She reads from trial documents in which she was accused of treason, and photographs of police attacking workers support her testimony. Although the workers won the right to unionize after a strike in 1946, Parent describes another strike in 1952 that was broken when the union signed a collective agreement against the workers' wishes. This historical material sets up a contrast between the activism of the past and the apparent lack of resistance in the present. But it also helps explain the current situation: the violent oppression of the Duplessis years has been replaced by a managerial culture in which employers, with the help of compliant unions, have developed more subtle methods of handling dissent. The effectiveness of these methods is underlined at the end of the film with a sequence depicting the meeting of a committee—made up of owners, union representatives, and politicians—failing to come up with any really constructive proposals.

The third thread follows Bertrand Saint-Onge, a young worker who sets out to educate himself about the causes of the industry's decline. In a key sequence, which derives from Arcand's original concern with technocracy, we see Claude Lemelin, an economist who was then the financial correspondent for *Le Devoir*, lecturing on the industrial and political context that has led to the closing of the mills. He stands in front of a whiteboard on which he has outlined the intricate relations of a multinational web of companies, of which Dominion Textiles in Quebec is only a small part. When the camera pans from him to reveal Bertrand sitting in an otherwise empty classroom, Lemelin points out that he, as an individual worker, belongs at the very bottom of this economic chain.

The development of these various materials filmed on location is punctuated by the shots of a teletype machine tapping out fragments of text taken from Herbert Marcuse's book *One-Dimensional Man*, originally published in 1964. Although Arcand has acknowledged his debt to Marcuse, the source is not given in the film so that these fragments function, as Craig Moyes has suggested, like "maxims, self-contained gnomic truths" (2006, 97). The first declares, "The web of domination has become the web of Reason itself," and later we are told, "The insanity of the whole absolves the particular insanities" (Marcuse 1991, 169, 52). At the end, the final fragment brings together the film's stress on the noise of the machines with its political implications, since, according to Marcuse, "the machine [is] the most effective political instrument in any society" (3). If these fragmentary statements had been presented in a fuller and more coherent way, they would have provided a theoretical or philosophical context to match the historical one that Madeleine Parent's testimony offers or the economic one provided by Lemelin. As it is, these intertitles may seem to offer ready-made "truths," but it is left up to viewers to figure out exactly how they apply to the other elements that they see or hear in the film.

However, there is one more thread—the most obtrusive one—that places the social and economic issues in the volatile context of Quebec after the Quiet Revolution. This thread consists of interviews conducted in English with Edward F. King, the president of Dominion Textiles, the company that owned many of the mills depicted. In one long sequence, he sits comfortably in his office and describes how he started out as an office boy and worked his way up despite not having any real understanding of what went on in the mills, referring to himself as an "interested spectator." Another sequence intercuts King's account of his career with Bertrand's description of how he came to work in the textile industry. King's cultured English voice contrasts with the colloquial French of the workers, reinforcing the impression that they are the victims of a system in which the politics of class can be mapped onto the politics of language. King even says that while he appreciates the difficulties facing the workers, they need to be "realistic" because, in his words, "We can't let one place drag us down." It is a "question of profits and investors," and "that's the way the system is built."

King had obviously collaborated quite openly with the filmmakers, apparently thinking they would paint a flattering picture of him and the industry; one interview is even conducted while he is being driven in his limousine. However, once he saw the finished product, he demanded that all the sequences in which he appeared be removed from the film. He claimed that he was "scandalized by the content of the film, based according to him on the class struggle" and outraged that the Canadian government would support "such subversive projects" (*La Presse* 1971, D9). Other mill owners also made representations to the NFB, pointing out "certain factual inaccuracies" (Evans 1991, 182). Arcand was told to remove all traces of King from the film, but by the time the reedited version was finished, Quebec was reeling under the impact of the FLQ kidnappings and the invoking of the War Measures Act.[4] The NFB then demanded the removal of another sequence in which FLQ sympathizers talked of violence as a possible solution to the workers' plight, and then, in March 1971, Newman decided that the film was so inflammatory that it would not be released at all and justified this action on the grounds that the documentary did not "fairly picture the textile industry it attempted to portray" (quoted in Evans 1991, 183). Two months later, Radio-Canada, the French-language service of the CBC, in collaboration with the Canadian Textile Institute, aired a series of films that presented a much more positive view of the industry (*La Presse* 1971, D9).

The politics of language in the film were echoed in a report on the ban in *Cinéma Québec* in which Newman's justification is printed in English, aligning the NFB treatment of the filmmakers with the attitude of the predominately anglophone bosses to their workers (*Cinéma Québec* 1971, 31). However, two copies of the film had "escaped" from the NFB: one was the full version, the other the edited version (in which King's interviews were replaced by Arcand's voice describing what was missing over a black screen). Many videotape copies were made from these prints, and it has been estimated that more than twenty thousand spectators saw the film (Perreault 1976b, D9), far more than it would likely have attracted if it had not been banned. Most of those who saw it were students, and the film, as well as its treatment by the NFB, became a propaganda tool for the separatist cause. *On est au coton* could thus be said to have provoked "a collective gesture of resistance on the part of the most progressive elements of the Quebec population against what could be called, euphemistically, the NFB's unfortunate decision" (Perreault 1976b, D9).

Arcand felt "bitter that the workers for whom it was made" still had not had a chance to see the film, and *Le Devoir* published a letter from the Secretariat for Political Action of the Confederation of National Trade Unions that "called for the release of the film and demanded that the workers be allowed to decide if it was realistic" (Evans 1991, 183). The NFB did finally release the cut version of the film in 1976, but it was not until 1992 that it created an English-subtitled version on video with the rather bland title *Cotton Mill, Treadmill*. The complete version, which had been preserved in the NFB's vaults, only became available in 2004, after King's son authorized its inclusion in a DVD set of Arcand's documentaries (Jean 2014, 313).[5]

The film's critical reception has clearly been affected by the controversy to which it gave rise. In his history of the NFB, Gary Evans takes a position sympathetic to the Board's viewpoint and dismisses the film as "a painfully long, cinematically clumsy piece (with the exception of impressive tracking shots on the floors of the factories)" (1991, 183), but Pierre Véronneau describes it as "one of Quebec's greatest political films" (1995, 16). As Craig Moyes has suggested, "*On est au coton* was simultaneously criticised for being both too radical and not radical enough" (2006, 91), and I have described it elsewhere as "a film that clearly presented itself as a political intervention but resisted the political categories into which critics tried to place it" (Leach 2003, 90). But this unsettling of expectations was precisely what Arcand was aiming for: Sydney Newman argued that the film did not live up to the NFB's reputation for "objectivity" and would clearly have been happier if it had an authoritative voice-of-God commentary; ironically, Gérald Godin, whose views were diametrically opposed to Newman's, thought that the film was "not didactic enough" and also thought it should have had "a narrator who could have explained the situation" (Arcand and Godin 1971, 33). From Arcand's point of view, a commentary would have sabotaged the film by discouraging viewers from thinking about the issues for themselves.[6]

At the end of the film, the overwhelming noise of the machines gives way to music being played at the opening of the provincial legislature, and the camera follows politicians into the chamber and mixes with guests filing into the visitors' gallery. The formal clothes (and medals) of the all-male politicians and the small talk of the guests make clear that the plight of the workers will not be effectively addressed in this session. Music (seemingly coming from an off-screen parade) is again heard over a shot of men and women walking along a city street, interrupted by a brief shot of a black slave, apparently taken from an American Civil War film, walking toward the camera at the same pace as the people on the street. This shot is an almost subliminal allusion to the controversial book *Nègres blancs d'Amérique* (*White Niggers of America*) by Pierre Vallières, originally published in 1968 by Éditions parti pris, in which he discussed his involvement with the FLQ and likened the situation in Quebec to the United States where "to be a 'nigger' . . . is to be not a man but someone's slave" (1971, 21). Even if the film wants us to think for ourselves, it is clear that the problems it addresses are dire, and this fragmentary but obtrusive metaphor seems to emerge from the filmmaker's frustration and as an effort to nudge our thoughts in the right direction.

"DUPLESSIS IS STILL ALIVE": *QUÉBEC: DUPLESSIS ET APRÈS . . .*

Before *On est au coton* had even been edited, and before the uproar began, Arcand had begun work on another feature-length documentary. He was approached by Pierre Maheu, one of the founders of *Parti pris* and now a producer at the NFB, who wanted to make a series of films on "four great men" of Quebec culture (Arcand, quoted in Tadros 1972a, 19)—namely, the hockey player Maurice Richard, the singer Willie Lamothe, the cleric Frère André, and Maurice Duplessis.[7] Not surprisingly, Maheu offered the film on Duplessis to Arcand, who, equally predictably, agreed only "on condition that it would be concerned with the political consciousness of the Québécois rather than with the man Duplessis himself" (quoted in Bonneville 1979, 38). He chose to focus on the 1970 provincial election to explore the extent to which the Quiet Revolution had changed the political landscape since the days of the Great Darkness. As the title *Québec: Duplessis et après . . .* suggests, the film deals with the impact of the past on the present, although, as we shall see, this was not Arcand's preferred title.

The election provides the film's present tense. The filmmakers followed candidates from the four main parties: the Union Nationale, which had regained power in 1966 and had traditionally depended on the support of rural voters; the Liberal Party, whose victory in 1960 had precipitated the Quiet Revolution and which usually appealed to the urban middle class as well as Anglophones and immigrants; the newly formed Parti Québécois led by René Lévesque, a former Liberal cabinet minister with a separatist agenda; and the Créditiste (or Social Credit) Party, a highly conservative party with strong moral and religious convictions. As Arcand explained, "We had to choose ridings that were homogeneous enough as well as representative of the Quebec electoral map . . . in which there were relatively few anglophone or new Canadian voters who would skew the final count" and "without well-known political stars" among the candidates (quoted in Tadros 1972a, 20). They chose the Montreal riding of Maisonneuve (urban and working class), Joliette (a predominantly middle-class riding northeast of Montreal), and Portneuf (a rural riding on the Saint Lawrence River between Trois Rivières and Quebec City, which included Arcand's childhood home of Deschambault).

Arcand started out with the expectation that filming the election would show that the rhetoric of the candidates for all parties would demonstrate the enduring legacy of the Duplessis years and that, despite apparent differences among their platforms, there was little prospect of radical change. Unlike with *On est au coton,* he felt that these preconceptions were confirmed by what he witnessed during the campaign. He suggested that the film "clarifies the enigmatic ending of *On est au coton*" in that nothing much would change if the Union Nationale government lost power to the Liberals (as it did), and he believed, "It is not certain that Lévesque would change very much in the workers' condition" (quoted in Houle, Leduc, and Hamelin 1971, 25). In order to demonstrate his thesis, Arcand needed to provide a historical context, and as he had done in *On est au coton,* he added material in the editing stage that became an implicit commentary on what took place during the election.

The most straightforward of these elements is newsreel footage of Duplessis, whose speeches are juxtaposed with those of politicians in the present, and in one shot of Lévesque, seen from behind as he addresses a crowd, we hear Duplessis's voice superimposed on the soundtrack. Two other historical perspectives were introduced: English Canadian filmmaker Robin Spry reads extracts from the Durham Report on the state of Quebec in 1830, and actress Gisèle Trépanier (who had contributed the voice-over commentaries to *Champlain* and *Les Montréalistes*) appears on-screen as a schoolteacher reciting passages from the "catechism of electors," prepared by the Union Nationale for the 1936 election in which Duplessis first won power. Shots of the Deschambault church choir (of which Arcand and his wife were members) also provide a reminder of a past in which the Church dominated Quebec (as the presence of priests around Duplessis in many of the newsreels confirms). As Arcand pointed out, the shots of the choir performing the midnight mass on Christmas Eve required a reconstruction because "today we don't sing it any more" (quoted in Tadros 1972a, 21).

The editing of these different elements creates, even more than in *On est au coton,* what Arcand called "a mosaic of images" without apparent relation to one another that would, "with a little reflection," create meaning in the minds of the viewers (quoted in Scully 1972c, 15). As a primer for the kind of viewing the film requires, there is a precredits sequence that begins with a shot of a winter landscape and cars buried in snow, an archetypal image of Quebec but one that in the context of this film establishes the idea of a society whose development is blocked.[8] There is a cut to Durham/Spry reading the most notorious part of the report, which describes French Canadians as "a people with no literature and no history." A cut to a shot of running water, accompanied by the voice of Duplessis, is in obvious contradiction to Durham's views, praising the "ancestors" who established Quebec in "a vast land surrounded by enemies." Duplessis is then seen at a news conference calling an election while joking about his reputation as "a dictator," followed by a speaker introducing a candidate in the 1960 election. Later, the Union Nationale catechism is introduced in a classroom, where the pupils answer by rote the questions read by the teacher as in Catholic catechism classes. After the catechism berates the Liberal government "dominated by High Finance," there is a cut to hydro wires in the snow, followed by Durham describing the poor methods of farming in French Canada and then by the catechism also denouncing the state of farming in Quebec.

The film offers no overt judgment on any of these components. As we have seen, however, Arcand had more respect for Lord Durham than most Québécois, arguing that "his report remains the most just diagnosis that has yet been made of Quebec society" and adding that "while Quebec is under foreign domination, everything that Durham said remains valid" (quoted in Perreault 1972b, C9). For Arcand, Durham was "motivated by a sincere desire to improve the condition of French Canadians" (quoted in Bergeron 2012, 116), but the passages quoted in the film, read in Spry's halting French, are often patronizing in their assumption of the superiority of Anglo-Saxon culture. The report refers, for example, to the "peculiar language and manners" of the French Canadians and describes their desire for independence as delusional. As Carl Bergeron suggests, Durham plays "the role of the cynical observer" (2012, 19), and Arcand implies that many of his observations still hold true. Thus when Durham refers to the "lack of education among the habitants," we are shown a number of modern signs with obvious spelling errors.

Just as he gave Durham his due, Arcand also thought the catechism was "a marvelous political program" and said he wanted "to confer on this reading a sort of nostalgia . . . as with the singing of the mass" (quoted in Tadros 1972a, 22). As a historian, however, he must have known that most of the charges against the previous Liberal government contained in the catechism were precisely those brought against the Union Nationale government during the Duplessis era. The catechism insists that big business does not work in the public interest, but Duplessis later speaks of his reliance on "private enterprise"; the catechism accuses the previous government of giving away Quebec's resources to foreigners, but Duplessis later declares that he is seeking American, English, and French capital to create new industries (foreign ownership is also shown to be a key issue in the 1970 election). When the teacher recites the catechism denouncing the nonexistence of freedom of opinion under the Liberal regime, she is standing in an editing room at the NFB, an ironic context that suggests the NFB's suppression of *On est au coton* is analogous to the repressive tactics of the Duplessis administration outlined in Madeleine Parent's contribution to that film.

Arcand's own interpretation of the material he gathered in this film was that there were "negligible differences between a René Lévesque and a Duplessis" and that there was a clear continuity from Durham's diagnosis of the culturally deprived French Canadians to the electors who supported Duplessis and to those who have responded to "the different hopes raised in the 1970 campaign" (quoted in Scully 1972c, 15). According to Arcand, the film "became, through Duplessis, a film on the Québécois man of politics" (quoted in Tadros 1972a, 19), taking for granted what stands out when viewing the film today—namely, that all the politicians and organizers are men. Apart from the schoolteacher and two women who speak from the floor at a PQ meeting, the only women in the film are voters being wooed by male candidates. We see these men making passionate speeches, shaking hands, and visiting groups of housewives in their homes, and it is their rhetoric and body language, as much as anything else, that points to the political continuity between past and present in Quebec.

The key issues all involve the fallout of the Quiet Revolution, which had been spearheaded by Lesage's Liberals, who had been ousted in 1966 by the Union Nationale thanks to electors who apparently felt that the changes had come too quickly. However, the momentum of change was such that the new government was able to do little to reverse it and had even kept on most of the technocrats appointed by the Liberals (Godin 1991, 148). As we have seen, the most visible sign of the Quiet Revolution was the removal of the Catholic domination of Quebec culture, and another issue in the campaign was the replacement of "confessional" schools with state-run schools, an issue that had once been important to the Union Nationale but now mainly concerned the Créditistes. The other issue that troubled many voters was the FLQ's campaign of violence, apparently inspired by the Liberal promise of becoming *maîtres chez nous* and from which the PQ had to dissociate itself if it wanted to appeal to mainstream voters.

One similarity between the elections of 1936 and 1970, which the film does not overtly acknowledge, is the effect of new parties on the political status quo: in 1936, Duplessis had just founded the Union Nationale, and in 1970, Lévesque's Parti Québécois was contesting its first election. Arcand compares the intervention of these two "men of politics" when he superimposes Duplessis's voice over Lévesque's speech, but this provocation did not go unchallenged: thus Luc Perreault in *La Presse* objected that this device makes us "think automatically: the two men are saying the same thing. . . . Fundamentally the comparison does not hold because . . . the ideology of the Parti Québécois explicitly aims to break with the status quo to which Duplessis adhered" (1972a, C9). It is not clear, however, whether Arcand wanted the viewer to conclude that there was no difference between the two men or that he was simply making a point about their style of campaigning. He commented, "It is difficult to be clear and precise when the political situation in Quebec is so confused," and he insisted, "What is essential is not to know who was elected. What is essential is to pose the question of the collectivity" (quoted in Tadros 1972a, 22). Yet despite his later disavowals, it clearly did matter to Arcand who would win this election.

As it turned out, the three ridings on which the film focused chose candidates from three different parties: the PQ won in Maisonneuve, the Liberals won in Joliette, and the Créditistes won in Portneuf. Overall, the winners were the Liberals led by Robert Bourassa, and Arcand was clearly disappointed. He pointed out that two weeks before the election, it looked as if the PQ was going to win, or at least do well, but "this hope was slowly extinguished." To counter the depressing effect of this outcome, he included a parade in support of Robert Burns, the PQ candidate in Maisonneuve: he called this sequence "a moment of hope . . . before the catastrophe" (quoted in Tadros 1972a, 22). When Burns's victory is announced, we hear the choir singing "Donna Nobis Pacem" (Give us peace), followed by Bourassa speaking in English of the challenge to the Liberal Party to show that Quebec can stay in Canada; we then hear Duplessis, also speaking in English, celebrating Canadian prosperity and Durham, in French, referring to the "hopeless inferiority" of French Canadians. However we read this enigmatic montage, Arcand tempered his sense that the PQ offered a new hope for Quebec by insisting that he could not support the party "unconditionally" because even the PQ "has been infiltrated by opportunists" (quoted in Tadros 1972a, 22).

The result of the election reinforced Arcand's initial pessimism about the state of Quebec after the Quiet Revolution, and while he was editing the film, he was also coping with the outcry that led to the banning of *On est au coton*. His new film was not banned, and Arcand's explanation of the difference was typically cynical. In the earlier film, he said he was "making an almost Marxist analysis of the facts" that showed "the true holders of power were not the men of politics but the bosses of big business," whereas *Québec: Duplessis et après . . .* "at worst only makes fun of a few politicians," so the NFB could accept it (quoted in Tadros 1972a, 22). However, the released version had been censored in ways that, he felt, made the film weaker and its meaning less clear.

The first act of censorship was the NFB's rejection of Arcand's preferred title. He wanted to call the film *Duplessis est encore en vie* (Duplessis is still alive), a title that evoked a horror film and cheekily equated Duplessis with Dracula.[9] Along with this toning down of the title, the precredits sequence suffered a major cut. Originally, it was to have opened with shots taken when Arcand and his crew hid in a school auditorium to film an election address by Rémi Paul, the minister of justice in the Union Nationale government. After the introduction of the local candidate (which is still in the film), the minister walked over to the side of the stage, "took a wad of bills from his pocket and started to distribute them," at which point the title would have appeared: *Duplessis est encore en vie* (Arcand, quoted in Jean 1989b, 50). According to Arcand, this cut harmed the film because "it is not clear where it is going" at the beginning (quoted in Perreault 1972b, C9).

Ironically, because *Québec: Duplessis et après* . . . was not banned, it had much less impact than *On est au coton*. The editing process was so complicated that the film was not released until 1972, when the political situation had become even more divisive because of the events of October 1970. While critics in Quebec did try to interpret the implications of its "mosaic" structure, Gary Evans thought that Arcand had "reworked (if not abused) history to prove the tenuous cliché that history repeats itself," and he reported that "to no one's surprise, Radio-Canada rejected it in May 1972, on grounds that it was too long, its title was false, it was difficult to programme, and interest was hard to sustain" (1991, 187). The film remains important, however, as a document testifying to the tensions in Quebec after the Quiet Revolution that would lead to the election of a Parti Québécois government in 1976 and then to the 1980 referendum on independence.

"THE POLITICIANS WE DESERVE": *LE CONFORT ET L'INDIFFÉRENCE*

After finishing *Québec: Duplessis et après . . .* , but before either that film or *On est au coton* had been released, Arcand decided he wanted to add a third long documentary to follow up on the concerns raised in his previous films. He felt that since "*On est au coton* finished in a sort of cul-de-sac; *Duplessis* also, but on a political level," he needed to deal with "another cul-de-sac, which was terrorism" (quoted in Tadros 1972b, 27). However, as it turned out, he submitted his proposal for *Les terroristes* to the NFB in October 1970 on the same day that Pierre Laporte, a Liberal cabinet minister, was kidnapped by the FLQ, and the project was "understandably set aside" (Arcand, quoted in Bonneville 1979, 41).[10] Because he had been working at the Board on a freelance basis, he now found himself unemployed, but after making fiction films in the private sector for several years, he would eventually make a third feature-length documentary when he temporarily returned to the NFB in 1977. The project was now to make a film on the referendum that the PQ had promised in their election platform the year before.

Arcand began shooting the film that became *Le confort et l'indifférence* in September 1977 (La Rochelle 2005, 148). As with *On est au coton,* he had to change his original conception of the film, although in this case, it was not because he found the reality he was filming different from his preconceptions but because events beyond his control intervened. He originally intended to shoot the entire film in a factory that manufactured hockey sticks, depicting the chain of production that resulted in a finished stick while recording the workers' reactions to the unfolding campaign; "but then the company workers came out on strike" (Arcand, quoted in La Rochelle 2005, 149–150). If he had been able to carry out this plan, the film would probably have been made more securely within the direct cinema tradition, but in the event, it followed the "essay" format that Arcand had adopted in the earlier documentaries.

After his first plan collapsed, Arcand was casting around for a new approach to the referendum campaign. He credits his brother Gabriel with giving him the idea of using extracts from Niccolò Machiavelli's *The Prince,* a treatise on the methods needed by a ruler to retain power first published in 1532, to provide a kind of commentary on the political debates of 1980 (La Rochelle 2005, 150). The historical Machiavelli (1469–1527) has been called "one of the foremost cynical philosophers of modern times" (Borghini 2017), and his ideas would thus have been quite congenial to Arcand. Played by the French actor Jean-Pierre Ronfard, his interventions in the film are more frequent and more apparently authoritative than those of equivalent figures in the earlier documentaries (Madeleine Parent in *On est au coton*; Lord Durham and the schoolteacher in *Québec: Duplessis et après . . .*). Indeed, it is tempting to identify his voice with that of the filmmaker: Léo Bonneville thus referred to "the fake Machiavelli" as "the double of the auteur who speaks through an intermediary" (Bonneville 1982, 19), and Michael Dorland saw the film as "Arcand-Machiavelli's judging of Quebec society and the dream of democratically achieving independence by referendum" (1982a, 32).

To a large extent, this interpretation is convincing, and in an article devoted to the representation of Machiavelli in the film, Roger Bourdeau concludes that by the end of the film, "Machiavelli's comments take on more than ever the weight of moral statements that in some way summarize the referendum campaign" (1987–1988, 30). As Bourdeau points out, however, "paradoxically, *The Prince* is dedicated to someone who Machiavelli would like to have seen bring about the unification of Italy at that time, which could lead one to believe that the Machiavelli of the film is defending the unity of the country" (29), and many of his observations bear on the need for a strong prince who can command the support of his people. The two leaders during the campaign who might qualify for this title were René Lévesque, the PQ leader, and Pierre Trudeau, who after a brief period out of power had just won a federal election with an overwhelming number of seats in Quebec.

In one sequence, after we see Lévesque appealing to his audience to have "confidence in us [the PQ]," there is a cut to Machiavelli who states that people want to be "represented by a man they esteem." Next, the film cuts to Trudeau shaking hands in a crowd and then back to Machiavelli explaining that a prince needs "the affection of the people," followed by Trudeau rejecting the "pessimistic nationalism" of the separatists. Although this passage might seem to be quite evenhanded in its depiction of two leaders competing for popular esteem and affection, Arcand was, as we have seen, definitely not an admirer of Trudeau, and Machiavelli's assumption of an Olympian superiority and his ironic smile liken him to Trudeau, who was often thought to be aloof and cynical. The extent to which we can take Machiavelli as speaking for the filmmaker is thus rather complicated. Arcand's final assessment of the referendum campaign was that Lévesque was "a man of an irreproachable honesty and sincerity" but, unfortunately, "a lamentable politician," unlike Duplessis, who was "an authentic Machiavellian . . . who would never have been fooled by Pierre Elliott Trudeau" (quoted in Bergeron 2012, 116).

Since Arcand had come close to identifying Lévesque with Duplessis when giving him the voice of the Union Nationale leader in *Québec: Duplessis et après . . .*, the question of the implications of the historical cynic's response to the present-day political situation becomes quite complex, to say the least. To complicate matters even more, Machiavelli delivers his observations "ensconced in an office high at the top of Place Ville Marie" (La Rochelle 1995b, 40) looking down on the city of Montreal, a setting that anticipates the sequence in *Jésus de Montréal* in which an unctuous lawyer tempts Daniel, the actor portraying Jesus in a new version of the Passion play, with wealth and fame; when the lawyer and the actor look down on the city spread out beneath them, the situation is comparable to the biblical account of Satan's attempt to seduce Christ in the wilderness by taking him to the top of a mountain. Although Véronneau refers to the film's "non-diegetic 'commentary'" (1995, 21), Machiavelli is actually half in the world of the film (since he is in contemporary Montreal) and half outside (since he comes from Italy in the past), and his words do not refer directly to the referendum. He appears on-screen much more often than his counterparts in the earlier films and comes to dominate the structure of the film, but a character who is part Arcand, part Trudeau, and part the devil can hardly be said to be speaking with a single voice.

Like the lawyer in *Jésus*, Machiavelli seems quite self-satisfied, and he delivers his prescriptions in a calm and composed manner that contrasts with the impassioned speeches of the sweating and gesticulating campaigners. Unlike the on-screen commentators Arcand had introduced into his previous films, he has no stake in the situation that the film depicts, and it is perhaps best to see him not simply as the filmmaker's spokesman but as a persona invented by a mischief maker, depicting the referendum through the eyes of the philosopher often seen as the originator of modern power politics. Unlike Machiavelli, Arcand did have a stake in the outcome of the referendum, but the outcome and the experience of making the film led him to declare, "The problem of Quebec was finished for the rest of my days" (quoted in Jean 1989b, 50). The figure of Machiavelli thus became a way of distancing himself from his own frustration and a displacement of the filmmaker's alleged cynicism onto the whole political arena depicted in the film.

According to Véronneau, Arcand "adopted a mocking tone, insolent or frankly amusing, using satirical and often brilliant editing . . . to convey a reality that pained him deeply" (1995, 21). As Dorland points out, "*Le confort et l'indifférence* only makes sense in the light of the No victory," and it would have been a very different film if the Yes side had won (1982a, 32). The introduction of Machiavelli helped Arcand deal with the problem that faced him in organizing the materials he had filmed during the campaign, which was that its viewers would, of course, know that the No side had won the referendum with nearly 60 percent of the votes. Arcand could not have known the outcome while he was filming, but once the campaign was over, he was faced with the task of rethinking the film to take into account his own response but also the fact that its viewers would know the result.

The structure he came up with, apart from the involvement of Machiavelli, was relatively simple. There is a clear chronological progression: the introduction establishes the prereferendum situation, the central part of the film depicts the referendum campaign itself, and a final section deals with the aftermath. Although he has said he knew from the beginning that the film would "displease both the Federalists and the Sovereignists" (quoted in La Rochelle 2005, 148), it clearly makes a distinction between the two sides. Both are seen to have their shortcomings, but whereas the federalists are accused of fearmongering, exploiting the anxieties raised by the FLQ's tactics in the 1960s and suggesting that a Yes vote would lead to a decline in the standard of living in Quebec, the Yes side is simply seen as being naive and unrealistic. As a supporter of the Yes side claims after the result is known, the sovereigntists were just "too honest," and the film strongly implies that their opponents stole victory from them.[11]

The film opens with a caption quoting from the U.S. Declaration of Independence: "All experience hath shewn that mankind are more disposed to suffer, while evils are sufferable, than to right themselves by abolishing the forms to which they are accustomed." These words foreshadow Arcand's explanation for the defeat of the Yes side but also leave open the possibility that the Québécois

"There is nothing more difficult than to introduce new institutions": Machiavelli sits comfortably above the city in *Le confort et l'indifférence.*

may eventually opt for the independence that the Americans achieved in 1776. The first shot is a pan across Montreal, seen from a high-rise building, which comes to rest on a man in period costume identified as Machiavelli. After he also speaks of people's fear of what is new, the first ten minutes of the film intercut among shots of Machiavelli making cynical observations, Lévesque on a visit to France in 1977 trying to rally support for his cause, and ceremonies in Ottawa during Queen Elizabeth II's state visit to Canada also in 1977. As he so often does, Arcand uses crosscutting to suggest connections and oppositions: Lévesque's earnest appeals to the French to support Quebec—as he puts it, the biggest French-speaking country in the world—are juxtaposed with the pageantry in Ottawa and Machiavelli's interventions. After Lévesque speaks of the need for his people to assert themselves, Machiavelli suggests we should ask if the reformer is an independent agent, and when Lévesque speaks of the need for arms to maintain power, there is a cut to ceremonial troops marching in Ottawa.

After setting out the opposing forces, Arcand introduces the campaign with a shot of Lévesque reading the referendum question at a PQ convention. As many Yes supporters will say during the campaign, the question does not ask people to vote for or against independence but rather to give the Quebec government a mandate to negotiate an agreement with the rest of Canada for an "economic association," with another referendum being held when an agreement is reached. The wording was intended to win over those who feared outright separation, but it allowed the federal side to point out that there could be no guarantee of a subsequent agreement and that the honest question would have been, "Do you want to remain in Canada?" Arcand seems to have felt that the question was too much of a compromise, but as we shall see, the film also makes clear that a more straightforward question would not have allayed the fears of those who were resistant to change.

In his depiction of the campaign, Arcand's mocking tone tends to reduce the whole thing to farce, with politicians making emotional pitches and voters exchanging insults. One sequence depicts a boxing match, billed as the "referendum match," in which a boxer representing the Yes side easily defeats his opponent. Sometimes the film's satire seems fairly evenhanded, as in a rapid montage of Trudeau, Lévesque, and other politicians from both sides throwing out figures about the costs that separation would supposedly incur. In each brief shot, all we hear is a dollar amount called out by the passionate speaker, reducing the campaign to a confrontation of monetary insults but also suggesting that the Yes side got drawn into their opponents' tactic of appealing to people's materialistic concerns. At other times, Arcand's frustrations are very apparent, as in a cut from No supporters singing "O Canada" to a shot of a flock of sheep, an apparent allusion to a montage effect in Charlie Chaplin's *Modern Times* (1936) that juxtaposes sheep and workers leaving a factory. The targets here are clearly those who voted No, but the film does also reveal Arcand's disappointment with the PQ, who, he said, "no longer spoke of changing the country but rather of changing the administration and symbols" (quoted in Jutras, La Rochelle, and Véronneau 1987–1988, 7).

Afterward, Arcand commented rather sourly, "It was the discourse of the majority that I heard in filming *Le confort et l'indifférence*. I can't go against the majority, it would be anti-democratic" (quoted in Jean 1989b, 50). In the film, some people express concerns about the possible loss of their federal pensions and other benefits, and others are depicted as "uncultured beer-drinking boors" (Dorland 1982a, 32–33). One sequence in the final section depicts a revivalist meeting in Montreal's Olympic Stadium, where crowds respond enthusiastically to a preacher standing in front of a Videotron sponsored by the grocery chain Miracle Mart. The implication is that the No voters were like the people in the stadium who respond en masse to the manipulations of a fundamentalist preacher. Clearly, Arcand had little faith in the democratic process, and he declared, "We have the politicians we deserve, which means that it is also our fault. It is not they who con the people, it is the people who want to be conned by them" (quoted in Gural and Patar 1982, 56). It is hardly surprising that one critic could complain that Arcand "says to people that they are stupid and cowardly and makes himself appear to be courageous for saying it" (Bissonnette 1982, 76).

Filming continued sporadically for a year after the referendum, and *Le confort* was not released until 1982. During the campaign, Arcand had invited several luminaries of direct cinema, including Gilles Groulx and Pierre Perrault, to film some of the subjects of their earlier films responding to the campaign as a sort of "homage to Quebec documentary" (Bourdeau 1987–1988, 31). In the aftermath of the very divisive campaign, these filmmakers returned to record the feelings of their subjects about the whole experience. Their emotional responses to the sovereigntist defeat only highlighted the gulf that existed between intellectuals, like Arcand and his colleagues, and those people who had voted against independence.

Although the film "played for six weeks in the big Comedie Canadienne" theater in Montreal (Godard 1971, 33), Arcand's approach, and his apparent contempt for the people "duped" into voting No, did lay him open to charges of misrepresenting the campaign. In his review, Bonneville pointed out that the film does not even mention the phenomenon of the Yvettes, a group of women formed after Lise Payette, a PQ minister, used this name to characterize submissive women as opposed to emancipated modern women who, she implied, would vote Yes; as a result, a group of women calling themselves "the Yvettes" campaigned on the No side, organized a rally that brought fourteen thousand women to the Montreal Forum, and as Bonneville points out, "undoubtedly influenced the vote" (1982, 19). As in *Québec: Duplessis et après . . .* , the film depicts men dominating positions of power in the campaign, while women are mainly depicted raising questions about the economic impact of separation. Nor does the film pay much attention to the changing demographics in Quebec, although it does include an interview with a Greek Canadian woman who explains that she voted No because while she felt she had been welcomed in Canada, the Québécois looked on her with suspicion.

Although he agreed with other critics that the film was manipulative and "hypocritical," Dorland thought that it was "a film that invites the most serious *self*-questioning" and "that alone makes it totally worthwhile" (1982a, 33). Similarly, Véronneau saw it as a prime example of the way Arcand "uses films to dismantle the codes of the representation and the ideologies that manufacture social consent" (1995, 22). The question remains of whether in its attempt to expose the way in which the No side played on people's fear of change, the film ends up suggesting that those who voted No were "duped" (Bissonnette 1982, 75). Those who, like Arcand, resisted the status quo argued that the people's resignation to their condition was the result of Quebec's colonial status, much as the Frankfurt school blamed "mass culture" for blinding people to their own true interests. The problem then becomes how to argue against the power of the dominant ideology without reducing the people who accept it to the category of "cultural dopes."[12]

In *On est au coton,* even if Arcand was shocked to find the workers resigned to their situation, the editing of the film's different materials left the viewer to decide how things fitted together. Similarly, the "mosaic" structure of *Québec: Duplessis et après . . .* raised complex questions about the political life of Quebec that went beyond Arcand's evident dismay that the voters had opted for the Liberal Party. In both films, of course, the "essay" format meant that the filmmakers had been selective in those aspects of the situation that they chose to include and responsible for the way in which these were organized, but there was no overriding voice that provided a predigested response to what the films showed as in the classical documentaries produced by Grierson at the NFB. Arcand's subjective documentaries seek to activate the spectator's own subjectivity in responding to the complex issues raised in the films. Ironically, *Le confort,* the film that is arguably the least "balanced" of Arcand's documentaries, did not run into the problems at the NFB that its predecessors had provoked, which may say something about the Board's evolution in the intervening years or simply perhaps that the No victory made the federal institution feel more comfortable and indifferent.

One other aspect of Machiavelli's presence in the film is perhaps even more unsettling to the "codes of representation." As Bourdeau suggests, the scenes with Machiavelli work "to refresh the documentary genre by integrating elements of fiction in order to find a hypothetical 'third way' which is a perfect hybrid of the two genres" (1987–1988, 29). Strictly speaking, of course, Machiavelli is not a fictional character, but wearing period costume and played by an actor, he participates in what Arcand has referred to as the "fraud" of the historical film. He had done something similar in *Québec: Duplessis et après . . . ,* but there it is not clear whether Robin Spry is supposed to be playing Lord Durham or simply reading from his report just as the schoolteacher recites the questions from the catechism. In *Le confort,* a caption identifies Ronfard as Machiavelli but also provides his dates, thereby confirming that his living presence is fictional. As La Rochelle points out, "For Arcand, there is a very fine line between documentary and fiction" (2005, 149) even though the filmmaker had argued that they are two separate modes. Arcand had already crossed this fine line in the fiction films of the 1970s that will be the subject of the next chapter, most notably in *Gina,* and the tension between documentary and fiction would continue to be a key element in Arcand's subsequent work.

3 • DIRTY MONEY

Arcand's Crime Films

As a spectator I love action movies, with chases, fights and so forth.

—Denys Arcand

The problems Arcand experienced with his first two feature-length documentaries left him in a state of depression at the beginning of the 1970s. He felt that he was "in an ideological cul-de-sac" and wanted to perform "an act of revolt, rather like the terrorists of the same period, but from the comfortable position of an artist" (quoted in Coulombe 1993, 25). As we saw in the previous chapter, his projected documentary on terrorism was aborted because of the October Crisis, and he turned to the private sector and to fiction filmmaking.

In fact, the final version of *Québec: Duplessis et après*... was not released until June 1972, by which time Arcand had shot and edited his first fiction film, *La maudite galette* (*Dirty Money*; 1971), which received its premiere at the Cannes Film Festival in May of the same year.[1] It was made thanks to fellow filmmaker Jean Pierre Lefebvre, who, following the example of Jean-Luc Godard in France, had made a series of very low-budget features in quick succession and had established his own production company, Cinak.[2] Arcand and Lefebvre had met at university, and Arcand had appeared in a small role in Lefebvre's *Mon oeil* (My eye; 1966), at which time Lefebvre had invited him to make a feature film for his company (Coulombe 1993, 24). The eventual result was *La maudite galette*, and although this film and the two others that Arcand made in the 1970s can be described as crime films, they pushed generic conventions almost to the breaking point.

In moving from documentary to fiction, he was following the example of many other Quebec filmmakers, including Michel Brault and Gilles Groulx, but this transition was not viewed as a positive move by those who believed that documentary was a more effective way of representing the new situation in Quebec. Arcand remembered Pierre Perrault "affirming that a work of fiction was morally contemptible," and he himself thought it was "a handicap for a fiction filmmaker to come from documentary" (quoted in Jean 1989b, 52–53). He pointed out that unlike in documentary, "in dramatic film . . . each movement is defined in advance" (quoted in Bonneville 1979, 41) and that "the approach of the fiction filmmaker, which is that of a novelist, is nearly opposite to that of the documentarist, who could be compared to an essayist" (quoted in Jean 1989b, 52). In Arcand's case, an additional complication was that he was making genre films rather than the more respected documentary-influenced "art films," such as Groulx's *Le chat dans le sac* and Brault's *Entre la mer et l'eau douce*.

In his comments on the number of filmmakers involved in making *Seul ou avec d'autres*, Arcand had demonstrated a commitment to the "auteur theory" as developed in France in the 1950s by critics writing for *Cahiers du cinéma*, who would later become the filmmakers of the French New Wave. According to this approach, a film should express the personal vision of its director, but whereas its French advocates admired many Hollywood filmmakers who worked from scripts written by others, Arcand (like many of the theory's later proponents) felt that the director should be responsible for the screenplay as well as its cinematic realization, hence, as we shall see, his reservations about *La maudite galette*, for which he did not write the initial screenplay. However, Arcand's attitude toward genre in the crime films he made in the 1970s also shows the influence of the more radical critics who took over *Cahiers* at the end of the 1960s and rejected what they saw as the romantic and individualistic underpinnings of the auteur theory. These critics called for a new approach that would deconstruct the dominant ideology for which conventional narrative cinema was supposedly nothing more than a vehicle.

In accordance with this ideological critique, Arcand thought of his films as antigenre films in that they did not produce "a dramatic narrative seeking to envelop the spectator in the fascination of its mechanics" (Niogret 1979, 100) but instead distanced the spectator from the action in order to expose the underlying ideology.[3] Although this attitude proved enormously fruitful in his three crime films, they still function, like many more conventional genre films, as ways of exploring controversial issues that could not be dealt with in a more direct way (as Arcand had found through the censorship of his NFB documentaries).

"A FILM ON EVERYDAY VIOLENCE": *LA MAUDITE GALETTE*

In many ways, *La maudite galette* grows out of Arcand's documentary work at the NFB, and in particular, it was an offshoot of his proposal for *Les terroristes*. His reason for turning to the crime film was apparent when he pointed out, "There is a lot of blood and violence . . . but it is really an abortive film on terrorism" (quoted in Wright and Magidson 1974, 24). The implication is that he would have preferred to make a documentary, and as noted, he also distanced himself from his first fiction film on the grounds that he merely filmed someone else's screenplay (Tadros 1973, 18). The writer in question was Jacques Benoît, whom Arcand had met at university (Coulombe 1993, 25) and whose novel *Jos Carbone,* published in 1967, depicts the intrusions of violence and eroticism into everyday life in a way that anticipates the film, although in a fantastic rather than criminal context. Arcand's reservations stemmed from his belief that an auteur should be solely responsible for the screenplay if a film was to express his own vision, but it was he who had commissioned Benoît's script, and he did make some important changes to it (La Rochelle 2005, 125, 129).

In his review of the film in *Le Devoir,* Robert Guy Scully (1972b) detected signs of the film's divided authorship, but the conclusions he drew were rather surprising given Arcand's reputation for cynicism. Scully cited an interview in which the director spoke of feeling "more and more on the margins of society," with the result that he felt "sympathy" for the petty criminals who also exist on the margins (quoted in Houle, Leduc, and Hamelin 1971, 29). The critic thus attributed to Arcand those aspects of the film that arouse sympathy for the characters, while he felt that Benoît's screenplay was responsible for the use of caricature and generic conventions in order to develop an absurdist vision of life. He concluded that Arcand had cast "actors who cannot rest at the level of caricature" and had directed them "with a care that presupposes a love for the characters." Whoever was responsible for the different aspects of the screenplay, there is a clear tension in the film between the distance from which the characters are mainly viewed and a sense that they are victims of the impossible social conditions in which they live.

Arcand was certainly fully responsible for the distinctive style that characterized the film and for the extent to which it broke with generic conventions. After the collapse of his documentary project on terrorists, he was "in a dark state" and prepared to make "a very dark film," which would "depict quasi-terrorist actions" (quoted in Bonneville 1979, 41). The film's working title was *Calibre 45,* evoking the gunplay and violence expected of a crime thriller, but Arcand's strategy was to set up a tension between the genre and the environment in which the crimes take place. The robbery that sets the plot into motion originates in the frustrations of a poor family, and in depicting their specific circumstances, Arcand was able to draw on the resources of his own family. As well as giving a small role to his brother Gabriel, who would go on to become one of Quebec's leading actors, he was assisted by his brother Bernard, an ethnographer, and especially by his sister Suzanne, a criminologist who collaborated on all three crime films (La Rochelle 2005, 134). Although there is no overt reference to the FLQ or the October Crisis in the film, it is clear that the terrorist acts of the last ten years in Quebec are here translated into what the director called "a film on everyday violence" (Arcand, quoted in Perreault 1971, D 9).

As with *Seul ou avec d'autres,* although to a very different effect, the story is much less important than the way it is told. Working on a shoestring budget of $142,817, made possible by a minimal crew, deferred salaries, and a twenty-day shooting schedule (Latour 1979, 14), Arcand drew on the example of the B films produced by Hollywood's "poverty row" studios in the 1940s and 1950s for release as second features in the double bills that were staples of film exhibition at the time.[4] Instead of filming in black and white, however, like these American forebears, Arcand decided to make his film in color and widescreen. Although the scenario of *La maudite galette* recalls "the plot of a good crime novel in the style of James Hadley Chase" (Perreault 1972c, C9), as Arcand explained, it is "a gangster story, but shot in a way contrary to gangster films" (quoted in Tadros 1972b, 29). He wanted to make a film "in contempt of all cinematic rules" (quoted in Bonneville 1979, 41), which would be "insidiously subversive" (Arcand 1972, 11).

Although Arcand admitted to enjoying the rapid editing and exciting action sequences that involve the spectator in the world of Hollywood genre films, *La maudite galette* is made up almost entirely of long takes and sequence shots, using the widescreen technology of Panavision, with a mainly static camera observing the characters from a distance. Arcand apparently told the actors that he was using sequence shots to save money (Guilbeault 1987–1988, 46), but even if this was the case, he also justified the strategy as a kind of Brechtian distancing effect as demanded by the new *Cahiers* critics. The intention was that the viewer, rather than becoming involved in the action through suspense about what will happen next, would be encouraged to ask questions about "the society that produces this sort of individual" (quoted in Tadros 1972b, 29).

The credits sequence begins by establishing the specific location with several long shots of the industrial east end of Montreal, and we then see a workman silently digging and moving stones and sand with a wheelbarrow in a fenced-in yard. When he sits down to eat his lunch, the advertising on the billboards over the fence evokes the consumer society from which he is cut off and introduces the feeling of deprivation that drives the criminal plot. In the next sequence, we learn that the worker is Ernest (Marcel Sabourin), an employee in a scrapyard owned by Roland (René Caron). He rents a room from his employer, and a lengthy sequence now takes place inside the house. Roland's wife Berthe (Luce Guilbeault) is working in the kitchen, drinking from a large gin bottle as she prepares food for their two children. In the background, a radio broadcasts commercials and an interview with Pierre Trudeau in which he speaks of the War Measures Act of "last October" and "the need to move on from the trouble last year." When Roland arrives home, Berthe tells him that his uncle Arthur

(J. Léo Gagnon), whom they have not seen for years, has come to visit. There follows a long take in which the uncle is the focal point as he sits in the living room beneath a framed print of dancers in a rural setting, which suggests the couple's aspirations to a more genteel life. He tells them he has brought them a gift of $500, and they then sit around the kitchen table eating a meal. The conversation becomes more intense when Arthur takes offense at one of Roland's jokes, and Berthe attacks him for hoarding the money that he has inherited from his wife.

Because of the uncle's visit, Ernest is told to eat in his room, and when Berthe takes him his meal, he is watching television.[5] The long takes of the family are, however, punctuated by two close-ups of Ernest in the shadows, listening to their conversation, and he hears Roland and Berthe telling stories about the stupidity of their hired man. At the end of the meal, Berthe gets so angry with Arthur that she returns the money and orders him to leave, and the sequence ends with a close-up of her face as she seethes with anger. The close-ups of Ernest and Berthe break up the long takes and draw attention to themselves because of their abrupt insertion. Although what has occurred so far has no obvious associations with crime or violence, these close-ups foreshadow the action that emerges from the characters' frustrations. When Roland leaves to drive Arthur home, Berthe immediately goes to the telephone to call a babysitter and to ask two youths (Jean-Pierre Saulnier, Gabriel Arcand) drinking in a tavern to come over, and when Roland returns, she persuades him to join them in robbing his uncle's house. As they drive off, Ernest can just be seen in the darkness climbing into the back of Roland's truck, unnoticed by the others.

Although the robbery takes the characters (and us) out of the house, it is, in its way, equally claustrophobic. The journey is filmed through the windscreen of the truck, with the headlights only just illuminating the road, and is accompanied by the film's first nondiegetic music, an upbeat but melancholic folk tune.[6] When they arrive at the house, a dog starts barking and continues to bark throughout the robbery until Ernest shoots it when he leaves. The four robbers enter the house wearing hoods and try to make Arthur tell them where his money is hidden. When they hear someone else in the house, they start to investigate but are picked off one by one. Ernest reveals himself and shoots Roland before pouring hot coffee on Arthur's chest until he reveals that the money is hidden under the stairs. After he finds a sack of money and puts Arthur's body in the truck, Ernest sets fire to the house and drives off with Berthe, the only other survivor, before dumping the body in a river on the way to a motel.

At the motel, Ernest finds an empty suitcase and pours the money into it; then he and Berthe have sex in the dark, filmed in a long take, silently except for the creaking of the bed. In the morning, Berthe quietly gets up, evidently planning to leave with the money, but Ernest shoots her, wounding her in the shoulder. He leaves her lying naked, facedown on the bed with blood streaming from the wound, and escapes over the motel roof. He carries the case through the sunlit countryside, which offers a release from the confined spaces that have dominated the film so far, but he then goes for a drink in a tawdry bar where the waitress (Mireille) wears a skimpy nightdress, which she takes off when she dances to music from a jukebox. After he sits down at a table next to a couple he has earlier seen drive past in a large car, the other man (Maurice Gauvin), clearly assuming that Ernest is a bum, offers to pay for his drink. He starts to boast about his wealth, shows off the expensive rings he is wearing, and says his car cost $9,400. Jokingly, he tells Ernest that he would sell the car and his "broad" for $20,000, and Ernest calmly opens the case and places the money on the table.

After Ernest drives off with the young woman (Andrée Lalonde), there is a cut back to the motel, where the owner (Charlie Beauchamp) is bandaging Berthe, who tells him that she plans to search for Ernest in Montreal. Meanwhile, Ernest takes his new companion to a luxury hotel in the city, but the man from the bar sends his thugs after them, and a shoot-out ensues in which she dies. After shooting the thugs and escaping from the underground parking lot, Ernest drives to a poor neighborhood and goes into one of the houses. He finds his parents sitting at a table and pours out the money, telling them, "It's all yours." They are rigid and silent, and Berthe appears from her hiding place behind the open front door with a shotgun. Ernest senses her presence, and they both fire at the same time in a long shot in which they are just out of sight on each side of the screen, as if these marginal characters, at the time of their deaths, cannot fit even on a Panavision screen. Their bloody bodies lie on the kitchen floor, and while the mother (Hélène Loiselle) kneels in grief beside her son, the father (Julien Lippé) calmly starts carrying the money to the washing machine. She eventually gets up and helps him hide the money before the police arrive. Arcand then draws attention to his use of the widescreen during the shooting by having two detectives (one of them played by himself) measure the distance between the bodies, solemnly announcing that they are eight feet apart. The parents decide to go to Florida, and the final shot shows them driving out of Montreal accompanied by the jaunty music that preceded the robbery.

This ending has been called "the most cynical and the darkest scene in Quebec cinema" (Lévesque 1979a, 95). For some critics, it was shocking because of its subversion of a genre that normally "takes the point of view of law and order," whereas *La maudite galette* ends "with a caustic humor, proving that crime pays . . . even for those who have not committed it" (Latour 1979, 13). Of course, crime has not paid for those who did commit it, but what is more important to the effect of the ending is the refusal to involve us with the psychology of the characters. Arcand described his approach as "phenomenological" and spoke of trying "to understand people by what they do, without rummaging through their psychology, but looking coldly at them as they act" (quoted in Lévesque

1979b, 97). Thus although Ernest's actions may be "the revenge of an outcast," as Léo Bonneville suggested (1979, 49), his arrival at his parents' house comes as a complete surprise. If the characters are motivated by their desire to escape from their miserable social circumstances, the film's precision about the amounts of money changing hands, as in the discussion of Ernest's meager wages and the dealings with the rich man in the bar, suggests a society whose values are solely materialistic. Rather than being seen as a realistic (or cynical) depiction of a particular social class, the film could be interpreted as a critique of "the American Way of Life" (Marcorelles 1979, 99).

Once *La maudite galette* was made, the problem became how to distribute it. It was invited to Critics' Week at the Cannes Film Festival (La Rochelle 2005, 130), where it received its premiere, and was also screened at festivals in Berlin and London. However, France Film, the distributors in Quebec, played down its art film credentials and framed it as a genre film, replacing its original poster with one that was "supposedly more commercial" (Scully 1972a). Despite their efforts, the box office during its initial release was disappointing, but although Arcand thought that television had put an end to the B movie and the double feature "in America at least" (1972, 11), the film was rereleased in France Film's network of second-run cinemas as a supporting feature with foreign films, and in this way, it remained on screens in Quebec for seventy-five weeks (Latour 1979, 14).

Critics in Quebec were generally enthusiastic and saw the film as more than a commercial genre film. In his review for *Québec-Presse,* Robert Lévesque declared it was "an event in Quebec cinema" equivalent to Michel Tremblay's *Les belles-soeurs* (1968) in Quebec theater, both works depicting "utterly dispossessed Québécois, beings who have nothing to lose, the detritus of a capitalist society, the waste product of a more and more inhuman world" (1979a, 94). The welcome the film received in Quebec echoed its earlier reception in France despite the need for subtitles due to the colloquial French spoken by its characters. In *Le Monde,* Louis Marcorelles called it "the first masterpiece of Quebec fiction cinema" (1979, 99), and in *L'Express,* Claude Mauriac declared, "There is no need for subtitles. The images speak. They cry out" (1979, 100).

As Mauriac's response suggests, the film, despite (or perhaps because of) the frequently noted coldness of its style, does have a powerful emotional effect. Lévesque argued that it captured "the Québécois essence (or soul)" (1979b, 97), and the film could be seen as exploring the frustrations and anger generated by "our life in a cul-de-sac" (Gay 1972, 26), which Arcand had already addressed in his documentaries. Although the film is not overtly political, at this stage of his career, Arcand still clung to the hope that the situation in Quebec as he saw it could improve, insisting, "My films . . . are there to change things a little, because it is impossible to live like this" (quoted in Lévesque 1979b, 97). In his next film, he would make the political subtext much clearer by shifting the focus from the bottom to the top of the social hierarchy.

"A DESPERATE WAKE-UP CALL": *RÉJEANNE PADOVANI*

According to Arcand, the budget for his next film, *Réjeanne Padovani* (1973), was $135,000, slightly less than for *La maudite galette*, which, as he said, "poses practical problems, especially when you want to make a film . . . set in an affluent milieu, with 24 principal actors" (quoted in Tadros 1973, 21). He suggested that if he had had a larger budget, he would have filmed in more locations, but as it was, the action was largely confined to the home of the character Vincent Padovani (Jean Lajeunesse), who is giving a dinner party to celebrate the completion of the first section of a new highway his company is constructing in Montreal. In order to introduce events that occur elsewhere, Arcand explained that he had "recourse to the telephone, which is much cheaper" (18), but the enforced confinement to the space of the home adds to the impact of the comfort and indifference of a small group of the power elite. Once again, Cinak produced and Arcand started from a script by Jacques Benoît, but in this case, he thoroughly rewrote it and felt that the film was fully his own work (La Rochelle 2005, 131).[7]

He again called it a film on "everyday violence" (Arcand 1975, 11), but this time the violence is committed by those who have power and is a product of the nexus of business, politics, and criminality that Arcand saw as dominating public life in Quebec. Just as *La maudite galette* grew out of his unrealized documentary project on terrorism, the inspiration for this new film came from his experiences when filming *Québec: Duplessis et après . . . .* While he was making that documentary on Quebec politics, Arcand had become aware of the links between organized crime and politicians, notably involving members of the Union Nationale in east Montreal (Élia 1998, 15). As we have seen, the NFB forced him to cut the opening sequence depicting a politician giving money to his aides to hand out at a public meeting, and he knew that he could not adequately address these acts of corruption in a documentary.

Despite Arcand's insistence on the difference between documentary, in which the filmmaker must react to unexpected developments, and fiction films in which "each movement is defined in advance" (quoted in Bonneville 1979, 41), it was still possible for one critic to describe *Réjeanne Padovani* as "a film that describes the way of life of our public men in an almost documentary manner" (Perreault 1973). In the 1970s, Montreal was undergoing a construction boom, and a highway much like the one in the film was one of the more ambitious projects of the time. The film was thus very topical, especially since it coincided with a government inquiry into political corruption in the awarding of contracts for lucrative construction projects. Critics were quick to notice parallels between the film's characters and their counterparts in the real world. Thus the alleged "godfather of the Montreal mafia was named Vincent Cotroni" (Poirier and Thériault 2012, 5), and Padovani's guests include the mayor of Montreal and the minister of highways, played by actors who resembled then mayor Jean Drapeau and Bernard Pinard, the equivalent minister in the provincial Liberal government led by Robert Bourassa.[8] Most tellingly, the final sequence in which the mayor and the minister officially open the completed section of the highway was clearly modeled on a photograph published in newspapers of Drapeau and Pinard cutting a ribbon to mark the opening of a section of the real new east-west highway (Élia 1998, 15). Beginning with a close-up of a grid in the concrete under which Réjeanne is buried, the camera then tilts up to reveal the men in the distance preparing to cut the ribbon as in the photograph.

It was hardly surprising that to English Canadians, the film reinforced the existing image of Quebec politics in which corruption was allegedly "accepted as perhaps regrettable, but nevertheless, an unavoidable condition of community life" (Shuster 1974, 45). However, despite Arcand's mischievous allusions to actual public figures from Quebec, he pointed out that the "same facts can be found in most so-called 'developed' countries" (1975, 11), and he insisted, "Quebec is not enough. . . . I make films for an international market" (quoted in Hofsess 1975, 145). For this reason, he said he "did not want people to relate the film to the October crisis or to Quebec nationalism," which, he felt, would confuse the issues with which the film deals (quoted in Tadros 1973, 22).[9] Rather than explicitly evoking recent events, his historical training led him to reread Tacitus and Suetonius and to draw on the Roman historians' accounts of the execution of Empress Messalina, Caligula's unfaithful wife (Bonneville 1979, 43); a similar fate befalls Réjeanne (Luce Guilbeault), Padovani's estranged wife, who tries to return home and ends up buried under the construction site. As Lévesque put it, Arcand turned the local events into "a universal tragedy" (1975a, 10) but one in which, as we shall see, there is an unsettling subtext of black humor.

The film opens with a disclaimer that it is "a fiction film" in which "any resemblance to people living or dead would be a coincidence," an ironically disarming claim that links it to the direct cinema tradition of "playing on the border between fiction and non-fiction" (Poirier and Thériault 2012, 5). In the opening shot, a limousine draws up in front of a luxury home, and the camera picks out the small Quebec flag flying from its hood, asserting the local context for what is to come. When the chauffeur opens the door, the man who gets out is Georges Bouchard (J. Léo Gagnon), the provincial minister of highways, who is late for a party at the home of Vincent Padovani. Dominique Di Muro (Pierre Thériault), Padovani's right-hand man, comes out to greet Bouchard and shows him into the house before returning to direct the driver (André Melançon), identified as a police constable, to the basement, where the various bodyguards and servants are gathered. The opening thus sets up the alternation between upstairs and downstairs that will drive the first part of the narrative, allowing Arcand to pursue his favorite strategy of using montage to bring out social differences and contradictions. As the French critic Pascal Bonitzer put it in an article in *Cahiers du cinéma*, "The metonymic relation . . . between the scenic space and the political order underpins . . . the general dynamic of the film" (1974, 40).

Réjeanne Padovani has been aptly described as "an anti-thriller which uses a cool, formally controlled eye to expose political corruption" (Harkness 1989, 235). However, the "cool" surface is punctured three times in the second half of the film: first when a reporter (Paule Baillargeon) and photographer (Attila Dory) arrive at the house and take an unauthorized picture of one of the bodyguards; then when a radical citizens' committee makes plans for a protest at the formal opening of the new section of the highway; and then, most centrally to the film's plot, when Réjeanne returns and asks to see her children. The first intrusion is dealt with when the bodyguard slaps the reporter and takes the photographer's camera, the second by a brutal attack on the committee's headquarters, and the third when the wayward wife is shot down in the middle of a fireworks display. Although the attack on the reporter requires a discreet call to the editor of the newspaper, these violent actions hardly disturb the calm surface of Padovani's evening, and in the final sequence, the opening ceremony goes ahead as planned, with no evidence of wrongdoing to spoil the occasion.[10]

Apart from a few brief sequences that take place elsewhere in Montreal, the film is constructed like a classical tragedy, obeying the unities of time (one evening) and space (the house). The two levels of the house represent the social order, and the segregation is breached only once, when Padovani asks Stella (Margot MacKinnon), the wife of his lawyer and a former opera singer, to perform for his guests. She sings an aria from Gluck's *Orpheus and Eurydice* in which Orpheus laments the loss of his wife, an ironic foreshadowing of Padovani's situation at the end of the evening. As the music begins, the servants in the basement move up the stairs to listen, led by Carlo (Gabriel Arcand), a reclusive killer who has remained almost silent during the chatter among his companions. Later, he will be the one who calmly guns down Réjeanne, but he seems genuinely moved by the music, in contrast to minister Bouchard, who continues wolfing down his food. Arcand here seems to be illustrating his comment that he has "always been fascinated by opera and especially by the fascination that opera exercises upon the Québécois" (quoted in Bonneville 1979, 45). If, as he says, "opera is the pastime of the rich" and "an art for the elite" (quoted in Tadros 1973, 19), this moment seems to suggest its appeal crosses class lines but

The opening of the highway proceeds without a hitch at the end of *Réjeanne Padovani*.

in doing so, helps the upper class maintain control over those beneath them. At the end, after the ribbon-cutting ceremony for the new highway, the aria is again heard on the soundtrack as the camera tracks beside houses being demolished to make way for further construction, evoking what Arcand called "the abyss that separates those who remain there from those who have precisely gone to the opera" (quoted in Tadros 1973, 19).

Rather than a conventional arrangement of climaxes, the steady escalation of the film's narrative structure is largely due to the accumulation of detail relating to the central theme of corruption. In one of the most illuminating accounts of the film's style, Pierre Vallières, a former FLQ leader and author of *Nègres blancs d'Amérique* (*White Niggers of America*), argued that the use of a "strategy of slowness" allowed it to reveal "the very often unexpected depths of individual and collective alienation" (1973, 8). The effect of this strategy is, as a French reviewer suggested, to "add to the weight of things not said so that the least half-gesture takes on a resounding importance" (Boury 1975, 107).

This approach was the polar opposite to the films of Costa-Gavras, which had inspired a lively debate in the 1970s around their use of the conventional techniques of the thriller to convey their political message. Arcand distanced himself from the Greek filmmaker, who according to Arcand, "tries to be attuned to the pace of his audience . . . whereas I never think of the audience" (quoted in Ibranyi-Kiss 1974, 57). This claim must be taken with a grain of salt, given the film's calculated strategies to unsettle its audience, but not all critics thought that Arcand's methods worked to the benefit of his film. In a rather strange interview, Arcand found himself defending the film against English Canadian critic John Hofsess's judgment that *Réjeanne Padovani* did not measure up to Costa-Gavras's *État de siège* (*State of Siege*; 1972), which came out at about the same time, and he was pushed into trying to define his own sense of film style: "To a great extent—to an extent that surprises me—a sense of style is important. *How* a thing is said is as important as *what* is said—in fact, those two things are frequently inseparable" (1975, 152). Unconvinced, Hofsess objected to the lack of characters with "redeeming value" in Arcand's film and to what he saw as the manipulation of the audience so that, as he said, "they can't form any judgment of your characters outside your own" (151–152).

Hofsess's complaint is perhaps surprising given that Costa-Gavras had often come under attack for manipulating his audience's responses in his earlier films, but he was presumably responding to the more ambiguous depiction of the political situation in *State of Siege*, in which South American guerillas kidnap and execute an American "advisor" with ties to the country's oppressive regime. At the beginning of the interview, Hofsess reacts skeptically to Arcand's claim that he is "primarily a satirist" (147), and he is thus able to ignore the fact that satire is a genre that hardly lends itself to ambiguity. The more relevant question is whether Arcand's approach allows for complexity, an issue that can be addressed by examining the response of another English Canadian critic. Martin Knelman offered support for the director's characterization of his work when he argued that the film's "purpose is to use satire of manners to contrast the surface circumspection of his scenario and its underlying horror" (1977, 77).

According to Knelman, Arcand's satiric intent means that "caricature suits his purpose wonderfully," but other critics thought there was more to the characters than this. Vallières insisted that the film refuses "caricature or superficial spectacle" (1973, 8), and a French critic suggested that Arcand presents his characters "with a harshness without cynicism" and "reveals them in their complexity" (Fléouter 1975, 102). These opposed impressions of the film stem from Arcand's "phenomenological" approach, already seen in *La maudite galette*, which eschews psychology for what as the director calls "the description of people through their actions" (quoted in Scully 1973, 21). This approach does not deny the characters' complexity but, contrary to Hofsess's complaint, leaves the spectator to infer what they are thinking from their behavior and to disentangle the real meaning behind their words.

It is clear that Arcand views the world he depicts in the film as hopelessly corrupt, but he engages the spectators in drawing out the full implications of what they witness. In doing so, he confronts them with a moral challenge, especially in view of the film's unstable tonal shifts between tragedy and comedy. He told Hofsess that his films are "very funny but hardly anybody laughs" (1975, 147), presumably because the context makes laughter seem an inadequate response. Although he insisted that his exposure of corruption was intended to be taken seriously, he added, "Yet—and this is completely compatible—I also view these same events from a longer range view of human comedy" (153). Thus the execution of Réjeanne is presented as tragedy, but the burial of her body under the highway so that her murder does not impinge on the opening ceremony is also, according to Arcand, "a good joke" (149).

The uncertain ground between tragedy and comedy also complicates the film's relation to the gangster genre. Arcand insisted it is "the story of a gang, not one character in particular" (quoted in Scully 1973, 21), and the cinematography creates a "shadowy aesthetic" that led critics to evoke *The Godfather* (Francis Ford Coppola, 1972). Yet the slow pace and lack of action create a "distantiation," in the manner of Bertolt Brecht, designed to create a detached, critical perspective on the crimes in which the gangster film usually involves the spectator. One critic felt that the fast cutting during "the scenes of repression . . . rather evokes Hollywood excitement than Brechtian reflection" (Chevrier 1987–1988, 35); however, the violent action in these sequences is viewed dispassionately, and the fast cutting works to remind the spectator of the brutality that lurks beneath the polite conversations of the people who authorize it.

If the film's style clearly invites a critical perspective, opinions differed as to its political implications. Vallières called it "the most accomplished work until now, and therefore the most political, in Quebec cinema" and argued that it called for "nothing less than a profound and radical cultural revolution" (1973, 8). Another critic called the final image of "the grey gutted city . . . the most political image in the whole of Quebec cinema" (Lévesque 1975a, 10). However, there were concerns that the film "demoralizes the spectator because of the lack of ways to intervene" (Chevrier 1987–1988, 35). As Harkness suggests, "It is a cold political analysis in a dramatic frame, designed to demonstrate the unlikelihood—indeed the impossibility—of political reform within the current system" (1989, 236). Arcand essentially agreed with this assessment of the film, expressing his sympathy for the "healthy forces of opposition" in the film but holding out little hope that they could bring about meaningful change (quoted in Bonneville 1979, 47). He wanted the film to leave the spectator with "the impression that we are governed by madmen; by evil madmen who are manipulated by all kinds of profiteers" (quoted in Tadros 1973, 18). Nevertheless, while he admitted, "My cinema is not mobilizing, it is desperate" (quoted in Lévesque 1975b, 100), this dystopian vision, as I have suggested earlier, functions to shift the audience out of its comfort zone and to become aware of the forces at work in Quebec politics.

The critique of political corruption is reinforced by the treatment of sexuality. During the course of the evening, we learn that Stella was once Padovani's mistress; Jeannine Biron (Hélène Loiselle) tries to make love to Jean-Pierre Caron (Jean Pierre Lefebvre), the minister's secretary, while he is making an important telephone call; and Caron's wife, Hélène (Frédérique Collin), seduces Padovani in order to get her husband a job in Montreal instead of Quebec City. Meanwhile, Bouchard receives sexual favors from Manon (Céline Lomez) and Micheline (Guylène Lefort), waitresses from Padovani's restaurant, who have been serving drinks behind the bar in the basement. As Arcand admitted, "All the female characters are prostitutes" (quoted in Perreault 1973), but he also pointed out that while the women "come across only as physical objects . . . you must remember that the men appear as total swines [*sic*]" (quoted in Wright and Magidson 1974, 27). The men also live off "immoral earnings," and one reviewer aptly referred to them as "technocrats of moral prostitution" (Daigneault 1975, 101).

The one partial exception to this corrupt assembly is Réjeanne. Arcand called this character "a catalyst" because her unexpected arrival, late in the film, "unleashes things and forces the characters to reveal themselves" (quoted in Bonneville 1979, 46). Yet she is not simply an innocent victim. After leaving Padovani, she has been having an affair with Lennie Tannenbaum (Stan Gibbons), the son of the boss of a rival gang—Jewish rather than Italian—and living with him in the United States, where she hates having to speak English. He is now dying of cancer, and she offers to betray the gang's secrets if she is allowed to come back, an offer that leads Di Muro to assume she must have betrayed "us" to "them." Referring to a classic of Quebec literature, Olivier Lemieux refers to her as "a counter-model to the French-Canadian woman as guarantor of the nation, an anti-Maria-Chapdelaine who chose individual happiness over the future of her family" and who, "in the image of the Quiet Revolution . . . has left her past without the hope of a better future" (2016).[11] However, it is clear that in her case, the past was no better than the present, and she dies because she has no power to change things.

Like *La maudite galette*, *Réjeanne Padovani* received its premiere at the Cannes Film Festival, was enthusiastically reviewed in the French press, and was described as the "underground hit" of the festival (Ibranyi-Kiss 1974, 57). Its success at the box office in Montreal and Paris even led Cinépix, its distributor, to release it in English Canada, unusual for a Québécois film at that time (or, unfortunately, today). As we have seen, its political vision was not always welcomed in Quebec, but Luc Perreault in *La Presse* called it "a desperate wake-up call launched against a system that makes possible all these scourges that riddle public administration in a society like ours" (1973). In a more recent article, Christian Poirier and Mélissa Thériault, while taking issue with Arcand's pessimism, conclude that the film's value might be seen in "the questions launched at Quebec society, questions that call for potentially varied responses" (2012).

"THE RAPE OF CONSCIOUSNESS": *GINA*

In an interview given just before he made his third fiction film, Arcand announced, "Now I'm going with this big outfit. They offered to produce anything I'd like so I just submitted *Gina* and they said fine, what about $300,000, maybe more?" (quoted in Ibranyi-Kiss 1974, 57). The outfit in question was Carle-Lamy, a production company set up in 1971 by director Gilles Carle and producer Pierre Lamy. Lamy, who had been credited as coproducer on *La maudite galette*, was impressed enough with the young filmmaker to offer to produce his next film, but the offer came too late to change the plans for *Réjeanne Padovani*. Arcand had told Hofsess, "I never bother with commercial considerations" (1975, 149), but the involvement of Carle-Lamy must have raised some suspicions that he was changing his outlook. Although Lamy insisted that his decision about whether to produce a film was based not on the scenario but the director (quoted in Perreault 1974, E13), *Gina* (1975), which included a striptease number, a gang rape, bloody action, and a chase sequence, would lead some critics to accuse Arcand of surrendering to the demands of the market.

Carle was a director with a very different sensibility, whose films are far removed from the "strategy of slowness," stuffed as they are with action and, most notoriously, erotic sequences usually featuring his then wife Carole Laure; however, his dark vision of the contradictions in Quebec society was fully as pessimistic as Arcand's.[12] Just before making *Gina*, Lamy had produced Carle's *La mort d'un bûcheron* (*Death of a Lumberjack*; 1973), in which Laure starred as a woman, named after Hémon's Marie Chapdelaine, who is searching for her missing lumberjack father. She strips for old men and performs topless in a bar to pay her way, only to find that the lumber company has covered up her father's murder during a labor dispute. Arcand probably had Carle's film in mind when he expressed some discomfort at the prospect of making a film about a stripper and having "to shoot some sequences where she's doing her job," insisting that he did not want to make a film that is "supposed to denounce exploitation and yet shows a girl undressing in a very seductive way" (quoted in Ibranyi-Kiss 1974, 58).

Arcand's misgivings about the sexual aspects of his new film were perhaps surprising given the article called "Cinema and Sexuality" that he had contributed to *Parti pris* in 1964. In this article, he had argued that "if the freedom we seek is social, religious and political, it must also . . . be sexual" (quoted in La Rochelle 2005, 307). After discussing what he saw as the sexual repression in Quebec cinema, he came to a conclusion that might have been written by Denis

Héroux to the effect that "a cinema that is at once free and fiercely national" could be achieved only when "our filmmakers manage to . . . undress their neighbour called Yvette Tremblay or Yolande Beauchemin, in broad daylight with a well-focused wide-angle lens" (313–314).[13] Despite this sexist recommendation, the brief sex scenes in Arcand's first two fiction films had been quite restrained, and although Bart Testa suggests that Gina (Céline Lomez) "inhabits a Carole Laure persona" (1987, 215), Arcand's treatment of the potentially sensational materials of his plot is quite different from Carle's.

The film's final budget was $360,000 (Latour 1976, 13), still a very small amount by Hollywood standards but more than twice that of each of his two previous films, and this increase certainly led to brisker editing and more fluid cinematography. Yet the cool and detached tone of the earlier films is still present, even in those sequences that draw on the generic excitement of much of commercial cinema. Its overall effect is best summed up by Harkness's description of it as "a perverse combination of lurid plot and austere style" (1989, 236). Although Arcand had told Hofsess that he was looking forward to making his "*warmest* film to date," the final product was far from the "*happy* film" he'd apparently envisaged (1975, 157).

The credits acknowledge contributions to the screenplay from Jacques Benoît, Jacques Poulin (another novelist), and Alain Dostie (the cinematographer who had collaborated with Arcand since his documentary days), but the director insisted that it was 95 percent his own work (Perreault 1976a, 116). As in the previous fiction films, he drew on his experience of making documentaries, in this case dealing even more overtly with the troubled production of *On est au coton*. While making that film, he had stayed with his crew in a hotel in Coaticook, where "they made the acquaintance of a stripper called Brigitte" (Perreault 1975, D13). Although Arcand took the story of the gang rape from two news stories about other strippers, he claimed that the rest of the scenes involving Gina were based on what actually happened at that time he was making his documentary (2005, 102–103). According to Réal La Rochelle, the early versions of the scenario did not include a documentary film crew (2005, 131), but the project came together when Arcand had the idea of making the film more autobiographical.

For most of the film, Arcand adopts the method he used in his documentaries and structures the narrative as what one reviewer called a "network of relations" (Gay 1975, 12), bringing together Gina and the thugs for whom she works, the film crew, the mill workers, and the members of a snowmobile club. These groups interact with each other, and the editing, at least for the first three-quarters of the film, is less concerned with advancing the plot than with bringing out the implications that emerge from their interaction. The main setting is Louiseville, an industrial town between Montreal and Quebec City, where the filmmakers have come to interview the workers at the local mill and where Gina is to be the star attraction at the hotel-motel in which they are staying. Violence breaks out after Gina's performance, when the snowmobilers burst into her cabin and rape her, provoking her to exact a bloody revenge. Much to the dismay of some critics, the film seems to turn into an action thriller when thugs attack the snowmobilers in their headquarters on an abandoned ship and Gina hunts down those who escape in a long chase sequence.

In the first half of the film, however, any hint of violence remains below the surface. It opens with a shot of a station wagon belonging to the "Office National du Cinéma" (in French, the NFB is the ONF, or the Office National du Film). The film crew are loading the vehicle while the producer (Gilles Marsolais) explains to the director (Gabriel Arcand) that the commissioner is having doubts about the project.[14] However, the director insists on leaving for Louiseville to finish the film he is making on the textile industry in Quebec. Arcand thus sets up the film as his revenge on the NFB, which had still not released even the expurgated version of *On est au coton,* casting his brother as the character who represents himself and replicating the sequence from the documentary in which a policeman issues the director a ticket for filming without permission. During the film, we will see extracts from several interviews (filmed in black and white and 16 millimeter) in which actors appear as workers, often using exactly the same words as the actual workers in the documentary. Edward F. King's role in the NFB's decision not to release the documentary is alluded to in an interview (conducted in English) with the manager of the mill who mentions that the filmmakers have already interviewed "our president Mr. Prince," and the producer will later arrive to tell the crew that the commissioner has decided to shut down the production after dining with "the president" at the Canadian Club.

After the filmmakers leave for Louiseville in the opening sequence, an abrupt cut takes us to the second strand of the narrative. A woman (whom we will soon learn is Gina) calmly prepares a bowl of cereal in a kitchen while noises and cries are heard from off-screen. The next shot shows another stripper being held facedown on a table while her boss (Donald Lautrec) berates her for running off with a man and missing her scheduled performances.[15] Gina continues eating but finally intervenes, and as she helps the weeping woman from the room, her boss reminds her that the train for Louiseville leaves in half an hour. The credits then appear over her train journey, during which a ticket collector greets Bob (Claude Blanchard), the owner of the snowmobile club in Louiseville, who boasts that he is returning from having negotiated a government grant of $85,000 to create trails, pointing out that the money will be especially welcome since three-quarters of the people in the town are unemployed.

Gina and the filmmakers arrive at the hotel-motel at the same time as the film crew, and they soon become friends. She sits at their table in the bar, and when the assistant cameraman (Serge Thériault) asks if her show is any good, she replies that she hopes it will be, in her words, "to your taste." Since she is apparently from a Hispanic background, she helps the filmmakers by acting as a translator when they interview two of the Colombians who have been brought in to work the night shift at the mill. When Bob and Titel (Jocelyn Bérubé), another snowmobiler, challenge the assistant cameraman and Gina to a game of billiards, the two outsiders easily win in a bravura sequence in which the actors make their own shots and that, as a set piece, matches the later striptease number. The defeat contributes to the snowmobilers' growing resentment of the newcomers, which had already become apparent when they disrupted the preparations for an interview with a former mill worker about a strike in the 1950s that was violently repressed. After the filmmakers get permission to film inside the mill, there are shots of workers at their machines amid deafening noise that imitate those in *On est au coton*, and the snowmobilers (who probably once worked in the mill) produce a similar "infernal" noise.[16] Their aggression is thus seen as a perverse response to the oppression from which the workers suffer.

Gina's presence enables the film to set up parallels between sexual and social exploitation: a shot of the stripper putting up a poster for her act is cut into an interview in which Dolorès (Frédérique Collin), a worker who is modeled on Carmen from *On est au coton*, explains how she got started in the mill, and this is followed by Rita (Paule Baillargeon), the wife of the hotel owner, explaining how she ended up there. These three female characters become friends with different members of the film crew: as we have seen, the assistant cameraman enjoys Gina's company; the director brings Dolorès to see Gina's act; and the cameraman (André Gagnon) is clearly attracted to Rita. The only "happy" moment in the film is when Rita, Gina, and the filmmakers skate on a small rink outside the hotel and then on the frozen river, where members of the snowmobile club shout insults at them from their ship. There is a genuine warmth that briefly emerges in these relationships between the crew and the women, which are not sexual but based on a shared need for companionship.

While the audience is gathering for her performance, Gina sits with the filmmakers, much to the disgust of the snowmobilers sitting at another table. When the assistant cameraman points out that the blouse she is wearing was probably made in a sweatshop by someone like Dolorès, Gina jokingly tells him she will be taking it off shortly. Before her performance, she has to fend off advances from the manager of the mill (Roger Lebel) and from Bob as well as insults from Carole (Louise Cuerrier), Titel's girlfriend, who says she dislikes seeing the cellulite on the thighs of strippers. When Gina retires to the washroom to prepare for her number, she and Dolorès stand in front of a mirror, and they discuss their different circumstances. While they both know they are being exploited, Gina proudly insists she is earning much more than the mill worker.

"How much do you earn per week?": Gina and Dolorès compare their situations before the striptease in *Gina*.

Gina dances to rock music from a jukebox, and after she takes off her blouse to reveal her breasts, she asks the filmmakers if this is, as she puts it, "to your taste." Although as Testa argues, "Arcand shoots the strip show quite awkwardly, with the camera either too far away or too close to the actress" so that "the viewer is not invited to join the on-screen audience" (1987, 217), the most disconcerting device occurs when there is a sudden cut to a long extract from the film within the film in which Dolorès describes the fatigue she feels after a long day at the mill. The interruption teases the viewer into thinking the interview will replace the rest of the strip, but there is a cut back to Gina, finishing her act and asking Carole if she can see any cellulite. A close-up shows Dolorès watching, and the performance ends anticlimactically with desultory applause before Gina stoops to pick up her clothes and leaves the stage.

During the rape sequence that follows, the snowmobilers wear their masks, and the whole thing is shown as a very mechanical act that "deliberately replicates similar scenes in lots of low-budget American biker movies" (Testa 1987, 216). There are cuts to the cabin next door, where the soundman, the almost silent member of the crew who has left at the beginning of the performance, is reading a book and listening to classical music, quite oblivious to Gina's plight.[17] When the rapists burst into her room, the television is on, and at the end of the evening's broadcast, it is showing a Canadian flag accompanied by the national anthem, as was then customary at the end of an evening's broadcasts. This symbolic juxtaposition led one critic to suggest, "'Of rape considered as the condition of a people,' that is the sub-title that should be given to *Gina*" (Gay 1975, 13). In his review in *Le Soleil*, Claude Daigneault similarly argued that it is "symbolic of the rape of consciousness that is apparent throughout the film" and, echoing Arcand's pessimistic outlook, that it represented "the opposite of the frenetic enthusiasm of the revolutionaries who think they can count on a mass of supporters behind them" (1976, 113). This symbolic reading of the rape is reinforced when Gina's boss and his thugs arrive at the hotel to take revenge, crossing paths with the producer who is just leaving, after telling the filmmakers that the commissioner has decided to stop the production of their film.

The violent revenge for the rape is also placed in a political context when Rita tells Gina's boss that making trouble never does any good, and he responds by asking if she has seen the statues in parks, which are of figures, such as Duplessis, Churchill, de Gaulle, and Napoleon, whom he calls "a whole gang of killers." However, for many reviewers, the film's ideological concerns were undercut by the shock of the means that it used to express them, a reaction that was only heightened by the violence that follows the rape, when the thugs from Montreal break into the ship and attack the snowmobilers with baseball bats. When Titel and Bob escape from the slaughter on their snowmobiles, Gina drives after them in her boss's car. Titel falls from his machine, and she deliberately drives over his leg before forcing Bob to drive head-on into a large snowblower, his blood shooting into the air as the blades chew up his body.

Unlike the previous two films, *Gina* was not invited to the Cannes Festival, and Arcand reported, "The foreign critics who had defended *Réjeanne Padovani* were ashamed of me and asked how I had been able to make such a horror" (quoted in Jean 1989b, 53). Quebec critics were divided between those who felt "the chase is deliberately prolonged to create suspense, but it has the contrary effect, because the chase is not plausible" (Scully 1975, 13) and those who argued that it set out to draw the audience into the mode of the action thriller, only to frustrate them when "this approach does not produce the emotional impact that the direction taken in this last part leads them to expect" (Gay 1975, 14). Arcand was quite unapologetic, suggesting that *Gina* is "a film that's as divided as I am" (quoted in La Rochelle 2005, 136) and insisting that he loved both "Jean-Luc Godard and *The French Connection*" (1976, 17). It is highly unlikely that Arcand was trying to direct a Québécois version of *The French Connection* (William Friedkin, 1971) but rather to draw attention to the tension between art cinema and genre filmmaking that is apparent in all his crime films. This dividedness that drives the film's style was well captured by Richard Gay, who argued that the rape and its revenge "reside midway between a cold and distanced cinema of the look and a cinema without any distance at all that vibrates to the rhythm of the action" (1975, 14). One way of eliminating this tension was adopted by Cinépix, the film's distributors, who reedited the film in a version without the film crew "as a short film for drive-in screenings in the United States" (La Rochelle 2005, 138).

The film ends with an ironic epilogue in which Arcand juxtaposes the three main strands of the plot that are left after the elimination of the snowmobilers. After the chase ends with a long shot of the snowblower, accompanied by the horrified cries of its operator, there is a cut to Gina walking calmly along a corridor in an airport with Mexican music on the soundtrack. After she checks in and takes her boarding pass, the camera pans to the left to reveal a mariachi band performing in front of the waiting room. While Gina waits for her flight, presumably to Mexico, there is a cut to a city street, where a police car drives up and a cop confronts a woman with a shotgun, who is standing over a man's body and explains, "I killed him because I loved him." The camera again pans to the left and reveals the film crew working on a crime film starring actors whom the Quebec audience would recognize as familiar stars from cinema and television (Donald Pilon, Denise Filiatrault, and Marcel Sabourin) playing cameo roles in Arcand's film.[18] A quick shot of a plane taking off is followed by a shot of a wedding group, on which the camera tracks in, and the image freezes on a radiant Dolorès with her husband as the end titles start to roll, accompanied by the mariachi music.

As Gilles Marsolais puts it, "Gina takes refuge in Mexico, Dolorès in marriage, and the filmmakers in commercial cinema" (2011, 164). But the ending leaves the viewer to figure out the implications of the characters' decisions. The triple exposure of the apparatus—in the revelation that the apparently nondiegetic Mexican music is actually being performed at the airport, the crime scene that becomes a film set, and the film image that turns into a wedding photograph—is designed to unsettle the viewer and provoke reflection. Arcand explained that he ended with the marriage as a perverse happy ending because, in the prevailing economic system, "marriage is the tomb of the working-class condition" and that, while Gina is free "because she earns five times as much as Dolorès, and because she loves nobody," both she and the filmmakers are "marginal figures" who cannot bring about social change (1976, 18).

This ending, like the ironic "happy endings" of Arcand's other crime films, derives from his self-confessed "love of subversion" and his belief that "a good film is always pulling the rug out from under people's beliefs and prejudices" (quoted in Hofsess 1975, 149). Marsolais argues that this subversive intent led Arcand to make "false fiction films": *La maudite galette* "develops a false criminal plot and exploits a false suspense"; *Réjeanne Padovani* is "a false *Godfather*"; and *Gina* is "a *false* skin flick" (2011, 156). While this is partially true, it rests on a suspicion of popular cinema common to many Québécois filmmakers and critics, which assumes that "its primary purposes [are] escape and simple entertainment" (165). Arcand, to some degree, shared this point of view, as shown in an interview from the time he was making *Gina* in which he wondered if, in making fiction films, he was "reinforcing the position of the Establishment" (quoted in Perreault 1975, D13). Yet these films were made at a time when a Hollywood "art cinema" was beginning to emerge. The films of Robert Altman, Arthur Penn, and others were made with resources far beyond those available to the Quebec director, but they certainly cannot be described as simple escapist entertainments. In fact, Arcand's crime films could be seen to anticipate, again with due allowance for their different economic contexts, the spate of disillusioned crime films that have emerged in Hollywood in the twenty-first century.

4 • FALL AND RISE

Arcand and the American Empire

The past is immutable, the future unforeseeable, all that counts is the fugitive present moment.

—Denys Arcand

Although Arcand's first two fiction films had received appreciative reviews in France, they were very much regarded as dealing with matters that were of mainly local interest. The same was true of the documentaries. Nothing pointed to the international acclaim he would experience in the 1980s, but before his rise to stardom, he had to go through another low period in his career.

After the lukewarm reception of *Gina,* it was not surprising that he found it difficult to pursue what he considered his personal projects. However, in this, he was not alone. Many Quebec filmmakers (and their English Canadian counterparts) found themselves shut out thanks to the new production circumstances that followed the federal government's implementation of the Capital Cost Allowance Act in 1974. As discussed in the introduction, the emphasis on supposedly commercial projects at this time led to films that, in pursuit of international success, tried to conceal their Canadian origins, cast minor American stars, and adopted the conventional cinematic style of mainstream Hollywood films. Of course, these films had to be made in English, so the impact of this policy was especially disastrous in Quebec. Several filmmakers left the province to make television films in English for the CBC, which had at that time a commitment to original and socially conscious drama that was lacking at its French-language counterpart. This migration produced such important, if now largely unknown, work as Gilles Carle's *A Thousand Moons* (1975) and Claude Jutra's *Dreamspeaker* (1976), both of which dealt with the relations between indigenous people and modern urban society. Television also figured prominently among the projects to which Arcand turned during this difficult period, but he did not leave Quebec.

The one project, apart from *Le confort et l'indifférence* (see chapter 2), that really interested Arcand during this period never came to fruition. In the early 1980s, Pierre Lamy offered to produce an adaptation of Louis Hémon's novel *Maria Chapdelaine*, and Arcand wrote a screenplay. Hémon was a Frenchman who had moved to Quebec in 1911, and he wrote his novel while working on a farm. It tells the story of a young peasant woman who falls in love with a man who leaves to work as a lumberjack and dies in a snowstorm when he tries to return to her during the Christmas season. She is then courted by two men, one of whom offers to take her to the United States, but she decides to stay and contribute to the building of French Canada. Arcand was attracted to what he called the novel's "foreign gaze on Quebec" (quoted in Gural and Patar 1982, 56), and he wanted to make "a very small, low-budget film, and with adolescents forced too young into adult situations" (quoted in Jutras, La Rochelle, and Véronneau 1987–1988, 12). However, Telefilm Canada preferred a rival screenplay written by Gilles Carle that, as Arcand ruefully commented, had "far more glamour than mine" (quoted in Loiselle 1995, 150), in that it was a star vehicle for Carole Laure, who was then much older than the character in the novel.

After spending five years working on *Le confort*, Arcand felt very disappointed at Telefilm's decision, which confirmed his sense that his career was on hold. However, he did manage to work on three projects during this period, which, despite his misgivings, would prove very useful when he was finally able to work on his own project, *Le déclin de l'empire américain*. Like the aborted screenplay for *Maria Chapdelaine*, all these commissioned assignments drew on his background as a history student. First, he wrote the screenplay for a seven-part television series called simply *Duplessis*, a biographical account of the career of the controversial politician, which was directed by Mark Blandford and broadcast on Radio-Canada in 1977. Second, with Blandford as producer, he directed three episodes of an English-language miniseries for the CBC called *Empire, Inc.* (1982), dealing with the life of a fictional Anglo entrepreneur in Quebec during the Duplessis years. Third, he directed *Le crime d'Ovide Plouffe* (*The Crime of Ovide Plouffe*; 1984), a theatrical film adapted from Roger Lemelin's novel and set in Quebec City in the years after World War II.

"I BECAME A COMPETENT FILMMAKER": FROM *DUPLESSIS* TO THE PLOUFFES

In his script for the *Duplessis* television series, Arcand offers a rather more nuanced account of the controversial politician than he does in his documentaries. The first episode depicts Duplessis while he is still the leader of the opposition, playing to an enthusiastic public as he accuses the Liberal government of corruption at a meeting of the "public accounts" committee and thereby provoking the 1936 election in which the Union Nationale is swept into power. His popular appeal is seen to stem from his sincere commitment to defending Quebec's traditional values against the threat of the modern world, but the series also brings out his government's use of the same corrupt methods that he had denounced in attacking the Liberals, as well as his flirtations with fascism, including his ties to Adrien Arcand, the Quebec fascist leader who was Denys Arcand's uncle.[1]

As Carl Bergeron suggests, Arcand's Duplessis (Jean Lapointe) is "cynically playing with populism but sincerely indignant at the fate of his people" (2012, 35). According to Blandford, the idea was to depict "the things Duplessis did from *his* point of view" and to "demystify the man" (quoted in Irving 1977, D16), but the popular success of the series in Quebec, thanks largely to Lapointe's engaging performance, suggests that the myth was still very potent. However, *Duplessis* came under attack, from "an ultraconservative group headed by the Jesuit Jacques Cousineau (who had been ecclesiastic consultant for *Séquences* when it demolished *Champlain* and *Ville-Marie*)" (La Rochelle 2005, 146), because of its depiction of Duplessis's alcoholism and other weaknesses. There was especial concern about one sequence in the final episode when, after Duplessis's death, some of his former colleagues discuss rumors that he frequented brothels, which are then called into question when his doctor reveals that the great man suffered from "a severe malformation of the penis."[2]

For Arcand, the most important benefit of working on this series was that it taught him how to direct "characters who talk," and as he explained, "Writing seven hours of dialogue for TV, where there is no action, no crowd scenes, no car chases forced me to overcome a barrier" (quoted in DeGryse 1987–1988, 42). The discipline he learned proved very helpful in a few years' time, when working on the dialogue-heavy screenplay for *Le déclin*.

Another step toward that film came with *Empire, Inc.*, conceived by the CBC as a modest challenge to the dominance of such American prime-time soap operas as *Dallas* (CBS, 1978–1991) and *Dynasty* (ABC, 1981–1989). It set out "to do for the memory of Anglophone Montreal what the hugely successful *Duplessis* series did for Quebec's pre-1960 politics: consecrate its official demise" (Dorland 1982b, 46). The empire that the title most obviously refers to is the business enterprise built up by James Munroe (Kenneth Welsh) from the 1920s to the 1960s, but the focus on a wealthy English Canadian family brings out the enduring influence of the British Empire as it is gradually replaced by the rise of the American Empire. The family also lives through the changes in Quebec society during this period that led up to the Quiet Revolution.

The idea of declining empires had been on Arcand's mind at least since his use of Suetonius in *Réjeanne Padovani*, when, he told Léo Bonneville, "I hypothesized that we were living in a period that was very much analogous to the fall of the Roman Empire" (1979, 43). *Empire, Inc.* must have reinforced this line of thought, and one of the three episodes that Arcand directed is especially relevant to *Le déclin*. Episode 2, "Brother, Can You Spare $17 Million?" was cowritten by Jacques Poulin as well as Douglas Bowie (who received solo credit on all the other episodes, suggesting that Arcand was more involved than with his other episodes). It is set at the end of the 1920s, when Munroe needs $17 million to save his companies from going bankrupt during the Depression. His son announces that he is going to marry the daughter of an English lord, and Munroe sees a chance to get the money he needs. When the lord (Robert Clothier) comes to visit and asks to speak to Munroe in private, the businessman fears that he has heard the truth about his dire financial situation, but it turns out he only wants to know about Montreal's brothels. Munroe takes him to the one where his own mistress works, not knowing that some friends have brought his son there to give him sexual experience before his marriage. Munroe opens the door to his mistress's room and finds her in bed with his son, and he is then even more shocked to discover that the English lord has no money. The whole tone of the episode suggests a more elaborate version of the sexual escapades described by the assembled friends in *Le déclin*.

Ironically, Arcand owed his return to the big screen to the fact that Gilles Carle won the contest to make *Maria Chapdelaine*, but the circumstances were very unusual. There were by this time tentative signs of a revival in the Quebec film industry, which Arcand attributed to the success of Carle's *Les Plouffe* (*The Plouffe Family*; 1980; Dorland 1986, 19). Based on the 1948 novel by Roger Lemelin, which had already spawned a radio adaptation (1952) and an enormously popular television series (1953–1959), Carle's new version of this story about a working-class family in Quebec City in the 1930s and 1940s was a hybrid text, released both as a feature film and a six-part television series.[3] It was so successful that Lemelin was persuaded to write a belated sequel to his novel called *Le crime d'Ovide Plouffe*, which was duly published in 1982, and inevitably, plans to adapt the new novel were quickly developed. However, since Carle was filming *Maria Chapdelaine*, Denis Héroux, who had produced *Les Plouffe*, asked Arcand to direct a feature film based on the last section of the new novel. Two years later, Carle turned the rest of the novel into four episodes of a television series, with Arcand's film as the final two episodes.

Le crime d'Ovide Plouffe is set in 1949 and thus violates Arcand's vow not to make historical fiction (as did his episodes of *Empire, Inc.*). It centers on Ovide (Gabriel Arcand), the middle son of the Plouffe family, who has become a prosperous jeweler and an advocate for the modernization of Quebec. He is accused of murdering his unfaithful wife by placing a bomb on a plane but, after a long and sensational trial, the real culprit is discovered, and Ovide leaves for Paris in search of a young Frenchwoman he met after leaving his wife.[4] The result was a sequel that was almost as popular as *Les Plouffe*, but the critics were much less enthusiastic. Arcand himself thought the novel was "abominable" (quoted in Coulombe 1993, 73), and Bonneville lamented, "The clinical and critical Denys Arcand is entirely at the service of the novelist" (1984, 34). However, Michael Dorland disagreed and wrote a very positive review for *Cinema Canada* in which he argued that the film was a worthy successor to the director's previous work, calling it a "marvelously cynical film." He saw the film as concerned with the impact of "modernity" on the Plouffe family, depicting "an entire society's poisoning by modern commercial relations that Arcand's features and documentaries have hitherto relentlessly sketched class by social class" (1984, 24). If few critics—or the director himself—shared Dorland's enthusiasm, his review suggests that this neglected film is a missing link between Arcand's earlier and later works.

Despite his dislike of the subject matter, Arcand valued the experience he gained from making this film, and he, modestly or ironically, declared, "With *The Crime* I became a competent filmmaker" (quoted in Loiselle 1995, 150). While the general opinion (with which Arcand would have agreed) may have been that *Le crime d'Ovide Plouffe* represented "the lowest low in a career that had witnessed its fair share of downs" (Loiselle 2008, 5), two years later, that career would soar to its highest point so far. However, the project that resulted in *Le déclin de l'empire américain* had very modest beginnings and had to overcome many obstacles.

"INVOLVEMENT AND DISTANCE": *LE DÉCLIN DE L'EMPIRE AMÉRICAIN*

The idea for *Le déclin* was developed as part of an initiative at the NFB devised by Roger Frappier, who had produced *Le confort et l'indifférence*: in order to combat the downturn in the Quebec film industry, he persuaded the NFB to fund a series of very low-budget 16-millimeter fiction films.[5] Arcand proposed a film that was initially called *Conversations scabreuses* (Indecent conversations), inspired by Louis Malle's *My Dinner with André* (1981); it was to consist entirely of a group of people from various walks of life talking about their sexual experiences. In researching this project, Arcand interviewed many people and collected four hundred anecdotes, and his first scenario already included the idea that the conversations would take place while the men were preparing a meal and the women working out at a gym (Carrière 1997, 38). Much like the belated addition of the filmmakers in *Gina*, it was only when he had the idea of making the characters history professors that the eventual narrative structure began to emerge (Sklar 1986b, 49). The thesis about the decline of the American Empire was the final addition, and although Arcand claimed it was not "a real thesis" but "a thesis for movie purposes" (quoted in Posner 1993, 221), it provoked much of the later commentary on the film.

Frappier was so impressed with Arcand's proposal that he decided to seek outside assistance to increase the budget so that it could be produced as a 35-millimeter feature film. He reached out to René Malo at Montreal's Max Films, and eventually, they cobbled together a budget of $1.8 million, with the major portion coming from Telefilm Canada even though the government body "told the producers that they thought the film was elitist, and doubted that it could work commercially" (Posner 1993, 222). According to Arcand, Telefilm was reluctant to invest in a film that had "no dramatic action, interminable elitist allusions and disgusting characters," but he took pleasure in pointing out that, when the finished film was released in Montreal, it took one week to "beat the record held by *Indiana Jones*" (2005, 125, 127). It eventually "surpassed *E.T.* . . . as the biggest box office success in French-speaking Quebec" (Loiselle 2008, 25), grossing $2.2 million domestically, $1.1 million in the United States, and attracting an audience of 1.2 million in France (Lavoie 2003, 18). Despite this unexpected international success (or perhaps because of it), the film generated at least as much controversy as any of Arcand's previous films, and it inspired more critical debate, often quite heated, than any other Quebec (or Canadian) film before or since.

Its popular success was held against the film by some critics in Quebec who thought it undermined Arcand's credentials as a director of art films. Louise Vandelac, a feminist sociologist, saw it as "nothing but a remake of *Deux femmes en or*," the most popular of the soft-core films that followed Héroux's *Valérie* (La Rochelle 2005, 183).[6] Another critic emphasized its box-office success and insisted that it could not be compared to "the artistic quality [of] 'authentically Québécois' films" (Renaud 2002). The film's appeal to international audiences also made it suspect in the eyes of critics who argued that the "superior French" spoken by most of the characters was a ploy to enable foreign audiences to understand the dialogue more easily than in films using colloquial Québécois French. This was indeed Arcand's intention (Posner 1993, 221), and the film was marketed and received abroad as an art film rather than a commercial product. Andrew Sarris even called it a "European art film" (quoted in Bachand 2006, 100), and Arcand himself saw it as proof that Quebec should be making "*films d'auteur*, modest films that could prove very accessible to the international market" (quoted in La Rochelle 2005, 238). *Le déclin* certainly fitted into such a strategy, but its commercial and international success, along with the strategies that it used to unsettle audience expectations, muddied the waters and led to a wide range of critical responses.

The opening sequences belong firmly in the art film mode. The first image is of a young woman, presumably the one that Rémy (Rémy Girard) will later identify as his attractive Vietnamese student, looking attentively in front of her. What she sees is Rémy lecturing to his class on the meaning of history, telling them that it is not "a moral science" and that it is primarily concerned with "numbers." He does not refer to Quebec but predicts that the black majority in South Africa will inevitably gain power, while the minority in North America probably won't. There is a sudden cut to the credits sequence, in which the camera slowly tracks along a spacious hall (filmed at the Université de Montréal), accompanied by stately music (Handel). The camera eventually comes to rest in front of two women sitting on a window ledge at the end of the hall. Diane (Louise Portal) begins to record a radio interview with Dominique (Dominique Michel) about her new book called *Variances de l'idée du bonheur* (Variations on the idea of happiness). As the two women walk around the university, Dominique, the chair of the university's history department, expounds her thesis that the decline of the American Empire, like that of the Roman Empire before it, is the outcome of a society that promotes the pursuit of "individual happiness."

The tone changes in the next long segment of the film, which cuts back and forth between four men preparing food in Rémy's summerhouse beside a lake, close to the border with the United States, and four women working out in the university's sports center, their respective activities suggesting the breakdown of traditional gender stereotypes.[7] Both groups share risqué anecdotes about their sexual experiences, some of which are illustrated by flashbacks. Although the conversations are generally lighthearted, there is already a sense that the good humor masks an underlying anxiety, and the mask slips occasionally, most notably when Claude (Yves Jacques), a gay art historian, finds blood in his urine. Despite the implication that these men and women share a mutual interest in sexual adventures, the intercutting between the different locations suggests that they exist in opposition to each other. At one point during the preparations for the meal, Rémy beckons to Alain (Daniel Brière), a graduate student who seems bemused by the older men's accounts of their sexual affairs, and takes him to his study, where he shows him two apparently different animals pinned in a glass case on the wall. He explains that scientists only realized they belonged to the same species when they found a pair having sex. When Alain objects that one is an insect and the other a reptile, Rémy tells him that sex is the only thing they have in common, with the obvious implication that men and women are also otherwise totally different from each other.

This sense of two opposing forces is reinforced when the women finally arrive at the lake. The four men and four women face one another, and as the screenplay describes it, "There is a second of silence and immobility, like in a western before a duel" (Arcand 1986, 108). However, when they walk purposefully toward each

"They have one thing in common": the reunion of the men and women in *Le déclin de l'empire américain*.

other, the expected confrontation does not occur; instead, they embrace one another warmly, and the meal begins with a conviviality that maintains the generally comic tone. But there are discordant moments, as when Diane complains that, because she married young, she is now only a part-time instructor and thus lacks the benefits provided by "the best collective agreement in North America." The arrival of Mario (Gabriel Arcand), Diane's working-class lover, also unsettles the group, as he makes it clear that he is not impressed by their tastes or their intellectual posturing.

The thesis of decline reappears when the friends walk beside the lake, accompanied by an extract from Diane's recording in which Dominique argues that, despite the pleasures that modern society provides, "the decline of a civilization is as inevitable as aging is for individuals." Her pessimistic outlook later leads to a confrontation with Louise (Dorothée Berryman), Rémy's wife and the only nonhistorian present, which destroys the fragile sense of community. At the end of the day, Louise disagrees with Dominique's argument and suggests that it is the result of living alone and sacrificing her life to her career. Dominique immediately asks Pierre (Pierre Curzi) and Rémy, her two male colleagues, what they think of her book. When they remain silent, she suggests that it is because she has slept with both of them (as we have seen in earlier flashbacks). Louise is devastated, even though she was aware of the affairs her husband has had when away at conferences, and the afternoon's entertainment comes to an uncomfortable end. Pierre takes refuge in his chalet with Danielle (Geneviève Rioux), the student who is his current mistress; Dominique spends the night with Alain; and Louise seeks comfort from Claude.

If the endings of Arcand's first three fiction films were darkly comic epilogues to narratives that embodied his "tragic" vision, the ending of *Le déclin* undercuts the bawdy comedy that dominated the film to that point. Dominique's decision to destroy the atmosphere by seeking revenge for Louise's comments on her argument confirms that it is impossible to separate the private sexual behavior that excited so much critical discussion from the historical thesis of imperial decline. The result is a film that became "one of Arcand's most violently attacked films" (La Rochelle 2005, 182). On the one hand, feminist critics deplored what they saw as the misogynistic comedy that supposedly made it popular with uncritical audiences; on the other, the historical framework came under attack for its reiteration of the filmmaker's pessimistic outlook that made social change seem impossible.

Novelist Louky Bersianik started a lively debate in the pages of *Le Devoir* when she accused Arcand of having "reproduced all the clichés of sexual politics" and of making a film that "reintroduces sexism from the beginning through to the end" (1988, 49). In particular, she singled out the characters of Diane and Danielle as being unrealistic and misogynistic representations of female experience. Diane is having a masochistic affair with Mario, which she enjoys and claims to control, but Bersianik maintains that this relationship "lacks credibility" because it is not "logical" that an otherwise "autonomous and apparently well-balanced woman" would behave this way (50). Danielle is a student who works in a massage parlor to pay for her studies, and the services she provides for her male clients include the option of bringing them to orgasm (which is how she first meets Pierre). Bersianik simply calls her a prostitute and claims that she is not a credible character because "real prostitutes aren't able to practice their trade without drugs" (51).

Whatever the merits of Bersianik's case that the film is sexist and antifeminist, her normative judgments are at least questionable and certainly imply a less complex view of human nature than Arcand's. In a reply to the article, Barbara Godard argued that Bersianik's argument tended to confuse "story and discourse," thus ignoring the ways in which the characters are placed in a narrative context, but Godard also ended up concluding that the film did not go far enough in distancing itself from the sex talk that forms much of its content (1988, 131). In particular, she found that the conversations in the gym lacked "verisimilitude" because of "the coldness and detachment of the women's speech about sex" (133–134), and she was not impressed by Arcand's claim that his female cast members had persuaded him to make their scenes more racy to match the men's conversations and to reflect the way that women really talk among themselves (Arcand, quoted in Sklar 1986b, 49). A more consistent response to Bersianik's article came from Véronique Dassas, who argued that her critique was mistaken in that it proceeded "as if the satire was not there, as if the cool gaze of the auteur was not a critical gaze," and she suggested that if the film was "vulnerable," it was because "Arcand's universe is closed, dark and without escape" (1987–1988, 57).[8]

As we have seen, Arcand's view of history, as inspired by Maurice Séguin, is indeed a dark one, and he has described the historians in the film as being "lucid enough to know that history is a kind of blind force that advances like a glacier" (quoted in Dorland 1986, 18). At the end of *Le confort et l'indifférence*, a caption quoting Aleksandr Solzhenitsyn laments, "Our lives are so short compared with the slow unrolling of history," which points forward to *Le déclin*, in which the same feeling is created even though the earlier film's specific political concern with the future of Quebec is suppressed. The history of Quebec thus becomes the "structuring absence" that gives the later work its tension. However, Peter Wilkins objected to readings of *Le déclin* that attributed meaning to things omitted from the film because they "convert an absence into a presence allegorically; there is no way of verifying their claims from structural elements within the film" (1995, 120). Yet, as Richard Dyer has explained, the idea of a structuring absence "does not mean things which are simply not in the text, or which the critic thinks ought to be in the text"; rather it refers to "an issue . . . that a text cannot ignore, but which it deliberately skirts round or otherwise avoids" (1993, 105). The fact that these historians have no evident concern with Quebec's past constitutes such an absence.

Arcand told Michael Dorland that he had tried to "remove all reference to the fact that these are French-Canadians or Québécois" apart from "the fact that [they] are Canadian and on the borders of the empire." He did so, he said, because he did not want to "demand of a foreign viewer any specific knowledge of the Canadian situation" (quoted in Dorland 1986, 17), but for Canadian audiences at least, the omission of any reference to Quebec's recent history is highly significant. It is not that Quebec is absent from the film—most international audiences would recognize its setting—but that it is almost completely and noticeably absent from the discourses of the historians.

As we have seen, the precredits sequence confronts us with Rémy's lecture on history as a matter of "numbers," which conforms to Arcand's own understanding of Séguin's teachings but leaves unspoken Séguin's concern with its implications for the Québécois, who, as a minority in Canada, do not have sufficient numbers to achieve independence. Next we hear Dominique outline her thesis on the decline of the American Empire, which is clearly applicable to the pursuit of individual pleasure to which the characters (including Dominique) seemingly devote their lives, but again she makes no reference to Quebec. Later in the film, there is a brief flashback to one of Diane's lectures in which she points out that history usually deals with "winners," partly because there are "more documents on the Egyptians than on the Nubians, many more documents on the Spaniards than on the Mayas, and, of course, many more documents on men than on women." Diane's analysis here reflects her own sense of her marginal position in the History Department, but she also does not bring out how her argument applies to Quebec's situation as a loser after the British won their imperial war with the French. The links between the personal and political remain beneath the surface, but Diane is, in effect, showing how Rémy's concern with "numbers" can be applied to the gender wars that shape the treatment of sexuality in the film.

Despite Arcand's concern to downplay the Quebec context, several critics identified *Le déclin* as a "postreferendum film" (see, for example, Larose 1987, 15; and Weinmann 1990, 146). Though Arcand's response was that he did not think of the film this way, he added, "But it is not at all impossible that I had absorbed a number of current ideas and feelings that are reflected in my film" (quoted in Coulombe 1993, 84), suggesting that his own thought processes in preparing his film mirrored the way in which the Quebec situation inhabits the film's unconscious. The argument of those who saw it as a response to the failure of the 1980 referendum framed the characters as disillusioned members of the lyric generation, which had come of age during the Quiet Revolution (see the introduction). In this respect, the comparison with *The Big Chill* (Lawrence Kasdan, 1983), often made at the time, is illuminating. The Hollywood film depicts a similar situation—a group of men and women from the 1960s generation who become aware that their lives have not fulfilled the hopes of their youth—but Arcand omits any backstory that would suggest the characters in his film were politically engaged in the past. Thus Robert Sklar describes the lack of reference to the characters' personal histories as the film's "absent cause" (1986a, 47), and Bart Testa suggests that *The Big Chill* "exemplifies what *Le déclin* brings under critique, the dissolution of politics into personal happiness" (2002, 192).

As we saw in the introduction, one of the two overt allusions to the history of Quebec occurs, very unexpectedly, near the end of the film: Mario gives Diane a gift, which turns out to be Michel Brunet's book *Notre passé, le présent et nous* (Our past, the present and us; 1976), a collection of essays and conference presentations, most of which consist of angry denunciations of Quebec's historical servitude with the implication that concerted action might bring about a political solution. The book's presence in the film is important mainly because of its title, which points to issues of community and historical continuity that these historians choose to ignore.[9] Its inclusion, as a homage to his former teacher, in a film that tried to suppress all references that would not be clear to international audiences, suggests Arcand's underlying impatience with his characters, who express no interest in Quebec's future.

One way in which Quebec *is* present in the film is through its landscape. Shots of the autumnal countryside around the lake are inserted at several points, and the film ends with long shots of the summer cottages surrounded by snow, the silence contrasting with the endless chatter in the rest of the film. As Arcand put it, these images place all that has gone before in perspective, affirming that, "when they [are all] dead, there will still be the lake; another season; the falling snow" (quoted in Dorland 1986, 16).[10] The beauty of the geographical setting endures despite the historical events that have left its francophone inhabitants (or at least the intellectuals among them) alienated and unable to envisage a meaningful future. Arcand especially appreciated a review in the English Canadian magazine *Saturday Night* that emphasized the importance of the "nonverbal enunciations," which create a sense of "immanent happiness" (quoted in Loiselle 1995, 154), evoking a need to live in the present that is embodied in the friendship of the characters, however flawed they may be and however endangered that friendship may be at the end.[11]

This enigmatic ending, with none of the characters present, provides a moment to reflect on the significance of the comedy and anguish we have just witnessed. However, even more than Arcand's previous films, this is an extremely slippery text, and Bersianik begins her article by admitting that it is "difficult to get a grip on this film in order to analyse it" (1988, 48). This difficulty was apparent in the many diametrically opposed critical readings of the film. While one critic, echoing Hofsess's objections to *Réjeanne Padovani*, could accuse Arcand of creating "a monolithic discourse . . . terrorist in its intimidating force" (Bilodeau 1986, 70), another could praise him for setting up "a situation where viewers must constantly question and assess their feelings about the statements and attitudes of this élite in relation to its own decline" (Pérusse 1995, 74). Another critic casually referred to the "derision which Arcand heaps upon his characters" (Schwartzwald 1991, 175), but yet another insisted, "Arcand brings to all his characters an enormous compassion" (Harcourt 2006, 149). Such radical differences between critics, even in determining the film's basic procedures and effects, suggest we are dealing with an open rather than a closed text.

To a large extent, the divergent responses reflect the difficulty of pinning down the film's tone. As La Rochelle puts it, "No success of this scale has been so ambiguous," and he suggests that the popular acclaim "appears to be based on *The Decline*'s reputation as a sex comedy, albeit an intelligent one, although it is one of the most deadly serious films its author has ever made" (2005, 181). Arcand himself insisted that, despite all the jokes, "the basic subject is total anguish, particularly the ending" (quoted in Bonneville 1989, 14). The effectiveness of this tonal instability can be appreciated by comparing *Le déclin* with Marcel Dubé's stage play *Les beaux dimanches* (Lovely Sundays; first performed in 1965 and adapted as a film in 1974), with which it shares a pessimistic view of contemporary Quebec. The play starts from a basic situation that foreshadows *Le déclin*, a gathering of four middle-class couples who are apparently close friends but have little to live for apart from their sexual adventures. In order to escape from their "moral emptiness" (Pontaut 1969, 5), they drown their sorrows in drink, and although there are moments of comedy, the overall effect is extremely downbeat. Dubé's vision has been called "tragic and somber," depicting "a closed universe from which there is no means of escape" (Hamblet 1970, 79), and while, as Véronique Dassas suggests, Arcand's film also offers little prospect of "escape" for its characters (1987–1988, 57), its perspective on their situation creates a more active role for the spectator than Dubé's dour depiction of a society in crisis.[12]

What is crucial to understanding the controversial reception of *Le déclin* is how critics respond to the way in which the narration situates the characters. As we have seen, Arcand himself claimed to prefer "styles that don't call attention to themselves" (quoted in La Rochelle 2014, 11), and his critics often find his cinematic style unadventurous. Bill Marshall, for example, complains that the irony in *Le déclin* "refuses to comment on its own construction" (2001, 293), but the film's unpredictable tonal shifts are clearly designed to keep the audience off-balance. The film is, in fact, characterized by a "marked enunciation" (Testa 2002, 197), and Denise Pérusse has written two essays on the film in which she shows that "the narration . . . is far from effacing itself" (1987–1988, 49) and that "there exists a considerable distance between what the characters say and the discourse that the enunciator delivers" (1995, 83). The presence of a narrator is apparent from the beginning (in the elaborately choreographed tracking shot during the credits sequence), and the ironic and cynical perspective of the narration is then developed (in a less overt, more Buñuelian way) through such devices as cuts that abruptly juxtapose different viewpoints, as well as flashbacks that seem to simply illustrate the characters' stories but are often contradictory or reveal information that their words try to conceal.

One example of such contradictions occurs when, after Louise has told the women how she and Rémy went to a party in which couples exchanged partners, Rémy tells Claude that he has never been to such parties because he wants to avoid "confusing married life with sexual affairs." A flashback illustrates Louise's story, but the viewer has to choose between believing her version or assuming that she has made it up to impress her more adventurous friends. That Louise may not be as innocent as she seems is also suggested by the difference between her account and Rémy's of another event. He describes how Louise became unreasonably angry when his car got stuck in the driveway after a snowstorm, preventing her from getting out. He attributes her anger to her period, which transforms her into a "monster" every month, but she then explains to the other women that she was upset because she was going to miss her last chance to see her tennis coach before he left for a tournament in Ontario. She insists that nothing happened between them, but she ruefully notes that she had the impression that something might have been possible that day. Once again, a flashback seems to confirm her version, but we are left to wonder if she is embroidering on the truth.

The veracity of what we have heard and seen about the various accounts of past events is further called into question at the end of the film when the historians discuss an alleged affair that one of their colleagues had at a conference in Italy. Several different versions of the incident have been circulated, leading Pierre to comment, "I have the impression we will never get to the bottom of this story." The effect is to cast doubt on all that we have been told before in a narrative that may seem omniscient but that refuses to provide a secure basis for judging its own truth value. The narration thus offers a perspective that comes from outside the characters and comments on their behavior but, unlike the similar narratives strategies of much Hollywood cinema, its unreliability means that the spectators must figure out the meaning of that commentary for themselves. For Robin Wood (1989, 61) and Bill Marshall (2001, 293), the narration fails to conceal the filmmaker's "complicity" with characters he claims to criticize. In the opposite camp, for Carl Bergeron, "the camera says something completely different from than the characters, which probably explains the film's success" (2012, 118), a conclusion that echoes Pérusse's observation that "there is a considerable distance between what the characters say and what the narrator thinks (without saying it)" (1987–1988, 51).

What these different critical responses come down to is a judgment about how close Arcand is to his characters. While Arcand admitted, "Those characters are also me" and that his attitude to them was "very warm and the camera was warm too, close to them" (quoted in Dorland 1986, 18, 21), Jean Larose thought that "Arcand works *at a distance* and *on distance*" (1987, 10). Despite his warm feelings toward the characters, Arcand has insisted that their "hedonism is another dead end," claiming that he is "always ambivalent towards [his] characters"; he finds "some of their witticisms amusing, and others contemptible" (quoted in Loiselle 1995, 154, 152). However, since there are no overt markers to signal which are which, spectators must decide for themselves, and so critical interpretations often tell us more about the critic than they do about the film.

The film thus produces, as Peter Wilkins puts it, "an uncomfortable oscillation between involvement and distance" (1995, 121), and this is nowhere more apparent than in the treatment of Louise at the end of the film. Since she attacks Dominique's thesis, which closely conforms to Arcand's own view of history, the logic of the film would seem to endorse Bart Testa's view that "Louise's demolition is satisfying" and is necessary to avoid making her "a sentimental alternative to the film's central thesis" (2002, 186–187). Yet even though her aspersions on Dominique's personal life may be uncalled for and her optimism rather naive, her advocacy of simply enjoying the present moment comes close to making her "the most insightful character of the bunch" (Loiselle 2008, 78). Even Robin Wood, despite his dislike of the film, grudgingly admitted that "a certain complexity of effect arises from the fact that the two women who emerge as the film's most sympathetic characters embody directly opposite positions: the most 'progressive' and the most conservative" (1989, 61). Arcand may not have agreed with Wood's assignment of ideological categories to the two women, but although the "progressive" Dominique may speak for the director's viewpoint, so does the "conservative" Louise, with her insistence on the value of friendship and what Arcand called "the fugitive present moment" (quoted in Bergeron 2012, 114).

All the critical debates over the film's meaning and ideological significance did not prevent it from becoming an enormous commercial success, and as Arcand explained, it threw him into a "maelstrom of media attention" (quoted in Barker 1990a, 4), which he would reflect on in his next film. There were even discussions about a Hollywood remake, though these eventually came to nothing, because, according to Arcand, the extremely competitive environment in American universities made the idea of friendship between academics seem extremely improbable (Coulombe 1993, 98). It became clear that the challenge that Arcand's films presented to standard definitions of art cinema also applied to the requirements of conventional commercial cinema.

"ARE YOU LOOKING FOR JESUS?": *JÉSUS DE MONTRÉAL*

It is characteristic of the slipperiness of *Le déclin* that it has been described both as a postmodern text (Loiselle 2008, 63–64) and as a film that shows that Arcand is "anything but a postmodernist" (Testa 2002, 191n23); however, it is perhaps Peter Harcourt who most accurately describes it as "a thoroughly modernist film set in these postmodern times" (2006, 151). This description applies even more forcibly to *Jésus de Montréal*, which, as David Pike suggests, depicts "the encroachment of an international postmodernity into the just recently modernized landscape of Montreal" (2012, 147). Several critics have referred to the film's "postmodern techniques" (Wilkins 1995, 126), and Mary Alemany-Galway has devoted a whole chapter of a book to arguing that Arcand's film is an example of the postmodern approach that she finds in much Canadian cinema (2002, 119–139). There is little to be gained by splitting hairs over what distinguishes postmodern techniques from modern ones, but if postmodernism means the "breaking up of the grand Narratives" (Lyotard 1984, 15) that shaped human experience in the past, Arcand's work certainly bears witness to the decline of many such narratives (most notably, those of Christianity and Marxism, and perhaps even history). But his relationship to the "postmodern condition" is much more complex—even contradictory—than a simple acquiescence to its imperatives.

Arcand followed up the huge success of *Le déclin* with a very different film that proved to be equally popular but less controversial—perhaps rather unexpectedly in view of the furor generated by Martin Scorsese's *The Last Temptation of Christ* (1988) a few months earlier. It required a budget of $4 million, and this was raised partly from French producers, which only further alienated some critics who saw Arcand as moving further away from his Québécois roots. However, for Arcand, the comfortable production circumstances made possible by the success of his previous film would have only exacerbated the contradiction that already existed between, as he described it, "my childhood memories of being a choirboy in a faraway village, Catholic for centuries, and my daily experience of being a film-maker in a large cosmopolitan city" (quoted in Hunter 1990, 11). The new film was designed to explore this contradiction, and he saw it as a response to the ending of *Le déclin*, "where all the people are completely lost and don't know where to go," which encourages "reflection on the meaning of religion" (quoted in Sklar 1990, 16).

Jésus depicts the experiences of an actor who is commissioned to create a modern version of the Passion play performed each year on the mountain above Montreal and who then comes into conflict not only with the moribund, premodern clerical establishment, which is shocked by the production's treatment of the story of Christ, but also with the postmodern cultural environment that turns the production into the latest media sensation. Arcand felt that the film reflected his own "uncomfortable and contradictory position," which he then compared to that of an actor he met who played the role of Christ for tourists on Mount Royal in the evening, perhaps "between two sessions for commercials or dubbing" (quoted in Marsolais and Racine 1989, 5). The director's situation and that of the actor raised the question of what could be salvaged from Quebec's Catholic heritage, still so important to its claims for a distinct cultural identity, in the context of a city like Montreal—which, as Arcand had shown in *Les Montréalistes*, owed its origin to Christian missionaries but had become a thriving modern commercial metropolis.

The film's title functions as a kind of montage effect, setting up a collision between the religious past and the secular present. Just as the narrative in *Le déclin* was punctuated by shots of the landscape around the lake, here the drama on the mountain is punctuated by shots of the city, and as Arcand has pointed out, "everything is filmed from above looking down" (quoted in Bonneville 1989, 18). Even if these images, along with the title, place *Jésus* in a specific cultural location, Arcand wanted to address a broader concern than the impact of Quebec's Quiet Revolution, and he suggested that the film dealt with the impact of "the disappearance of religion" in the Western world (quoted in O'Brien 1990, 50). Although the film's satire is directed against organized religion (as well as the mass media), Arcand based his screenplay on the latest historical research on the life of Jesus, not in order to discredit Christianity but to restore the meaning of what he called "the very few words that we are sure Jesus said," which "still speak to me though I'm an atheist" (quoted in Hunter 1990, 12). He chose to follow the Gospel of Saint Mark because he thought it was "the oldest, the most narrative and the most brutal" (quoted in Bonneville 1989, 17).

If Quebec history is the structuring absence in *Le déclin*, here it is belief—but not just religious belief. The film suggests the media have become "the new institutionalized 'church'" (Nelson 1990, 26), but the information they circulate is so overwhelming and contradictory that it has a divisive rather than unifying effect. As many critics have suggested, *Jésus* is also about the role of art in the age of media simulations (a concern that has become even more urgent in the twenty-first century with the emergence of so-called social media). The focus on the dilemma of an actor playing Jesus becomes a way of exploring the relations of fiction and reality, both within the world of the film and in the process of creating it. If, in the film, Daniel Coulombe (Lothaire Bluteau) comes to inhabit the role of Jesus through painstaking research, so did Bluteau in preparing to play Daniel. For Arcand, this actor's persona was perfect for the role, because, while "most actors are heterosexual or gay . . . with him there is no sexuality at all" (quoted in Hunter 1990, 12), and he insisted, "If [Bluteau] had said no, I would not have made the film" (quoted in Bonneville 1989, 18).

As in *Le déclin*, the film begins with a precredits sequence: in this case, we are plunged into the middle of a dramatic confrontation between two men in a rustic cabin, one of whom accuses the other of killing their father. Before leaving, the accused murderer reminds the other man that it was he who wished their father dead and that he had once said, "We must destroy the idea of God in the spirit of man." Left alone, he soliloquizes, regretting that he has rejected the gift of love that Jesus offered him, and he hangs himself. The screen goes black, and suddenly we hear a theater audience applauding and realize that the overwrought altercation we have just witnessed was the final scene of a stage play.[13] In the lobby afterward, Pascal Berger (Cédric Noël), the actor who played the character who hanged himself, is surrounded by admirers, including Denise Quintal (Monique Miller), a publicity agent, who declares, "I want his head," and explains she is referring to her next advertising campaign. A critic (Pauline Martin) tells Pascal, "You are the greatest actor of your generation," but he moves away to greet a colleague he has seen in the crowd, who tells him he is about to play the role of Jesus.

This prologue introduces the main concerns of the film: the moral consequences of the loss of faith; the relations between the real, the theatrical, and the cinematic; and the biblical parallels that will emerge from Daniel's project (here, Pascal as John the Baptist, preparing the way for the coming of Christ, and the publicity agent as Salome, demanding the head of the Baptist). The credits sequence then begins with a shot of a conductor who directs two female singers in what appears to be a rehearsal for a performance of Pergolesi's *Stabat mater*, a reminder of a time when art drew its power from religion. Here it is performed in an empty church by young musicians, dressed casually, suggesting the possibility that art remains a potential source of spiritual experience in the modern world. During the rehearsal, Daniel enters the church and looks up at the singers before being welcomed by Father Leclerc (Gilles Pelletier), who takes him to see a video recording of the Passion play as it has been presented at Saint Joseph's Oratory, on the mountain above Montreal, for the last thirty-five years. The television monitor shows young actors intoning, with highly theatrical mannerisms, dialogue that is, as Leclerc admits, very old-fashioned. Daniel's task is to produce a new version that will bring the old story to life for a contemporary audience.

His first step, like that of Jesus in the Gospels, is to gather his disciples. He finds Constance (Johanne-Marie Tremblay), whom he has recognized as an actor in the old version, working in a soup kitchen. They recruit Martin (Rémy Girard) while he is dubbing a pornographic film in which he has to supply the voices for two men in an orgy, as well as René (Robert Lepage), who is recording the commentary for a planetarium spectacle illustrating the latest theories about the origins of the universe. Finally, Mireille (Catherine Wilkening) is discovered, dressed in what the screenplay calls "a few diaphanous veils" (Arcand 1989, 45), walking on water during the shooting of a television commercial for a perfume named after Milan Kundera's *The Unbearable Lightness of Being*.[14]

While recruiting his actors, Daniel is also conducting his research. He speaks to a theologian (Claude Léveillée) who describes new archeological discoveries and the results of computer analysis of ancient texts but points out that his faculty depends on the archbishop for its funding. Thus, unlike actors, whom he thinks can say anything, he and his colleagues cannot publish their findings. The next sequence shows Daniel in a library studying a book about the practice of crucifixion, when a librarian (Paule Baillargeon) brings him more books and asks, conspiratorially, "Are you looking for Jesus?" When Daniel, looks surprised and replies that he is, she solemnly assures him, "He will find you." The tensions among scientific research, ecclesiastical authority, and evangelical Christianity point to the minefield that Daniel is about to enter (which Arcand somehow managed to avoid with his film) and that will have tragic consequences for the actor.

Once the cast is assembled, we see what is evidently an early rehearsal, with the actors wearing their own clothes, but an abrupt cut takes us to a scene from the first performance, with the actors in full costume. This might initially be taken to be a "flashback" to the actual events on which the play is based, but then we see the on-screen audience and recognize the actors, who, apart from Daniel as Jesus, take on multiple roles in the production. The scene in progress depicts

Pontius Pilate interrogating Jesus, and when Pilate declares him to be "inoffensive," a Jewish priest draws him aside to talk in secret, their conversation heard by the film audience but, rather improbably, not by the play's spectators on the mountain. As in all the extracts from the production that follow, this sequence plays with the difference between theatrical and cinematic representations and the ways in which they each create an illusion of reality for an audience, both for the on-screen audience that moves after each scene between the different Stations of the Cross and for the film audience that follows the actors as they interact offstage and suffer the consequences of their artistic risk-taking.

The film thus juxtaposes different forms of representation, frequently unsettling the viewer and, as in *Le déclin*, further complicates matters by sudden tonal shifts. Here, the most startling such effect occurs at the end of the final performance, which the actors have decided to put on even though Father Leclerc has ordered them to cancel it. When Jesus/Daniel is on the cross, security guards intrude into the biblical scene in order to stop the performance, inciting a scuffle with members of the audience that causes the cross to topple over, seriously injuring Daniel. In this moment, "farce turns into tragedy in one brutal cut" (Alioff 1989, 16), and "tragedy emerges where we thought a comedy was being enacted" (Weinmann 1990, 215). While one critic complained, "drama and comedy destroy each other," thus undermining the director's "pessimistic approach to the world" (Roy 1989, 45), most audiences seem to have welcomed what Arcand calls "*my* style," which, he says, defies critical canons that insist on "unity of style" (quoted in Marsolais and Racine 1989, 8). His so-called pessimism is thus more complex (or more contradictory) than some of his critics have assumed.

The lack of stylistic "unity" is partly an effect of juxtaposing the mundane lives of the actors with questions of metaphysical import. One critic has accused Arcand of ignoring "the differences between the aesthetic perspective as an engrossment with surfaces, and the religious perspective as a concern with the really real" (Walsh 2003, 56–7), but the film's point is that these differences, while they may be important, are increasingly difficult to define. Thus at one point, a performance is interrupted by a Haitian woman who throws herself forward to ask Jesus to forgive her and has to be restrained by a guard. Is she to be seen as a naive spectator, confusing an aesthetic experience with a religious one, or is she simply responding to the convincing performances of the actors and the power of the story? A similar question arises with regard to Daniel, who increasingly seems to become Jesus outside the play as well as within it.

The audiences who have followed the Stations of the Cross respond to the production with enthusiastic applause at the end of each performance, much like the audience at the play in the opening sequence, but unlike the Haitian woman, they respect the boundary between art and reality. After the first performance, however, the production is released into a world of media hyperbole. The same critic who praised Pascal now tells Daniel he is the greatest actor of his generation, and we see radio and television personalities raving about the production, dispensing contradictory information, and offering interpretations masquerading as truth. On the other hand, Father Leclerc is far from congratulatory and asks Daniel if he is "completely mad," objecting in particular to the suggestion that Jesus may have been the illegitimate son of a Roman centurion. The priest thus reveals himself as a would-be liberal who wants to "refresh" the old play but has no interest in seeking new ideas that would conflict with the traditional teachings of the Church.

Daniel has updated the Passion play to bring out the modern relevance of Jesus's message, and Arcand's *Jésus* also presents itself as a modern reworking of the biblical story through the parallels it suggests between its characters and events and those depicted in the Gospels. Thus Leclerc is a Judas figure who betrays Daniel; as a single mother, Constance is an ironic version of the Virgin Mary (even more ironic in that she is having an affair with Father Leclerc); and Mireille can be seen as Mary Magdalene, saved by the production from a life in which she sells her body in the media marketplace. It is his disgust with the way Mireille is treated at an audition for a beer commercial that leads Daniel to overturn equipment and physically attack Denise Quintal, who is running the audition, an allusion to Jesus driving the moneylenders from the temple. Just as Satan offered Jesus material power during the temptation in the wilderness, Richard Cardinal (Yves Jacques), an unctuous lawyer and agent, takes Daniel to the top of a high-rise building, shows him the city below, and offers to make him rich. And while Daniel does not literally die on the cross like Jesus, he succumbs to the injuries he sustained there and is (symbolically, at least) resurrected at the end of the film.

The miraculous resurrection in the Bible is here translated into modern terms through the device of organ donations, which enable others to go on living. For some critics, even some of those who admired the film, this ending pushes the allegory too far. Gilles Marsolais felt that it plunged the film "into the clichés that it had been able to avoid until then" (1989, 42), while Adam Barker found that it "risks tipping the metaphor into the risible" (1990b, 4). Arcand defended it as showing that Daniel "has not died in vain, despite appearances" (quoted in Marsolais and Racine 1989, 9), and we see the result of his sacrifice when doctors congratulate patients after successful operations. Since the recipient of Daniel's heart is "a 'damned Anglo'" and his eyes save an Italian woman from blindness, Heinz Weinmann argues that the ending, in the spirit of Jesus, represents "the gift of oneself to the Other, the foreigner, the enemy" (1990, 246), and Ian Lockerbie suggests the film offers hope for the future based on "Quebec's movement outwards towards others" (1996, 130).

However, while the ending does support such interpretations, there are, as usual with Arcand, possible alternative readings. One critic offers a more cynical interpretation of it as demonstrating that "there is no future for French-speaking Montreal" (Simons 2004, 163), and the events leading up to Daniel's death do at least make it difficult to accept that this is a straightforwardly optimistic conclusion. After the toppling of the cross, Daniel, his body still covered in the simulated bloody whip marks from the crucifixion scene, is rushed to the nearest hospital, where he is shunted off to a crowded corridor until a doctor becomes available. However, he seems to recover and walks out of the hospital to a Metro station, where he harangues the people waiting for trains with apocalyptic warnings, while the head of Pascal Berger / John the Baptist is visible on an advertising poster in the background. After he collapses on the platform, the medics take him to an anglophone Jewish hospital that is much less crowded and where he is immediately admitted, only for a doctor to tell Constance and Mireille that they have arrived just too late to save him.

Many critics picked up on the irony that the hospital that fails to treat Daniel is St. Mark's, named after the disciple on whose Gospel Arcand based his film, whereas it is a Jewish hospital that might have saved him. As Bart Testa suggests, "the collapse of socialized medical care" is seen as the product of a society that has lost touch with "humane reason and human charity," and the final irony is that Daniel, whose attempt to revive the spiritual power of Jesus's teachings had embroiled him in the machinations of "the commercial city," has become simply a dying body in "the suffering city" (1995, 107–109). Ironically, it is the Church that crucifies Daniel/Jesus and prevents the renewal of the message of the Gospels: the ultimate message thus seems to prefigure the recent argument of the Slovenian theorist Slavoj Žižek: while "the Christian legacy is all too precious and, today, more pertinent than ever," the Church is "the main anti-Christian force today" (2015, 77–78).

As the varied responses of the critics suggest, Arcand had again created an open text that invites the spectators to interpret the film according to their own backgrounds and experience. The ambiguous treatment of the "resurrection" also provokes questions about whether Daniel's disciples will continue his work. A montage sequence shows patients in hospitals recovering from their transplants intercut with Cardinal meeting with the actors and proposing that they should form a theatrical company to honor Daniel's memory. Martin, René, and Constance agree as long as it will be faithful to the kind of work Daniel would want them to do and not a "traditional and commercial theater," and the lawyer reassures them, insisting, with an ironic smile, that he has always believed that profit does not exclude experimental work. However, Mireille simply gets up and leaves, and as André Loiselle and Brian McIlroy put it, "By having one character refuse the lawyer's offer and walk away as empty and unfulfilled as she

"All this shall be destroyed": Daniel prophesies the Day of Judgment on a Metro platform in *Jésus de Montréal.*

was at the beginning of the film, Arcand forces both the optimist and the cynic to question their interpretation of the film" (1995, 6).

This sequence also speaks to Arcand's situation as a filmmaker in Quebec, one whose two latest films had achieved commercial success, leading some of his opponents to conclude that he had lost his integrity as an artist. Earlier in the film, when Daniel appears in court after his destruction of the equipment at the audition, the judge (played by Arcand himself) sends him for a psychiatric assessment. When the psychiatrist (Andrée Lachapelle) asks if Daniel's anger stems from being born in Quebec rather than in California, New York, London, or "even Stockholm where you could have met Ingmar Bergman," he replies that, while it is "inconvenient," it "could have been worse: I could have come into the world in Burkina Faso." Back in court, the judge reads the psychiatrist's report, which, he ruefully announces, concludes that Daniel is "better adjusted than many of the judges in this court."

This sequence captures Arcand's own uncomfortable position in his home province, where he feels deeply rooted but with whose culture he has, in his words, "a love-hate relationship" (quoted in La Rochelle 2005, 270). The fragility of his situation as a filmmaker became apparent soon after, when he went through another lean period in the 1990s.

5 · OF BEAUTY AND DEATH IN THE DIGITAL EPOCH

When you're facing death, ideologies tend to fade a little bit.
—Denys Arcand

After the extraordinary success of *Le déclin de l'empire américain* and *Jésus de Montréal*, Arcand's career took another downturn. The 1990s may seem, in some ways, like a parenthesis in Arcand's career, with apparently minor projects and another period of critical and commercial failure after those two Oscar-nominated films. The three films he made between *Jésus* and *Les invasions barbares* (two of them in English) were either rejected or ignored by most critics, who saw them as departures from his earlier preoccupations and ways of seeing. Yet *Love and Human Remains* (1993), *Joyeux calvaire* (*Poverty and Other Delights*; 1996), and *Stardom* (2000) were not, like the films he made between *Gina* and *Le déclin*, commissioned pieces undertaken because he could not find funding for his personal projects. This time the problems could not be so obviously blamed on the state of the Canadian film industry, though they could be partially attributed to difficulties in the filmmaker's personal life, since both his parents died during this period.

Although none of these films have provoked much critical interest, they do represent the filmmaker's response to cultural and historical developments at the end of the twentieth century in ways that anticipate the inflection of his characteristic themes and style in his film that would finally win an Academy Award. They could be said to grow out of the absence of Quebec history in *Le déclin* and the pervasiveness of the media in *Jésus*: if those films offered, as I have argued, a modernist perspective on a culture that has lost any sense of its past, creating "a visible tension between postmodernity and traditional Montreal" (Pike 2012, 99), postmodernity seems to have taken over in the new films to encompass the style as well as the worlds they depict. One symptom of this change is that all three films, in quite different ways, are set in "non-places," which, according to Marc Augé, are spaces that "cannot be defined as relational, historical, or concerned with identity" (1995, 77–78). Although, as I will argue, Arcand's capitulation to postmodern trends may be more apparent than real, in these films, he may be said to simulate postmodern techniques to explore the emergence of "the digital epoch," which he saw as "an extraordinarily important rupture" (quoted in Patry 2011b, 12).

As a result of these new developments, Arcand ventured into territory more often associated with Atom Egoyan, a younger Canadian director whose emergence in the 1980s benefited from the changes in Canadian film policy that helped revive Arcand's career at that time. Egoyan's early films explore the implications of the then new video technology for the relations between image-making and identity. His characters live in the anonymous modern cities that Northrop Frye once described as "obliterated environments" (1971, iii), and their lack of landmarks to shape their sense of the world often leads to retreats into fantasies shaped by media images. Just as Arcand's characters have lost touch with Quebec's past, Egoyan's suffer from the loss of their ethnic heritage (usually related to the director's own Armenian background), which, they imagine, would have provided a more defined cultural identity.

The two filmmakers crossed paths when they both contributed segments to the compilation film *Montréal vu par . . .* (*Montreal Sextet*; 1991), which consisted of six short films, by Québécois and English Canadian directors, commissioned to celebrate the city's 350th anniversary. Egoyan's "En passant" ("Passing Through") depicts a tourist whose only engagement with the city comes through nonverbal signs and a recorded guide that directs his movement through the streets. With typical perversity, Arcand's "Vue d'ailleurs" (Seen from afar), based on a scenario by Paule Baillargeon, is set in an embassy in an unnamed tropical country, where a woman recounts the story of her passionate affair in snow-covered Montreal at the time of the FLQ bombings.[1] This segment was shot mainly in Ontario with "the crew usually used by . . . Atom Egoyan" (Mietkiewicz 1991, F8), and as we shall see in discussing some of Arcand's later films, this brief contact seems to have inspired the older filmmaker to further pursue his concerns with the proliferation of media images that he had already begun to address in *Jésus*.

LIVING THROUGH "THE DIGITAL EPOCH": ARCAND IN THE 1990S

Many critics expressed surprise that Arcand would choose to follow up his two great successes with an adaptation of Brad Fraser's 1989 play, originally called *Unidentified Human Remains and the True Nature of Love*, which, apart from being in English, was set in Edmonton and dealt with people and issues that seemed far removed from the director's previous work. However, Arcand pointed out that the play, which depicted the interactions of seven characters who remained on stage throughout, lent itself to "the kind of ensemble film I do" and that with the action constantly moving to different parts of the stage, it was constructed like a "fugue," allowing for the comparisons and contrasts that had always characterized his narrative structures.[2] He first saw the play in Montreal, staged in French by André Brassard but still set in Edmonton. However, since, as Fraser put it, the Alberta Motion Picture Development Corporation decided "the project wasn't 'Albertan' enough" (1996, 6), the original plan to shoot the film in Edmonton had to be abandoned. The location was moved to Montreal, but Fraser's screenplay was still filmed in English.[3]

As well as its formal structure, what attracted Arcand to the play was its "universe of sexual ambiguity," and he thought of the characters as "modern archetypes," living in "complete uncertainty with regard to their work, their sexual orientation, and their pleasure" (quoted in Coulombe 1993, 41, 43). David (Thomas Gibson), an actor who once starred in a television series but is now working as a waiter, is the former lover of Candy (Ruth Marshall), with whom he still lives. However, he is now openly gay: he is attracted to his friend Bernie (Cameron Bancroft) and becomes friendly with Kane (Matthew Ferguson), his teenage busboy. Candy is unsure of her own sexual orientation; she is tempted when Robert (Rick Roberts), a bartender, asks her out on a date but also by the lesbian advances of Jerri (Joanne Vannicola), whom she meets at a gym. There is no specific focus, like the meal by the lake in *Le déclin*, and the narrative is held together mainly by the activities of an unseen serial killer preying on women in the city streets and by Benita (Mia Kershner), a dominatrix and psychic, who acts as a kind of choric figure, catering to and exposing the characters' secret desires. Her gory stories both reflect and possibly even produce the conjunction of sex and death by which the characters are surrounded.

These young people could be the children of the generation depicted in *Le déclin*, who were virtually absent in that film but would emerge in the foreground in *Les invasions*. In *Love and Human Remains*, they are as sexually active as Rémy and his friends, but their sexual orientation is much more fluid, and although they are younger, they are more troubled by the threat of death, partly due to the lurking presence of the serial killer but even more so due to the advent of AIDS. Fluidity is also a feature of the media culture in which they are immersed, inundating them with a constantly changing flow of information and images. Devices such as answering machines and television remotes lead not to better communication but to confusion and uncertainty. Thus near the end of the film, David switches off his answering machine just before a former lover completes the message that he has tested HIV positive, and Candy casually turns off the television just as a reporter is about to reveal a clue to the identity of the killer, although as it turns out this would have led her to suspect the wrong man. As we have seen, Arcand felt that the lifestyle of the characters in *Le déclin* was a hedonist dead end, and these younger characters have become what Réal La Rochelle calls "the living dead of hedonist techno-culture" (1995b, 49).

What struck many critics as a major departure for Arcand was the film's "postmodern aesthetic of abrupt connections . . . a little like the omnipresent zapping of television" (Bachand 2006, 104). The rapid editing, along with the "perpetual camera movement," was intended, as cinematographer Paul Sarossy explained, to mirror "the constant state of unease that the characters have in relation to the world and each other" (DVD). However, while the film's style may reflect the hectic pace of the culture it seeks to critique, the overall effect is simply an acceleration of the unsettling juxtapositions that characterize the director's earlier films.

Another "postmodern" element, partly enforced by the production difficulties mentioned above, is the anonymous urban environment in which the film is set, although unlike in many tax shelter films during the CCA era, it is clear that the city is in Canada, and there is at least one French-language television channel. The film was shot in Montreal, but Arcand deliberately "explored corners of the city that are not filmed very often" (quoted in Charbonneau 1994, 9) and created what La Rochelle calls "a *barbarian* metropolis" (2005, 199). Young people lost in a generic urban landscape is a staple of Egoyan's films, and David Pike even suggests that *Love and Human Remains* should be viewed as "an essay in Egoyanism" (2012, 100); after all, Sarossy was Egoyan's regular cinematographer, with whom Arcand had worked on *Montréal vu par . . .*[4] The influence of the younger director might also be detected in "the lack of affect" (Castiel 1994, 38) in the performances of the actors, a trait also often noted in Egoyan's films and that had earned him the reputation of being a cold and detached director (though similar comments had already been made about Arcand's French-language films).

The publicity for the film described it as a "comedy," but like most of Arcand's films, it is much more generically unstable than this suggests. Its depiction of characters drifting from one relationship to another, in search of a love that they doubt even exists, does lead up to a sequence that is worthy of a bedroom farce, when Kane, Jerri, and Robert turn up in quick succession in the apartment shared by David and Candy, creating embarrassment and confusion. However, the tone rapidly changes when Bernie climbs into the apartment through a window and threatens Candy, revealing that he is the killer. He escapes to the roof of the building, where he tries to explain his behavior to David, before falling backward over the edge.

It was hardly surprising that the film failed to match the success of Arcand's two previous films. Fraser attributed the disappointing response to this generic uncertainty, suggesting that "people were unsure whether they were seeing a suspense film or a Gen X slice-of-life kind of movie" (1996, 7), a problem similar to that Egoyan would face on the release of *Where the Truth Lies* (2005), which seemed to satisfy neither audiences expecting an Egoyan art film nor those expecting a crime thriller.[5] As usual with Arcand's films, critical judgments were deeply divided: while one critic ranked it "far behind his numerous masterpieces, whether documentary or fiction" (Lavoie 1994, 47), La Rochelle argued that it "belongs as profoundly to Arcand as its two predecessors" and that "together they form a great 'trilogy of Montreal'" (1995a, 20).

Montreal figures rather more visibly in Arcand's next film, in which he returned to French-language production, albeit in a modestly budgeted television film about two homeless people. The screenplay for *Joyeux calvaire* was by Claire Richard, an actress who had worked among street people (like Constance in *Jésus*), although there were rumors that her partner, the surrealist novelist Réjean Ducharme, had contributed to the script (La Rochelle 2005, 223).[6] The title can be literally translated as "joyous calvary," a contradiction that draws on the frequent use of religious terms in Quebec slang, but it is also a colloquial phrase meaning something like "a real mess." When the film was shown in a subtitled version on the English-language CBC network, it was called *Poverty and Other Delights*.

At this time, Arcand was struggling with his own screenplay for a film on beauty that eventually became *Stardom*, and he was trying to come up with ideas for a film about death, following the deaths of his parents. Directing this television film could be seen as his way of escaping from these more ambitious projects, but while *Joyeux calvaire* may contain little that is conventionally beautiful, the narrative is framed by death. It begins with a man, later identified as Stanley (Lorne Brass), jumping from a bridge at a Metro station and badly injuring himself when he lands on a platform, and it ends when he successfully commits suicide at the same spot. In between, the film depicts a day in the lives of two street people, Marcel (Gaston Lepage) and Joseph (Benoît Brière), as they wander through the city, apparently without direction; however, Marcel keeps inquiring of the people they meet if they have seen the suicidal Stanley.

Neither of these men was born in Montreal—Marcel comes from Caraquet in New Brunswick and Joseph from Abitibi in northern Quebec—but Marcel has lived in the city for some time and keeps up a running commentary on the people and places they encounter for the benefit of his companion, who has just arrived (and for the sake of the audience). The city through which they pass is filled with wastelands, ruined buildings, and construction sites, and more than one critic compared it to Beirut (Lavoie 1997, 43; La Rochelle 2005, 223). Yet as in most Arcand films, the pessimism is relieved by moments of humor, derived from the eccentric characters they meet, and by flashbacks to earlier times in their lives—some of which, as in *Le déclin*, may be tall stories.

One wry flashback implies the death of cinema—or, at least, Quebec cinema. After they pass a new building that, Marcel explains, used to be a cinema, he tells the story of how the manager once invited him out of the cold, and a flashback shows him sitting in the auditorium during a screening of Robert Lepage's *Le confessionnale* (*The Confessional*; 1995). Lepage's film had seemed to signal a revival in Quebec cinema a few years earlier, but the cinema is empty, and Marcel sleeps through the film.

Like *Jésus de Montréal*, *Le confessionnale* also depicts the death of Quebec's Catholic past, but Marcel and Joseph encounter a former lawyer who still thinks of Quebec as "a province whose cornerstone is religion." Joseph then introduces a flashback showing his attempt to climb the steps in front of Saint Joseph's Oratory on his knees while praying for a cure for injuries that he sustained after falling from a roof. However, he is wearing shorts, and with bloody knees, he gives up and walks away, convincing two tourists that he has been cured by a "miracle." In a further twist, this apparent mockery of residual religious practices is undercut when, back in the present, Joseph explains that he went back to complete the climb in long pants, and his injuries went away a week later, which the nurses at the hospital called a "miracle."

As these two sequences make clear, the tone is far from the gritty realism of the postwar Italian neorealist movement that depicted life in war-ravaged cities; still less is it that of an earnest political tract. Some critics held this against the film, and one complained that, while Arcand's early films focused on "the political and the social," he now "depicts individuals and, above all, marginals" (Beaulieu 1997, 48). Yet the individual and the social are not separate categories, and the apparent lack of anger with which these individuals accept their fate only provokes questions about why they are so marginal and why the city has declined to this extent. As usual, Arcand confronts the audience with unexpected juxtapositions and contradictions but none perhaps as bizarre as when the film aired on television, punctuated by commercials for consumer goods that emphasized the gulf between an affluent society and the suffering city depicted in the film.[7]

The few critics who reviewed *Joyeux calvaire* saw it as a return to Arcand's auteur vision in a minor key, but his next film, *Stardom* (once again made in English), was even more poorly received than *Love and Human Remains*. After a disagreement with Roger Frappier, Arcand had signed a contract with Robert Lantos, the head of Alliance, then Canada's largest production company, who offered to produce his next film with a higher budget than he had ever had before (La Rochelle 2005, 227).[8] The contract was signed in 1993, but Lantos was unhappy with Arcand's first version of the scenario, and the project was shelved, with the result that *Stardom* was only released in 2000. Although it was showcased at both the Cannes and Toronto film festivals, it received only a limited release in Canada and went straight to DVD elsewhere. In his *24 Images* review, André Roy dismissed it as a "succession of . . . more and more ugly and badly framed shots" (2000, 87), and the *Take One* reviewer dismissed it as "a limp statement from a talent in decline" (Townend 2001, 42).

After the success of *Jésus,* Arcand had announced that he was preparing "a film about fashion" (quoted in Barker 1990a, 4), but by 1994, he was calling it a film on "ephemeral beauty" (quoted in La Rochelle 2005, 227). The finished film addresses both these topics, but it is primarily a satire on (post)modern media culture, telling the story of the rise and fall of Tina Menzhal (Jessica Paré), a fashion model, entirely (almost) through a montage of clips from the extensive media coverage of her career. The film thus takes even further the channel-surfing aesthetic that Arcand had used in *Love and Human Remains,* offering a "pastiche . . . of the strategies of televisual seduction" (Mandolini 2000, 50). However, although the film set out to question "the hegemony of the image at the dawn of new millennium" (La Rochelle 2005, 237), it led some critics to wonder if it is possible to "expose a problem by merely replicating it" (Loiselle 2008, 104).

Stardom has subsequently received strong and cogent defenses, notably from Réal La Rochelle and Peter Harcourt, but most critics at the time objected to the device of narrating the story of the model through footage supposedly produced by the media entourage that surrounds her. The film begins with a long shot of a snow-covered parking lot in Cornwall, Ontario, and we first see Tina sitting in a car with her mother and sister, telling them how much she misses her father. She picks up her hockey gear and walks into an arena, passing a community television truck just as a man with a camera steps out. The credits then appear over shots of two women's hockey teams skating around the rink, accompanied by a waltz from Verdi's *La traviata,* creating a spirited opening that implies any of these women might have been cast into the media spotlight but also foreshadowing Tina's fall from grace, like that of the courtesan in the opera. When the credits end, the film camera tracks into the television camera, and the rest of the film (until the final sequence) consists of material taken from a variety of media sources: inept cable TV programs, frenetic MTV-style segments, news and talk shows, and most extensively, a documentary made by Bruce Taylor (Robert Lepage), who follows Tina everywhere as her fame grows. These sources record Tina's few brief moments of fame from her "discovery" by Montreal photographer Philippe Gascon (Charles Berling) to her return to the city of Cornwall where she started out.[9]

"You know the expression trophy wife?": Bruce Taylor films Tina before her marriage in *Stardom*.

Although Tina becomes famous as a top fashion model in New York and Paris, the film is not really about fashion (there is only one runway sequence) but rather about the impact of her beauty on her private life and on the men who become involved with her. She has affairs with Gascon, who is deported from the United States facing child pornography charges, and Barry Levine (Dan Aykroyd), a restaurateur who leaves his family to follow her to New York and is also sent back to Canada to face charges of fraud. It is not clear whether either man is guilty or whether the charges have been fabricated by Tina's agency to free her from lovers with whom she has grown tired. Her downfall comes when she marries Blaine de Castillon (Frank Langella), the Canadian ambassador to the United Nations. He turns out to be a very possessive husband, driving her to physically attack him; this apparently causes a concussion that results in what a television reporter calls a "rambling speech" at the U.N., in which he offends the delegates of many other nations. The negative publicity puts an end to Tina's career.

As this outline suggests, the film does have a linear narrative despite the fragmented way in which it is presented. In this respect, it differs from Robert Altman's *Prêt-a-porter* (1994), also known as *Ready to Wear*, with which it was often compared. Altman's film, in which the fashion world figures much more prominently, was also not well received, but like many of the director's other films, it consists of a multitude of small narratives, none of them dominating the others. Since, as Harcourt suggests, *Stardom* is a film "about loss—loss of self, loss of centre, of sincerity, and especially of moral purpose" (2003, 3), the focus on a central character seemingly works against this critique of postmodern culture.

Arcand himself admitted that his novelist friends told him he had "underestimated the power of narrative" because, "as soon as you begin to tell the story of a young woman, people are no longer interested in the orchestration, they want to know what happens to her" (quoted in Coulombe 2000, 6).

Tina may be the film's center, but she is an empty center—not because she is necessarily a shallow person but because the film refuses to allow us to identify with her. As Arcand puts it, the "filter between the subject and the spectator" amounts to "Brechtian distantiation multiplied" (quoted in Bergeron 2012, 119). The only clue to Tina's psychological state is her attitude to her absent father, a Czech hockey player who failed to make the NHL and lost contact with his family when he was sent to play in Cape Breton. Despite her tearful claim to miss him in the opening sequence, when he turns up as a surprise guest on a talk show after her rise to fame, she angrily denounces him and walks out of the studio. While her feelings about her father may explain her destructive relationships with older men, what the media images show is a superficial portrait that reveals the limitations of the culture that has turned her into a "superstar." On several occasions, we see her being asked questions in interviews or on talk shows and being interrupted before she can answer, and the viewer is left wondering whether she has anything to say. However, when an interviewer refers to "the superficiality of our time," Bruce points out that "superficiality never killed anyone," a view with which Arcand has said he sympathizes, suggesting that the real damage is done by "people who believe they have the truth" (quoted in Alioff 2000, 12).

Yet the filmmaker would no doubt agree with André Loiselle's comment that superficiality is "implicated in the violence it serves to shield" (2008, 104), a point that is made in the film when a television news item on a massacre in Algeria is interrupted by an apparently more important story about Tina's admission to the hospital and Barry's arrest for assault. The slipperiness of Arcand's approach is apparent in André Roy's dismissal of the film, in which he manages to attribute the insensitivity in this sequence to Arcand himself rather than to the target of his satire. He concludes that the director hides "behind the mechanical and successive arrangement of images to avoid giving his own point-of-view" (2000, 87). However, it is not that there is no point of view—it is very clear that an unseen narrator is organizing these images—but rather, as Harcourt suggests, there is no "settled point-of-view" (2003, 4). In this, the film is only a more overt demonstration of the unsettling tactics found in Arcand's previous films, as Carlo Mandolini's description of it as an "image-mosaic" implies (2000, 50).[10]

However, even Mandolini ends his generally positive review by regretting "the abdication of an auteur who distances himself from an art that he has served so well for years" (2000, 51). Although *Stardom* may have seemed like a major departure for the director of *Le déclin*, which was itself hardly universally acclaimed in Quebec, it was another sign of his work's ability to challenge the standard definitions of art cinema. The ending is typically ambivalent: after the film camera tracks out from the television camera, we see a pregnant Tina in her suburban home, an image that can be read as showing her "at peace with the world" (Alioff 2000, 9), as being "purposefully unconvincing" (Loiselle 2008, 104), or as another example of the filmmaker's characteristic "refusal of closure, the courage of open-endedness" (Harcourt 2003, 8). Of course, these interpretations are not mutually exclusive.

"THE GENTLEST DEATH ONE COULD IMAGINE": *LES INVASIONS BARBARES*

The title and the basic metaphor of *Les invasions* may have been inspired by a 1990 essay on "Americanity" in Quebec culture by Gilles Thérien. After referring to *Le déclin,* he argued, "If one speaks of empire and decline, there is always at the gates of any empire a horde of Barbarians ready to invade the territory," with the result that "to think of the empire is also to think of what undermines it, the thought of the Barbarian" (1990, 10). Whether or not Arcand was aware of Thérien's essay, the film presents itself as a belated sequel to *Le déclin,* with many of the characters and actors who appeared in the earlier work (and some from *Jésus*). As in *Le déclin,* the title places the personal interactions of the characters within a larger political or collective framework that draws attention to developments in the decade and a half between the two films. If, in *Le déclin,* the thesis of "decline" was mirrored in the sexual entanglements among the historians, here the idea of "invasions" is associated with the imminent death of Rémy (Rémy Girard), the most sexually active of the characters in the earlier film, now a patient in a crowded hospital, suffering from terminal cancer.

The idea of making a film about death was not a new one for Arcand. In the early 1990s, he had revealed, "For a long time I have wanted to make a film about someone who is going to commit suicide" (quoted in Coulombe 1993, 32), and after the film's release, he told Peter Howell that he had been working on the subject for twenty years (2003b, 29). This project became even more urgent, as he explains in the published screenplay, after he had watched his grandfather, father, and mother all die of cancer in the hospital (Arcand 2003, 7). He was unable to find a way of addressing his concerns that would not be "mawkish," "sombre," and "morbid" (quoted in Howell 2003b, 29) until he came up with the idea of using the characters from *Le déclin.* In his depiction of Rémy's last days, he was able to continue the critique of the Quebec health care system that he had begun at the end of *Jésus* but now with an even stronger personal dimension. As a result, "the whole shoot was very emotional for me," and he produced a film that (at least partially) went against the grain of his earlier work, which, as he was aware, has been "usually considered distant and ironic and all these sorts of things, and worse" (quoted in Howell 2003a, C1).

It should be noted that the film exists in two versions. The original version is 112 minutes long, and this is the version released in Quebec, but the French producer of this coproduction requested cuts to eliminate "certain Quebec particularisms" (La Rochelle 2005, 246). In the so-called international version, thirteen minutes were removed, most notably three darkly comic sequences in which Rémy's former mistresses invade his hospital room and accuse him of mistreating them. In keeping with his taste for films, like Buñuel's, that might conventionally be regarded as "'badly' shot" (quoted in Johnston 2004), Arcand has stated his preference for the original cut, which, he says, "includes the slow parts, the parts that wander, the comedy scenes that border on bad taste, but I like it" (quoted in La Rochelle 2005, 246), and this is the version I will discuss here. The screenplay includes a few other sequences that were cut or never filmed for dramatic or budgetary reasons.

As Arcand noted, the emotional power of the film might seem uncharacteristic, but the effect is all the greater in that the emotion creeps up gradually, and the opening sequences seem to introduce a seriocomic dissection of modern Quebec society of the kind found in many of his previous films. The first shot shows the trading floor of a private bank, which the screenplay describes as resembling a cathedral (Arcand 2003, 15), where Sébastien (Stéphane Rousseau) receives a phone call from his mother in Montreal. Louise (Dorothée Berryman), whom we may recognize from *Le déclin* as Rémy's wife, tells him that his father has been admitted to the hospital and asks him to come home to help her deal with the situation. Sébastien then calls his partner, Gaëlle (Marina Hinds), who is working at an art auction where the bidding, like the dealings at the bank, is conducted in English. When she agrees to go with him, there is a sudden cut to a woman working out, which is then located on a television screen being watched by a male patient (Denis Bouchard) in a hospital room where one of Rémy's former mistresses (Sophie Lorain) is loudly denouncing him, completely ignoring the three other patients in the room.

There is a cut to a close-up of hands preparing communion wafers, and the credits sequence begins with classical music, as in *Le déclin*. However, the music fades out as the camera begins a long tracking shot behind a nun walking down a crowded and noisy hospital corridor, filled with patients lying on gurneys. The nun turns out to be Constance (Johanne-Marie Tremblay), who was first introduced working in a soup kitchen in *Jésus* and who has evidently given up acting after Daniel's death, which was caused by lack of care in a similarly congested hospital. Described in the screenplay as evoking Dante's *Inferno* (Arcand 2003, 23), the claustrophobic effect of this shot contrasts with the cathedral-like space of the bank, and the whole sequence becomes a perverse remake of the tracking shot through the spacious hall in the Université de Montréal at the beginning of *Le déclin*.

As André Loiselle suggests, "By the end of the prologue, Arcand has already introduced his narrative strategy and the elements with which he will play for the rest of the film: generational conflict; disease; incommunicability among characters; but also humour, affection, and filial loyalty" (2008, 114). To this list might be added the tension between physical bodies and media images / virtual reality, introduced through the shot of the workout routine on the television screen and developed largely through the relationship between Rémy and his son. It quickly becomes clear that Sébastien has returned because of his mother's appeal and not because he has any affection for his father, from whom he has been estranged since his parents separated following the revelations at the end of *Le déclin*. Rémy complains that Sébastien is only interested in video games and has never read a book, and the son thus represents all that the father "refuses in the contemporary world, computers and video games, cell phones, speed, money, and power" (Barrette 2003, 4). The film depicts their gradual reconciliation, although in keeping with Arcand's usual irony, this only occurs because of the power of Sébastien's money and his skill with digital communications technology.

Despite his father's hostility, Sébastien immediately displays his willingness to use unorthodox methods to help him when he traces and cuts the cable to the television of the patient who spends all his time watching it with the volume turned up. He then takes advantage of an overworked nurse to steal Rémy's file and transmit it to a doctor friend in Baltimore. When he and his father travel together in an ambulance to Burlington, Vermont, for a scan that is not available in Montreal, Louise expresses her hope that the trip will allow the men to talk to each other, but there is a cut to inside the ambulance, where Rémy sits in silence while his son conducts a business conversation in English on his cell phone. However, Sébastien does contact his sister Sylvaine (Isabelle Blais), who is sailing in the South Pacific, and relays a video message from her to their father on his laptop, and he phones Rémy's friends to tell them of his condition.

Sébastien sends the results of the scan to his friend, who confirms that Rémy's illness is terminal and suggests that he could at least be made more comfortable if he came to the United States, but Rémy refuses to go into "exile." He insists that he voted for the "nationalization of hospitals" at the time of the Quiet Revolution and is prepared to suffer the consequences. Although Arcand admitted that Rémy is "a very bad character," a bad father and husband (quoted in Howell 2003a, C4), there is little doubt that the director identifies with his desire to remain in Quebec and with his distaste for the contemporary cultural and technological environment. As the filmmaker explained at the time of the film's release, "The constant acceleration of life and the media roar are repulsive to me" (Howell 2003b, 30), but just as Arcand allows Louise in *Le déclin* to challenge the "realistic" viewpoint he shares with Dominique, here he also allows the devil his due. Modern technology has made possible more precise ways of diagnosing and treating illness, although these developments have also widened the gap between the rich and the poor, since there are long waiting lists for access to this equipment in Quebec, and the only alternative, for patients who can afford the expensive treatment, is to go to better-equipped hospitals in the United States. As Sébastien tells a nurse, "money is not a problem" for him, and he makes use of his wealth, and his technological know-how, to improve the quality of his father's last days despite their differences and the overstretched Quebec health system.

A montage effect neatly sums up the gulf between the old libertine and his technologically savvy son: there is an abrupt cut from Rémy, eagerly anticipating a massage from a beautiful Bulgarian nurse, to high-speed action on a video screen in an arcade where Sébastien is playing a game. The juxtaposition of the nurse, who is a recent immigrant judging by her rudimentary French, and the video game also raises questions about the implications of the film's title and the identity of the barbarian invaders to which it refers. As André Loiselle points out, this title, like that of *Le déclin*, is taken from "a commentary from a 'specialist'" (2008, 119)—in this case, a television opinion piece on the terrorist attack on the World Trade Center on 11 September 2001, with the effect that the personal themes of sexuality and death are placed within a broader context that relates them to the political issues facing Quebec society and the Western world.

The most obvious "barbarians" to whom the title alludes are the terrorists, and the 9/11 attack is introduced in an abrupt cut to a shot of a plane flying into one of the towers. Some critics objected to the use of this disturbing image, and its unsettling effect is heightened by its unprepared-for invasion of the cinema screen following a heated argument between Rémy and Sébastien. It is quickly contextualized by a cut that reveals it is being shown on a television screen above the information desk in the hospital, where Sébastien has gone to report the theft of his laptop from Rémy's room, and it is immediately followed by commentary from a historian identified as Alain Dussault (Daniel Brière), the graduate student from *Le déclin*.[11] Citing his "old university professors," he argues that, in historical terms, the attack was "relatively insignificant," except that now the barbarians have struck at "the heart of the empire."

It is not clear how soon Alain's commentary comes after the event since images of the attack continued to appear on television for weeks afterward and commentators discussed its significance for even longer. As he points out, his view of history corresponds to Rémy's, but if the broadcast takes place in the immediate aftermath of the attack (as it does for us in Arcand's film), it seems rather pat and to fit too easily into his pose as "media expert." The shock cut to the plane flying into the World Trade Center is matched later by an equally sudden cut to the violent collisions in Sébastien's video game, evoking the (con) fusion of the real and the virtual noted in many commentaries on the media coverage of the 9/11 attacks.[12] In this sense, the intrusion of the image of the actual attack into the fictional world of *Les invasions* becomes an invasion comparable to similar montage effects in the everyday media environment, as Arcand had already shown in *Love and Human Remains.*

The other explicit reference to invasion in the film has to do with the recent waves of immigration that have threatened traditional definitions of the Québécois identity. According to Pierre Barrette, from the Quebec point of view, "the attacks of 11 September 2001 . . . appear as the localized symptom of a much larger confrontation with the Other, the immigrants, the foreigners whose proliferation in a once so closely-woven Quebec . . . has forced a fundamental question about what defines us as a society" (2003, 4). The changing demographics of contemporary Quebec are visible in the film in the figure of the Bulgarian nurse as well as a Hindu patient in Rémy's hospital room, but the word *invasion* is spoken by a police officer (Roy Dupuis) not in reference to recent immigrants but to dealers in illegal drugs. He tells Sébastien that, if the police arrest an Iranian gang, they will be "replaced by the Iraqis, or the Lebanese, the Italians, the Thais, the Chinese, the Cambodians . . . It is an invasion." In other words, the problem is not so much immigration as globalization, the drug dealers representing the dark side of the border crossing that Sébastien's devices enable him to perform so easily in his business dealings. It is a vision of a future in which, according to Arcand, "borders will be almost irrelevant" (quoted in Howell 2003b, 30).

Yet borders do still matter in the political workings of the American Empire. Arcand has suggested that in the future, "there will be American citizens on one side and non-resident aliens on the other" and, "seen from Washington, the French, the Bulgarians or the Japanese are one and the same thing: barbarians" (quoted in Howell 2003b, 31). However, he has also alluded to the roots of the word *barbarian* in ancient Greece, where, he says, it referred to "foreigners, that is, those who do not belong to the Greek culture," so that "the word is not pejorative. To be a barbarian is neither a quality nor a fault, it means that a person belongs to a foreign physical and cultural space" (quoted in La Rochelle 2005, 242–3). From this perspective, however, in the globalized and virtual culture of the contemporary world, it is possible that people can be seen as barbarians even if they occupy the same geographical space and come from the same cultural background. Thus Rémy views Sébastien and his former students as barbarians because their culture excludes books and history, and the film makes clear that the politicians and administrators who have destroyed the health system also deserve that title. Maurice Yacowar has even suggested, "Arcand's real barbarians are the sophisticates who converge on Rémy's hospital room" because "most of his problems stem from the society he helped to create" (2004, 93).

One further invasion is central to the film's concerns, and that is the cancer that has invaded Rémy's body. He tries to alleviate his suffering by adopting the intellectual detachment of the historian, and when Constance suggests they are living in a "horrible epoch," he tells her that the twentieth century was not "especially bloody" and enumerates the massacres committed in the past, many sanctioned by the Church, including those that took place during the colonization of North America. Nevertheless, he concludes that "the history of humanity is a history of horrors," and the next sequence consists of a montage of overhead shots of the men in Rémy's room in their beds at night, ending with a shot of a man whose face is completely hidden by an oxygen mask. Instead of alleviating the individual experience of dying, the hospital system only intensifies it, despite the efforts of many of the people working within it, and it is only Sébastien's wealth and devious methods that eventually ensure that his father's death will be "the gentlest that one could imagine" (La Rochelle 2005, 243).

After storming out of his father's crowded room when Rémy refuses to move to Baltimore, Sébastien runs downstairs and finds a floor that has been abandoned because of lack of funding. He then bluffs his way into the administration wing of the hospital, which, as described in the screenplay, is "clean, calm, and well decorated" (Arcand 2003, 67). He confronts the director general (Lise Roy), who responds to his request for a single room for his father with a string of managerial jargon to show that it is out of the question. When he offers her a dossier he has prepared, she opens it to find bundles of banknotes; at first, she responds indignantly, "We're not in the Third World here," but she then points out that he would need to clear any arrangement with the union. Sébastien says he will take care of the union, and he pays the union boss (Jean-Marc Parent) to have one of the rooms on the empty floor painted and furnished for his father. As usual, Arcand's depiction of a corrupt and inefficient administration and venal union officers (one of whom is played by the director himself) ensured that the film would displease many of those on both the right and the left.

Indeed, the film offers a scathing indictment of Quebec society forty years after the Quiet Revolution. The impact of the loss of Québec's traditional culture is brought out when the London gallery sends Gaëlle to evaluate a collection of religious art that the Catholic authorities want to sell. She visits a warehouse where she meets Father Leclerc (Gilles Pelletier), the struggling priest from *Jésus*, who tells her that the churches in Quebec suddenly emptied within a few months in 1966, "a strange phenomenon that nobody has ever explained." She informs him that the statues and icons that surround them may have value "on the level of the collective memory" but no material value on "the international market." The credits sequence has already reminded us of the Catholic past through the presence of a nun administering spiritual comfort to patients, but

Constance is an isolated and ineffective figure in a hospital where beds are labeled with the wrong names and many patients are not Catholic. She listens patiently to Rémy, gently reproving him for his philandering past, but tells him his view of history only means that God must exist in order to offer forgiveness.

Apart from securing a comfortable room, Sébastien's two most important interventions change the whole tone of the film. He informs Rémy's friends of his illness, and he seeks out a supply of heroin to ease his pain. Claude (Yves Jacques), who has evidently recovered from the illness that caused his bloody urine in *Le déclin*, flies in from Rome, where he lives with Alessandro (Toni Cecchinato), his Italian partner, and works for the Canadian government.[13] Sébastien's messages reach Diane (Louise Portal) in a house in the country with a man dressed as a cowboy in the background;[14] Pierre (Pierre Curzi) in his home with his young wife, Ghislaine (Mitsou Gélinas), and their children; and Dominique (Dominique Michel) on a cruise ship in Alaska. They all gather at Rémy's bedside and, despite the circumstances, try to resume the witty and amusing conversations they had in the past. They also talk about their memories, and Rémy traces his first sexual experience back to seeing an Italian film about Maria Goretti, a young Italian girl who was canonized after being raped and murdered. Although the film was shown to schoolboys for its edifying moral, the young Rémy was aroused by a shot of the girl wading into a lake, exposing the thighs of the actress Inès Orsini, an experience also remembered by the other men in the room. This shot appears on screen in Arcand's film, as do shots that document his later obsessions with famous young women: Françoise Hardy, Julie Christie, Chris Evert, and Karen Kain.

Despite the nostalgic pleasures offered by these memories, Rémy is still in real pain, and Sébastien, rather naively, decides to ask the police if they could put him in touch with a drug dealer. Not surprisingly, they refuse, suspecting him of being a journalist out to expose corruption on the force. However, Diane puts him in touch with Nathalie (Marie-Josée Croze), her estranged daughter, who had been briefly glimpsed in *Le déclin* when, in a flashback, she found her mother in bed with Rémy. She has become a drug addict (not, presumably, as a result of that experience), and she agrees to help, but she warns Rémy that she is not entirely reliable. When she first arrives with heroin, he tells her he was once close to her mother, and she remembers that "the married men left before morning"; he comments that it must have seemed sordid from a child's point of view but explains, "We called it sexual liberation." They develop a warm relationship, and his description of the horrors of history in his conversations with Constance is balanced by his outburst to Nathalie about how much he has loved life. As in *Le déclin*, the warm feelings of friendship do not cancel out the critical perspective on the state of modern Quebec, but they do offer a way of living (and dying) with it.

Although the Quebec context is more explicit than in *Le déclin*, Arcand did eliminate several references to Quebec politics and history. The screenplay includes a sequence in which Rémy receives a visit from another of his former mistresses, who is now the minister of culture, and he tells her, "I have not been able to endure politicians for at least twenty years." She replies with words that have been applied to Arcand himself: "We know the results of the disengagement of your generation" (Arcand 2003, 65). In this exchange, Rémy is confronted (as is Arcand) with the bitter thought that he and his friends were at least partly responsible for the current situation. Both the character and his creator are also concerned at the loss of a historical sense that has characterized post–Quiet Revolution Quebec (and the so-called postmodern condition, according to most accounts). In another sequence that was either cut or never filmed, Diane tells Claude that "Canadian history" is no longer taught in schools and has been replaced by "universal history" (99). In the film itself, the course that Rémy has to give up because of his illness is on American history, but the film version ends before a section included in the screenplay in which the teaching assistant who replaces him refers to xenophobes in nineteenth-century America who "were radically opposed to immigration, convinced that all new arrivals would support the Democrats" (133). In modern Quebec, of course, similar fears concern immigrants who will be unlikely to support the Yes side in any future referendum, but if Arcand had included these lines in the finished film, he would have left viewers to draw their own conclusions from the historical parallel.

As in many of his films, perhaps most notably *Jésus*, Arcand uses sudden shifts of tone to keep spectators unbalanced and alert. According to Pierre Barrette, the satiric elements associated with "the usually caustic Arcand" are still present but are "humanized and elevated by his confrontation with the theme of death" (2003, 4). The almost slapstick comedy in the sequences in which Rémy's former mistresses attack him in the full version of the film (the first mistress pays a return visit and a second also appears) coexists with the critique of the health system and with "Rémy's didactic exposés" (Bachand 2006, 111), leading up to the emotional final sequences. As we have seen, montage effects often lead to abrupt changes of tone: in his *Sight and Sound* review, Philip Kemp notes, "Frequently Arcand teases his audience by switching moods on us, from cynical to affirmative and back" (2004, 37). One example of this strategy occurs when Rémy receives a visit from three of his former students. Their appearance is surprising considering the apparent indifference of the class when he announced he would not be able to complete the course, but he tells his visitors that he is moved by their expressions of concern. In the next sequence, the revelation that Sébastien has paid them to come seems to cynically undercut the emotion generated by the previous sequence, but the effect of this revelation is itself somewhat canceled out when one of the students refuses her share.

Rémy's assisted suicide takes place at Pierre's summerhouse, beside the lake that was a key location in *Le déclin*. Earlier, Rémy had asked to be taken there during the return trip from Burlington and had sat beside the lake in his wheelchair; now it provides an idyllic natural setting for his death surrounded by his friends and family. The sequence begins with the group sitting outside the house, speaking of the different intellectual fashions the academics among them had embraced during their careers. Rémy starts off naming the political movements in Quebec during the 1960s and 1970s: "separatists, independentists, sovereigntists, sovereignty-associationists." The others chime in with a litany of "isms": anticolonialism, Marxism, Marxist-Leninism, Maoism, Trotskyism, structuralism, situationism, deconstructionism, and feminism. This list of discarded theories was calculated to divide Arcand's critics, with his opponents accusing him of another "ism" (namely, anti-intellectualism), while supporters like Réal La Rochelle, who had once described how the filmmaker always kept his distance from "isms" (1987–1988, 14), could praise "the memorable sequence of the 'isms'" (2005, 30).

The most obvious omission from this list is postmodernism. It could be argued that many of these discarded theories are "grand," seeking to explain everything, and that these academics are indeed postmodernists in their rejection of such totalizing systems. Does this mean that Arcand is a postmodernist? Once again, we come up against the problem of to what extent we should identify the characters with their author. As in *Le déclin*, their failings are viewed critically, but here they are situated within the context of a critique of the even more flawed worldview of managerial rhetoric and digital technology that characterizes what might be called postmodernity. If Arcand no longer has any faith in grand narratives, he clearly shares with Rémy a horror of the idea of a world without books and of a society that no longer responds to the needs of its citizens (which will be the topic of his next film). The sequence of the "isms" celebrates the value of friendship, but as usual, it challenges the viewer to respond to the contradictions that have emerged in the experience of the film.

The next sequence takes place inside the house, where the guests sit around a table, and Claude serves one of his elaborate dishes. Rémy cannot eat the food or drink the fine wine, but he enjoys listening to his friends talk, and he asks them to drink to his health and tell him how good it is. As Kemp puts it, "When all the creeds and isms have failed, Arcand reminds us, human companionship and affection remain" (2004, 37). During the meal, Pierre advances his theory that, "contrary to what people believe, intelligence is not an individual quality but a collective, national, and intermittent phenomenon": he refers to the coming together of great thinkers in ancient Athens and in Philadelphia at the time of the Declaration of Independence, and Alessandro chimes in with Renaissance Florence. According to Pierre, the present is a time when "intelligence has

"You have managed to pass on your appetite for life": Rémy, surrounded by his friends, receives his daughter's final message.

disappeared" and may not return for centuries. The implication is that stupidity as well as intelligence is collective, but Pierre's pessimistic discourse coexists with the warmth of the group's feelings in the face of Rémy's imminent death. As with Dominique's thesis of "decline," there is no need to take Pierre's thesis too seriously, but it does demonstrate the idea, found in Arcand's films throughout his career, that the individual and the collective are mutually dependent.

After the meal, the friends sit outside around a fire, creating what Yacowar calls "a tribal image," suggesting that in this outdoor setting, the former "sophisticates" have become "exuberantly primitive" (2004, 94). They share an elaborate joke about the "gentle death" of a nineteenth-century French president who supposedly died while being fellated by his mistress. When a nurse arrives with the equipment to administer an overdose of heroin, she reminds Sébastien to deny that she has ever been there if this illegal act ever comes to light. While Nathalie is preparing the heroin, Sébastien receives a second video from Sylvaine on her yacht, in which she tearfully says goodbye to her father, and thus the most moving moment in the film comes as a result of the digital technology that Rémy hates. As he slips into unconsciousness, he "sees" the thighs of Inès Orsini, and there is a fade to a low angle shot of trees swaying in the breeze, followed by a cut to storm clouds over the lake.

When she administers the fatal dose, Nathalie tells Rémy that it was a privilege to have known him, and the ending of the film is marked not only by his death but also by the prospect of her redemption. Their time together has inspired her to take a course of methadone, and at the end, Sébastien, who according to his father has never read a book in his life, invites her to move into

Rémy's apartment, which is filled with books. Nathalie is a proofreader—for Boréal, the publishing house that published Arcand's screenplays—and the camera follows her gaze around the bookshelves, picking out the titles of books that Arcand admires (taken from his library). The camera picks out four books in close-up: Primo Levi's *If This Be a Man* and Aleksandr Solzhenitsyn's *The Gulag Archipelago* because, as Arcand points out, "they are essential works on the great massacres of the twentieth century"; Samuel Pepys's "amazing" diary; and Emil Cioran's *History and Utopia* "because I like his twisted mind . . . and that strange Balkan world" (quoted in La Rochelle 2005, 263). This last title is especially significant since it presents an essentially pessimistic philosophy that privileges historical over utopian thinking, much as Arcand's cynical perspective rejects the hopes of the lyric generation, settling in the end for a life based on the enjoyment of the present moment.

These books constitute a map of Rémy's mind (and Arcand's), but it is left to Nathalie to piece together the connections between them. She has become the mediator between the generations and, perhaps, between Rémy and the future. At the summerhouse before Rémy's death, when she and Sébastien sit together outside, his phone rings, probably with yet another of his business calls, and she throws it on the fire. He responds only by saying, "Think you're funny?" (in English) and smiling. It is clear that they also have become friends, and when Sébastien is leaving her in the apartment, Nathalie pulls him toward her, kisses him passionately, then pushes him out to rejoin Gaëlle. After the young couple take a flight to London, and Diane and Dominique see Claude and Alessandro off at the airport, the final credits appear over shots of the lake, accompanied by Françoise Hardy singing "L'amitié" ("Friendship").

In an article in *Le Devoir*, Jean Larose, who had earlier attacked *Le déclin*, called *Les invasions* "a film about death that doesn't take death seriously . . . a curious combination of nihilism and sentimentalism" revealing a "kind of commitment to reducing the spectator to despair" (quoted in La Rochelle 2005, 253). Given the ending described above, this would seem to be one of the most perverse readings ever of an Arcand film, but other critics raised similar objections, in particular with regard to the film's depiction of the young characters. Although, as Bergeron recognized, "without Sébastien, without Sylvaine, without Nathalie, *Les Invasions barbares* would be only a geriatric version of *Le déclin*" (2012, 76), Jean-Philippe Gravel objected, "These young people are even more deprived of a political consciousness than their elders" (2003, 29). This may be true; both of Rémy's children have left Quebec, one for the heart of the American Empire (even if the bank is in Britain) and the other for the remote expanses of the Pacific Ocean. When she enters the film, Nathalie is in the process of destroying her life with drugs, perhaps because of her experiences as a child.

Yet the ending does offer the guarded hope that all three will now be able to avoid the mistakes of the previous generation.

Les invasions barbares received a twenty-two-minute standing ovation at the Cannes Film Festival and grossed "over $35 million at the box office world wide—a record for a Quebec film" (Loiselle 2008, 107). Of course, it also won an Academy Award, but as was by now predictable, while many critics in Quebec celebrated it as a triumph for Quebec cinema, its commercial and international success again raised questions for some about Arcand's status as a director of "art films." In an issue of *Ciné-bulles* that included an editorial stressing the need to "clearly establish the difference" between commercial and auteur cinema (Perron 2003, 2), a lengthy article discussed the film in the context of Arcand's career and argued, "It is rare that success, especially in Quebec, is not based on a misunderstanding" (Gravel 2003, 25). This idea of "misunderstanding" was taken up in the title of André Habib's mainly negative review, in which he called the film "a totally cynical vision of the world—not compensated by any cinematic invention to speak of." If many critics admired the film, he wrote, that only goes to show that, "in the land of criticism, the dupes are kings" (2004). By confidently positioning himself as one of the non-duped, Habib offers a cynical view of critics and audiences worthy of that often attributed to Arcand himself.

This kind of reception often seems to illustrate Arcand's point that he lives in a world full of contradictions, a claim that this issue of *Ciné-bulles* seems to illustrate. As proof that he is not opposed to "all kinds of theatrical success," Habib (2004) praises the "very appealing" *La grande séduction* (*Seducing Doctor Lewis*; Jean-François Pouliot, 2003), a Quebec film that received an enthusiastic review alongside Jean-Philippe Gravel's thoughtful but largely negative critique of *Les invasions*. *La grande séduction* is a gentle comedy, in the manner of the British Ealing comedies of the 1940s and 1950s, about a small community on a fictional island in the Saint Lawrence River, which organizes a cricket match to lure a doctor from Montreal who, somewhat improbably, loves that sport. It is indeed an appealing, if rather far-fetched, story—hardly an obvious example of an auteur film and hardly a distinctive representation of modern Quebec society and culture.[15]

At the opposite extreme is Michael Haneke's *Amour* (2012), which won the Academy Award for best foreign-language film ten years after *Les invasions* and which also ends with the death of a terminally ill character. This is very much an auteur film, mainly confined to the Paris apartment of an elderly couple, where the husband struggles to deal with the progressive decline of his wife after a series of strokes until he decides to end her suffering by suffocating her with a pillow. Compared to Haneke's austere and minimalist film—one review was titled "No Gentle End" (Porter 2013, 275)—Arcand's is a more diffuse and varied work, but equally true to its filmmaker's vision. Haneke's film, like most of the auteur's work, is much more difficult to watch, and arguably more likely to promote "despair," but its critics have not accused the director of being cynical. Arcand's film is certainly a more enjoyable experience, and as a result, it has reached a larger audience, but it certainly does not treat the idea of death less seriously.

Even Réal La Rochelle shared some of the concern expressed by Arcand's critics—that the film offers a despairing view of modern Quebec and of the human condition—and he too linked this pessimistic outlook to the depiction of younger characters. He argued that, while Rémy's generation is "dead or petrified in its emptiness and melancholic despair . . . the second generation, that of Sébastien and Nathalie, represents the 'barbarians'" (2005, 35). Although this assessment is true to the ideological dynamics of the film, it is false to the actual experience of viewing it. The mutual support among the older friends and the new maturity of their children do not cancel out the critical perspective on Quebec society and globalized culture, but they do provide a human warmth that has survived despite the system. If the characters in *Le déclin* tried to exclude their children from their lives, leading to apparent psychological damage, in the later film, the generations do come together and tentatively reconstruct a sense of family. La Rochelle suggests the following generation will mark "the beginning of the future," which will be "racially mixed (métissé), a little society of nations weaving the Quebec of tomorrow, French-speaking, multi-ethnic, artistic" (2005, 35). This generation is not seen in *Les invasions barbares*, but the ending points forward to the ways in which Arcand's later films will address the issues of globalization and the changing demographics of Quebec society in the twenty-first century.[16]

6 · LIVING IN THE SHADOWS

Arcand and Contemporary Quebec

My nostalgia is perhaps only the effect of the passage of time.

—Denys Arcand

In the first decades of the twenty-first century, it has seemed to many people in Quebec—as in other Western countries, including the rest of Canada—that there has been a "barbarian invasion" in the form of an influx of immigrants and refugees from the many impoverished and troubled nations around the world. At first, as in Jacques Parizeau's ill-judged speech following the 1995 referendum, the main concern was with the impact the changing demographics would have on prospects for an independent Quebec. However, the events of 11 September 2001, and outbreaks of violence in the Middle East that have resulted in many Muslim refugees seeking asylum elsewhere, have led to a more widespread fear that the newcomers represent a threat to Quebec's cultural identity. The campaigns against wearing hijabs and turbans (see the introduction) have often been justified on the grounds that these religious insignia conflict with the secular order of modern Quebec, to which immigrants should conform; on the other hand, exceptions are usually made for the wearing of crosses, not to mention the highly visible presence of the huge cross that overlooks the city of Montreal.

As *Les invasions barbares* confirmed, Arcand shares this anxiety about the state of the modern world but not the prejudices and chauvinism that often accompany it. In the preface to the published screenplay of his next film, *L'âge des ténèbres* (*Days of Darkness*; 2007), he suggests that "the end of the Second World War will one day be considered as the end of what will perhaps be called Western civilization," which was "based on faith and books." He explains, "We are entering a new, totally mysterious Middle Ages"; however, he insists, "I am not nostalgic for the past. There has never been a golden age" (2007, 7–8). As we shall see, the society depicted in the film is immersed in fantasies of a distant past as an escape from the frustrating realities of modern life, but the title evokes a more recent past in its suggestion that, for all its technological and economic transformations, Quebec has regressed to a state that is, in its way, as restrictive and conformist as the Great Darkness that the Quiet Revolution had supposedly swept away.

The three films he has made since his Academy Award winner in 2003 have all attempted to grapple with the director's disillusionment with the failed promise of the Quiet Revolution, and they have all encountered a resistance that has prevented them from receiving the attention that they deserve. It would be accurate to say that *L'âge des ténèbres* received a mixed reception, but *Le règne de la beauté* (*An Eye for Beauty*; 2014) was almost completely ignored, receiving only a very limited release outside Quebec. His latest film, *La chute de l'empire américain* (*The Fall of the American Empire*; 2018) has been greeted as something of a return to form but is unlikely to emulate the success of *Le déclin de l'empire américain*, to which its title suggests it should be seen as another sequel. None of these films deals centrally with the impact of immigration on Quebec society, although the subject is touched on in ways that typically seem to be designed to activate and call into question the clichés and stereotypes that abound in public discourses.

After the success of *Les invasions*, Arcand felt that he was in a position to make the films he chose, whenever he wanted to, and the three films he has made in the last fifteen years are indeed those of a veteran filmmaker making his own choices. As we shall see, however, they have suffered from comparison with his major international successes, disappointing some who had admired those films and providing ammunition for his detractors. Their relative lack of popular success and critical appreciation suggests that the director's vision is now out of sync with the evolution of Quebec society. However, they still have much to say about the issues that inspired his earlier films and about the state of Quebec sixty years after the Quiet Revolution; their critical reception testifies to the continued hostility that the awkward questions they raise still tend to provoke in some quarters.

"AN IMPLACABLE FILM": *L'ÂGE DES TÉNÈBRES*

Arcand attributed the decision to market his next film as the final part of a trilogy, following on from *Le déclin* and *Les invasions*, to the distributor's desire to cash in on the commercial success of the earlier films. He himself thought the new film had more in common with *Stardom* (Coulombe 2007), whose resounding commercial failure would not have made it a strong selling point. However, the idea certainly caught on with reviewers, one of whom called the film "the last part of a trilogy on what the filmmaker sees as the disintegration of western civilization"

(Castiel 2007, 35), and Arcand encouraged such thinking by introducing characters from the earlier films. Most notably, Pierre (Pierre Curzi) reappears, now as a destitute old man who has been abandoned by the young wife he had acquired in *Les invasions*, and Constance (Johanne-Marie Tremblay) and Father Leclerc (Gilles Pelletier), from *Jésus de Montréal* and *Les invasions*, make brief appearances at the end. None of these characters is named in the film, and it might be assumed that the actors are playing different (but related) characters, but the screenplay identifies them by their names from the earlier films. Another link among all three films is the casting of Gaston Lepage as a security guard (as in *Jésus* and *Les invasions*), who may be identified as a returning character—or possibly Arcand is just suggesting that all such functionaries are interchangeable.

According to Arcand, his new project began as a reaction to the "media orgy" that followed the release of *Les invasions*, which, perversely, provoked a desire to depict "the painful and not at all glamorous life of an individual whom nobody has ever listened to, and will ever listen to" (quoted in Laurendeau 2007, 38). A similar experience after the making of *Le déclin* had resulted in the satire on the media in *Jésus*, but this time, the focus on a downtrodden and resolutely ordinary man made it difficult for some critics (and presumably audiences) to be "interested in the fate of this clapped out character, an unloved husband and neglected father" (Barrette 2007, 4). Jean-Marc Leblanc (Marc Labrèche), whose very name evokes a blank sheet, is perhaps a nonentity in his everyday life, but the film also immerses us in his fantasy life in which he is a dynamic and virile male who attracts the kind of media attention that Arcand had just experienced. In one fantasy sequence, reporters pursue him after he wins the Goncourt Prize for his (presumably autobiographical) novel, *Un homme sans intérêt* (A man of no interest).

The title of Leblanc's novel echoes that of Austrian philosopher Robert Musil's unfinished novel, *A Man without Qualities*, but Arcand was perhaps more indebted to a fragmentary novel by Portuguese poet Fernando Pessoa, *The Book of Disquiet*, which Jean-Marc reads when he sits beside his ailing mother in a hospice. While Pessoa's central character can declare, "My imaginary world has always been the only true world for me" (1991, 93), he rarely describes this world, and the novel mainly consists of apparently random thoughts inspired by his humdrum existence as a lonely Lisbon office worker. Arcand's film, on the other hand, is punctuated by the colorful fantasies that offer Jean-Marc compensation for the frustrations of his everyday life and that gradually become difficult to distinguish from the absurd events in the "real" world. The result is a film that is "a mixture of genres that intentionally sets off in all directions" (Castiel 2007, 37), combining elements of comedy, satire, fantasy, and science fiction.

It is the last of these genres that provides the narrative framework for the film, which is set in the near future and, as in much science fiction, draws on what

Frederick Pohl calls the "extrapolative imagination," suggesting possible outcomes of tendencies in contemporary culture (1981, 26). Arcand's belief that history is important only for the light it throws on the present is here translated into the depiction of a dystopian future to address disturbing trends in the present. The main futuristic element is Jean-Marc's place of work: the government of Quebec has taken refuge in the huge stadium built for the Montreal Olympics in 1976 (and the site of the evangelical rally in *Le confort et l'indifférence*). This stadium, which dominates the city skyline, may once have been an iconic piece of modern—even futuristic—architecture, but it is now associated with the past and widely regarded as a "white elephant" (Bergeron 2012, 85) because of the enormous costs involved in building it and because it has not had a main tenant since the Expos, Montreal's former major league baseball team, moved to Washington, DC, in 2004. Its vacant status allowed the filmmakers to transform its interior into a vast network of supposedly temporary offices housing government departments with a bewildering array of acronyms.

Jean-Marc works for the Office for the Protection of the Citizen, or the OPDC, but unfortunately, when citizens come to him for advice, he can only explain to them the intricacies of a convoluted system of regulations and procedures that ensures their problems will never really be addressed. Thus when Pierre describes his impoverished state after his divorce and asks for help in getting public housing, Jean-Marc can only tell him that this is a municipal responsibility and send him to "the SDHM," which, he explains, is behind "the CDP." On their breaks from their futile jobs, Jean-Marc and his colleagues must elude the antismoking patrols and watch their language. When Jean-Marc jokingly refers to William (Didier Lucien), his black colleague and friend, as "working like a nigger" (*nègre*), his supervisor reports him, and as a result, he is subjected to a disciplinary hearing in which he is told that "the Office of the French Language" has decreed that this is a "nonword." Later, the entire department attends a motivation session in which a representative of "Humor Quebec" stresses the value of laughter and the festive in the workplace, but there is clearly very little to laugh about in this environment. Although the film is often broadly comic, Arcand's use of humor involves something very different, and more challenging, than the absurd motivator's advocacy of laughter as the only way "to survive in the present situation."

Jean-Marc's home life in the suburbs is equally unsatisfying. He lives with his wife (Sylvie Léonard), who is frantically trying to win an award as the top real estate agent in her company, and their two daughters, who are constantly plugged into a variety of electronic devices. He commutes to work by train among passengers wearing surgical masks or speaking loudly on their phones. It is a world in which technology isolates individuals from those around them but also offers, through the internet, an escape from the mundane reality of everyday life. Although many critics saw this film as another example of Arcand's focus on the individual rather than the collective, it is clear that he is in fact offering a critical vision of a society in which the state, which replaced the Church in the 1960s as the basis for a meaningful collective identity, has disintegrated into an uninspiring bureaucratic apparatus. Rather than simply expressing the filmmaker's cynical vision, the dystopian view of the near future depicts a society in which fantasy offers an escape from "the ambient cynicism of society" (Castiel 2007, 37).

The opening sequence immediately plunges us into Jean-Marc's fantasy world without having shown a "reality" with which it can be compared. We see a young man (Rufus Wainwright), dressed, as the screenplay puts it, "like a prince from *The Thousand and One Nights*" (Arcand 2007, 15), singing an aria from a baroque opera as he walks through an ornate room in which an apparently naked blonde woman (Diane Kruger) watches him from under satin sheets. The singer's face twice briefly morphs into that of an older man wearing glasses, before Jean-Marc wakes up to his wife calling him from downstairs. The voluptuous blonde (simply described as "Star" in the final credits) reappears several times in his dreams, as does a female reporter (Emma de Caunes) who excitedly drags him away to have sex with her whenever she interviews him about his great achievements, such as winning the Goncourt Prize for his novel and being elected leader of the PQ.[1] Both women are portrayed by French actresses, partly explained by the film's status as a Canada-France coproduction but also by Jean-Marc's respect for French culture.

The status of the fantasy sequences is undercut by several self-reflexive moments that call into question their origin in Jean-Marc's imagination. At the beginning, when the star joins him in the shower after his rude awakening, she turns to the camera and points out that the audience can see her thighs and a hint of a breast in profile, which she says is "perfect for the American censors." Later, she will complain about being the fantasy of a "loser" rather than someone like Roger Federer or Tiger Woods. When Jean-Marc imagines himself as a guest on a French television talk show, he is told that the show has been canceled in France and that the filming is taking place in Montreal, with the result that the studio audience consists not of "beautiful chicks" but entirely of lumberjacks. It is also clear that the fantasies are not simply those of a frustrated individual but extend into the so-called real world he inhabits. The houses in the affluent suburb in which he lives are all designed to look imposing, as if they were, as the screenplay puts it, "small chateaux" (Arcand 2007, 19). When he travels to work for the first time, the music used to introduce fantasy sequences accompanies the transition from his train journey to his arrival at the former Olympic Stadium,

"I have dreamed of this moment for a very long time": Jean-Marc is interviewed as the new leader of the Parti Québécois in *L'âge des ténèbres*.

suggesting that the idea of the Quebec government operating in this building is Arcand's fantasy. However, the difference is that this is not a wish-fulfillment fantasy but an extrapolation of present trends into an imagined future.

This future society is one that looks back to an imagined past, which offers a mythic escape from a dystopian present. When Jean-Marc's car is held up in traffic on his way to the station, he sees a large billboard advertising "a medieval spectacle" (Arcand 2007, 21) called *Quest for the Grail*, and when he visits his mother in hospice, he sees a group of men dressed as medieval knights walking across the street. His daughters play a video game featuring a battle between knights in armor, but the final blurring of the distinction between fantasy and reality comes after his wife moves to Toronto, when he attends a speed-dating session and has brief interviews with several obviously unsuitable partners before he meets a woman (Macha Grenon) who tells him that she is really the Countess Béatrice of Savoy. She boasts that she has seen *The Lord of the Rings* sixty times and thinks it is "the greatest work of modern times." He agrees to be her squire at a tournament where knights will fight for her hand in marriage, and when they arrive at a castle, they see people from various walks of life leaving their cars to play roles in this fantasy reenactment.[2] Inside, a man dressed as a monk (Jean-René Ouellet) proclaims that "the perfidious Arab" is threatening the West and reminds his audience of their ancestors who "cut the throats of a million infidels." His appeal to the spirit of the crusades and the fear of Arabs creates an uncanny fusion of past and present and reminds us of Rémy's description in *Les invasions* of the horrors that have been perpetrated throughout history in the name of religion while suggesting the function of this embodied fantasy as a compensation for the perceived decline of traditional values.

This imaginary past, and the other role-playing games seen throughout the film, offer "a reassuring clarity" (Bergeron 2012, 91) that contrasts with the complications and frustrations of modern life, but Jean-Marc finds this form of escape much less satisfying than his own fantasies. At the tournament, as a result of a series of farcical misunderstandings, he defeats the Black Prince in a tournament for Beatrice's hand in marriage, but the contest is officially declared a draw. He decides he has had enough and tells Beatrice, "Stuff your troubadours."

When he returns to work, he receives a second visit from Pierre, who suggests that Jean-Marc doesn't care about his clients because he has a "comfortable life"; this remark elicits an angry response in which Jean-Marc describes the achievements and hopes of his youth in a list that sounds very much like Arcand's curriculum vitae, and he walks out, telling the people lined up outside his department, "We have no solutions. Your lives are too complicated. The situation is too complicated." As he is leaving, he learns that his mother has just died, rams into another car in a road rage incident, and when he gets home, finds that his wife has returned. After another angry confrontation, he walks off down the suburban street, and the next shot shows him getting off a bus in the country.

Jean-Marc leaves behind a world in which the idea of public service has itself become a bureaucratic fantasy built around cheerful public relations announcements and absurd motivation sessions, masking the reality of red tape and political correctness. He installs himself in his father's old cottage beside the Saint Lawrence River, where he bids a fond farewell to his imaginary mistresses, is attracted to the simple life on a nearby commune, and has a brief reconciliation with his older daughter when she comes with her mother to deliver his possessions.[3] The film ends with a tranquil sequence in which he peels apples at the commune: there is a cut from an extreme close-up of an apple as he peels it to a bowl of apples that gradually dissolves into a Cézanne still-life painting of the same subject, evoking a harmonious balance of nature and art not found in the hectic and absurd urban environment that he has rejected. This serene ending might suggest a return to the traditional values of the ideology of conservation, but as Réal La Rochelle has pointed out, "any reference to the religious or the sacred" found in the early versions of the screenplay has been removed (apart perhaps from the presence of Constance and Father Leclerc) so that the ending "remains open, which says nothing about what the protagonist will become" (2014, 46).

This ending has a possible utopian dimension, affirming the value of life and art, but the relatively positive outcome for the individual character can be achieved only by the removal of the science-fiction elements from the film's narrative. The government for which Jean-Marc worked will presumably continue to proclaim its function of protecting citizens while entangling them in jargon and red tape. By casting off his fantasies, Jean-Marc has returned to "reality" but only after admitting that the dystopian world of the city cannot be changed. This is, of course, precisely what Arcand's enemies accuse him of doing, and we thus come back to the question of the filmmaker's relation to his central character. At the time of the film's release, he suggested, "[although] people prefer to dream . . . I would say rather I am a realist and a joker" (quoted in Coulombe 2007). The "joker" side of the director must have enjoyed depicting Jean-Marc's fantasy life, but while Labrèche makes the "man without interest" into an engaging character, the fantasies are clearly empty illusions that offer some respite from the disturbing reality that Arcand sees as only a slight exaggeration of the state of modern Quebec.

Predictably, the film provoked a wide range of critical reactions, many of them very negative. Carl Bergeron suggested the problem was that unlike *Les invasions,* in which "the acid critique of the Quebec situation . . . remained subordinate to the humanistic message of the film," *L'âge des ténèbres* is "an implacable film that avoids playing the card of seduction" (2012, 98). However, in an interview with the director in *Séquences,* Francine Laurendeau called it "an extremely seductive film" and told him she could not understand "the hostility of the critics" (2007, 38). Ironically, in view of the fun poked at Jean-Marc's obsession with French culture, the film premiered in France, and Arcand's opponents in Quebec made the most of its poor reception there. However, it did well at the box office in Quebec (La Rochelle 2014, 55) despite some scathing reviews that denounced its maker's "incurable misanthropy and cynicism" (Martin Bilodeau, quoted in La Rochelle 2014, 48) or, as was now to be expected, simply labeled the film as "reactionary" (Barrette 2007, 4).

The film's satiric targets certainly include some that are normally seen as signs of progress in modern society: the move toward more inclusive language, the laws against smoking in public places, among others. Jean-Marc's fantasy of kidnapping and making his female boss (Caroline Néron) into his slave, with the help of William dressed as an African chieftain, manages to be both sexist and racist. There are more such offenses, but these violations of political correctness function, like the clichés in *Le déclin,* as provocations that encourage us to think about how legislating progressive change can lead to bureaucratic control over people's lives, as Arcand felt had happened in Quebec after the Quiet Revolution.

The director called *L'âge des ténèbres* "his darkest film . . . and the funniest" (quoted in La Rochelle 2014, 48), and an English Canadian critic went so far as to declare that, although it is "arguably Arcand's most depressing film . . . it's also one of his greatest and, in a strange way, his most uplifting" (Howell 2007, H10). While critics and audiences had responded enthusiastically to the similarly complex tone of some of his earlier films, Arcand ruefully noted, "people who had adored *Les Invasions barbares* rejected *L'Âge des ténèbres*" (quoted in La Rochelle 2014, 54), much as French critics had turned against him earlier in his career when he followed *Réjeanne Padovani* with *Gina* (see chapter 3).

"THE POSTCARD EFFECT": *LE RÈGNE DE LA BEAUTÉ*

In 2011, the critic Robert Lévesque, once a strong supporter of Arcand's work, lamented that the director had "turned his back on his first, true films . . . and become an unwavering box-office filmmaker" (quoted in La Rochelle 2014, 53). Such a judgment depends on the confident assumption that there is a clear dividing line between art films and commercial cinema, which, as we have seen, Arcand's films have often called into question, even in the early days. It is certainly true that, since the tremendous success of *Le déclin*, Arcand (and his producers) have kept at least one eye on the box office, but he is clearly ambivalent about the hype that was generated around that film and his two other international hits. The critical enthusiasm generated by them aroused expectations that his more modest efforts could not fulfill, which at least partly explains the critical response to the films he made between *Jésus de Montréal* and *Les invasions barbares*. The need to balance his sense of himself as an art filmmaker and his awareness of the demands of the marketplace has created tensions that are very apparent in his two most recent films and their critical reception.

Le règne de la beauté certainly has its roots in the art film tradition. The director explained that he set out to make a film that would "resemble the last fifteen minutes of *L'Âge de ténèbres*" (quoted in La Rochelle 2014, 74). This ending reminded André Loiselle of a scene in Ingmar Bergman's *The Seventh Seal* (1956), in which a medieval knight "finds a refuge from a meaningless world of ignorance and disease in the simple pleasure of eating wild strawberries and drinking milk" (2008, 158), and it was Bergman's next film, *Wild Strawberries* (1957), which was in Arcand's mind when he began work on the project that would become *Le règne de la beauté*. The idea came to him when he received an honorary doctorate, like Isak Borg, the old doctor in Bergman's film: the ceremony at Montreal's McGill University in 2004 included a reading of each honoree's biography, and the reference to his childhood in Deschambault led him to plan an autobiographical work in which he would look back, as Borg does, on his own past (La Rochelle 2014, 69–70). However, while the completed film is largely set in Charlevoix, the rural area where Arcand grew up, the protagonist is no longer an old man or a filmmaker, as originally planned, but an architect at the height of his fame who has been honored with a prestigious award for his achievements.

In 2007, Arcand had announced that he was preparing "the last film of my life, in a completely different register," and he would continue to differentiate the new work from his previous films, explaining that its tone would be "more peaceful, more calm, more contemplative" (quoted in La Rochelle 2014, 69, 74). However, he came to regret this emphasis because it encouraged reviewers to see the film as an attempt to break from the cynical outlook of his previous films and not to look beneath its beautiful surface.[4] Looking back on its critical reception, he would complain, "People believed I wanted to do something different with this film, but that's not true," claiming that the "more contemplative tone" came about only because of the rural setting and the characters who are rather less garrulous than those in his previous films (quoted in Demers 2018). The tone is certainly very different from much of Arcand's previous work, although, as he has pointed out, critics have tended to ignore the moments of "tenderness" in many of his films (quoted in Coulombe 2007). As we have seen, he had already dealt with the topic of "beauty" in *Stardom*, a film that also met with critical disapproval on the grounds that it was an apparent departure from his earlier work. However, while the tone of *Le règne* could not be further removed from the hectic pace and hyperactivity of *Stardom*, which could also be seen as a product of its setting in the world of publicity and fashion, the underlying themes of the two films are not dissimilar.

Whereas Bergman placed the ceremony in *Wild Strawberries* near the end of his film, Arcand opens his with an awards ceremony in Paris in which Luc Sauvageau (Éric Bruneau) is celebrated for achieving the kind of success that Jean-Marc in his previous film could only fantasize about. The introduction of the recipient is in English, which is very much the language of power in the film, and the speaker praises the "quintessential purity, beauty and simplicity" of Luc's architecture, which projects "honesty and peaceful strength." Luc delivers his acceptance speech in French and declares, "A civilization is always judged by its architecture," which he calls "an activity of hope." He receives a standing ovation, and a woman in the front row, whom we assume to be his wife, smiles proudly. As he steps down from the podium, another woman calls out to him in English and seems to expect him to recognize her. She introduces herself as Lindsay Walker (Melanie Merkosky), and his sudden recognition cues a flashback to their first meeting in Toronto, when he was a member of a jury assessing architectural plans and she was the administrative assistant. He then flies to Charlevoix where he joins his wife, Stéphanie (Mélanie Thierry)—not the woman at the ceremony—who is entertaining friends in their modern house (presumably designed by Luc), built amid the beautiful landscape. His cynical account of how the Toronto jury was chosen to represent different interest groups in Canada, with himself as the token Francophone, amuses them, but he carefully omits Lindsay from his report.

The long flashback makes up the bulk of the narrative and situates its mainly young characters in settings of natural and man-made beauty. Arcand depicts the region in different seasons, with special emphasis on the Saint Lawrence River and the landscape surrounding it. Many reviewers in Quebec, including some who had criticized the supposedly poorly framed shots in the director's earlier films, now objected to the beautiful cinematography, which seemed to represent

"The most beautiful house on the North Shore": Luc and his friends celebrate the completion of a house he has designed in *Le règne de la beauté.*

an abandonment of the satiric vision for which Arcand was known (and frequently condemned). However, one of the fiercest attacks on the film came not from a Quebec critic but from a reviewer in the *New York Times* who claimed that it was "the cinematic equivalent of a photo spread in *Vogue* or *Architectural Digest* that taunts you with images of the rich, well-to-do beautiful people leading the tastefully glamorous life" (Holden 2016).

This critic pointed specifically to a sequence in which Luc declares, "Ugliness is a crime against humanity," as if this hyperbolic statement were the film's intended message. Once again, we come up against the question of how much we are expected to identify with the central character, here complicated further by the film's autobiographical origins. While Arcand certainly shares Luc's appreciation of beauty and distaste for ugliness, the film suggests the futility of a "reign of beauty" based on the exclusion of realities that would disturb the image of perfection. Although more attractive than the characters in *L'âge des ténèbres,* Luc and his friends are equally immersed in a utopian fantasy.

As usual, Arcand does not overtly judge his characters but places them in narrative contexts that invite us to see their limitations. In this case, for example, situating the narrative in rural Quebec excludes the reality of the province's changing ethnic makeup; all the characters enjoying the "reign of beauty" are white, as are those we see in the privileged milieus in Paris and Toronto, although none of the film's critics have pointed this out. What Réal La Rochelle calls the film's "'postcard effect,' in the best sense of the term" (2014, 109) may create a good deal of visual pleasure, but it coexists with an awareness of the underside of the depicted lifestyle. In a perceptive article in *Le Devoir* responding to the film's negative critical reception, Dominique Cornellier likened it to *Stardom* and suggested that both films explore "the injustice of beauty and the falseness of images" (2014).

The *New York Times* reviewer regretted that the film was not "a satire, which it should be" (Holden 2016), but despite the veneer of beauty and affluence, Arcand's satiric perspective on the decline of modern Quebec is still very apparent for those who want to see it. There is another depiction of the dilapidated, and ugly, state of the health system: Roger (Michel Forget), who has built many of Luc's houses, becomes seriously ill and is sent for tests to a hospital in Quebec City, where he spends days in a corridor, before returning home to die. Critics also come under attack: when Luc sits on another jury in Toronto, the other members use high-flown aesthetic jargon to put down student projects, and afterward, they meet in a restaurant where they pour scorn on the insidious effects of "mass tourism." At the end of the ceremony in Paris, two critics, much like those in *Jésus de Montréal*, compare notes and jadedly discuss where their next assignment will take them. Luc has become a member of an elite that uses its privileges to distinguish its tastes from those of the ignorant masses, and while he may not endorse all their views, he goes along with them in his pursuit of success. Far from presenting these people as role models, the film is, as Cornellier puts it, "a radical critique of contemporary society and its autistic hedonism" (2014). After he and Lindsay make love in a luxury hotel in Quebec City, Luc drives out of the city along a street filled with fast-food outlets, gas stations, and other examples of urban sprawl. It is clear that the buildings he designs, as beautiful as they are, can only be afforded by the wealthy and have little impact on the lives of most people.

One aspect of the new film that may have encouraged reviewers to see the film as a departure for Arcand is the youthfulness of most of its characters as compared to the regular cast of middle-aged actors familiar from his most well-known films.[5] Yet as we have seen, Arcand had previously insisted on a cast of mainly young actors in *Love and Human Remains*, and like their predecessors in that film, the characters in *Le règne* have been described as "the children of the heroes of *Le Déclin*" (Martineau 2018). More accurately, they might be the grandchildren of the lyric generation (see the introduction), which was described by François Ricard as a generation for whom "everything takes place under the sign of beauty, harmony and joy" (1994, 8). Compared to their unsettled counterparts in *Love and Human Remains* (or Nathalie in *Les invasions*), these characters live apparently comfortable existences in a circle of good-natured friends. They drink wine together (without the pretensions of Luc's colleagues in Toronto) and enjoy the products of the marijuana plantation hidden in Luc's garden. Their lifestyles are healthy, and they enjoy participating in many different sports.

Stéphanie is a physical education teacher, and Isabelle (Marie-Josée Croze), the local doctor in a modern clinic, treats patients with efficiency and compassion.

However, external factors point to the limitations of life in an isolated community: Isabelle does not have the resources to treat serious illnesses, Luc's aspirations as an architect can only be fulfilled by becoming part of the culture of globalization, and television and other media invade domestic spaces, bringing news of disturbing events in the outside world. Although the natural environment might connote a return to the real, like Jean-Marc's final abandonment of his fantasies and his urban life, the community is cut off from what passes for reality in the outside world. As a result, the characters seem to be lacking in direction, despite Luc's ambitions, and even the natural impulses of sexuality only complicate matters. Luc drifts into his affair with Lindsay (in which the sex is filmed more graphically than is usual for an Arcand film), but it lasts for only two nights.[6] Like Candy in *Love and Human Remains*, Stéphanie is unsure of her sexual identity, and Luc sees her kissing Mélissa (Geneviève Boivin-Roussy), who is in an apparently stable lesbian relationship with Isabelle. Later, she admits that she only thought she was attracted to another woman, much as Luc comes to realize he was not really in love with Lindsay.

The most serious sign of the insecure basis of this beautiful life occurs when Stéphanie suffers a breakdown. She already seems disturbed when Luc returns from Toronto at the beginning: as the friends listen to his description of his visit, she looks distracted, and a brief shot of Lindsay intrudes into the sequence. Her unease may have its roots in an intuitive awareness of her husband's infidelity, and perhaps in her attraction to Mélissa, but it comes to a head when she and Luc watch a television program about violence in the Middle East. The Arab protestors and soldiers are the only nonwhites we see in the film, and the shocking images provoke Stéphanie to ask, "Are we real?" and she tells Luc that she feels "panic" as gunfire is heard on the soundtrack. Her question goes to the heart of the film's depiction of the lives of these young people. Luc explains that the program is a "documentary," as if this might reassure her, but another panic attack occurs when she and Luc take a chairlift at a ski resort. She contemplates suicide when she is left alone while Luc is meeting Lindsay in Quebec City, and when she becomes increasingly withdrawn, she receives treatment in a nursing home.

Luc visits Stéphanie there, and he tells her about a commission from the Cistercians to design an abbey, which he likens to the monastery built by the British architect John Pawson in the Czech Republic. This raises the question of whether the "purity" of Luc's architecture has a spiritual dimension and how, if it does, the emphasis on the beauty of the countryside in the film relates to Arcand's attitude to religion at this stage of his career. In the way it blends in with the natural surroundings, Luc's modern architecture evokes the traditional iconography of rural Quebec, and we even see Luc and Stéphanie performing in the church choir at Christmas, as Arcand and his wife once did, evoking a similar sequence in *Québec: Duplessis et après . . .* (see chapter 2). Although, as we have seen, Arcand had expunged all religious references from the end of *L'âge des ténèbres,* he nevertheless gave Jean-Marc a name that combined those of two of the apostles, and Luc is named after a third apostle. Yet if the ideology of conservation lies behind the new film, the effect here is to act as a subliminal reminder of the loss of religion that has shaped the society in which the characters live. In the context of the film, it is more a historical than a nostalgic reference.

Perhaps critics would have been happier with the film if Luc had been punished for ruining his wife's life, but he and Stéphanie amicably agree to a divorce, sell their house, and she gets a job as "third assistant coach" to the Canadian women's soccer team. The film ends with a return to the present in Paris, where Luc introduces Lindsay to his new Spanish wife and receives a telephone call from Stéphanie, which makes clear that she has also remarried. The final credits then appear over a montage of shots of modern buildings, which are presumably "the work of Luc Sauvageau in the fifteen years, after the story came to its end" (La Rochelle 2014, 96), including a religious building that we must assume is the completed abbey.[7] Despite his personal failings, the beauty of these buildings suggests that Luc's award is well deserved, and the viewer is left to contemplate the relations between his creative work and the social and economic context from which it has emerged (perhaps suggesting, despite his acceptance speech, that a society cannot be judged by its architecture).

The film, like most of Arcand's recent films, was a Canada-France coproduction, and like its predecessor, it received poor reviews in France even before it opened in Quebec. Most reviewers in Quebec newspapers followed their French counterparts while the film journals, with one exception, ignored it. As the *New York Times* reviewer put it, the general impression was that the film represented a "low point in the director's career" (Holden 2016). In his review in *Séquences,* however, Pierre-Alexandre Fradet offered an illuminating assessment of the film, in which he argued that, if the main concern is with beauty, the subtext is "nothing other than the quest for personal joy and its profound instability" (2014, 59). As we have seen, Dominique Cornellier defended the film in *Le Devoir,* insisting that it is "not the superficial work decried by the critics of this world" and that it "unleashes clichés to make us see their political and sociological underside" (2014), a judgment that recalls Denise Pérusse's reading of *Le déclin* (see chapter 4). More recently, Richard Martineau, who had initially agreed with the film's detractors, revisited his opinion and decided that, although "it is minor Arcand . . . better a minor film by a major filmmaker than a major film by a minor filmmaker" (2018).

Both Corneillier (2014) and Martineau (2018) claimed that in *Le règne*, beauty has become a "trap" or a "prison," and Martineau goes so far as to argue that the characters are "so used to being surrounded by beauty that they no longer even notice it. They are the living dead" (2018). This is, I would suggest, a slight exaggeration, since Arcand clearly enjoys the beautiful things in life, and his film asks its viewers to take pleasure from its images but, at the same time, emphasizes the costs involved in creating beauty while ignoring the ugly things in the world around us.

"CRIME CAPER AND STATE OF THE NATION RUMINATION": *LA CHUTE DE L'EMPIRE AMÉRICAIN*

After *Le règne* was shown at the Toronto International Film Festival, where, according to Martin Knelman, it was "given the royal treatment, drawing packed houses" (2015), its planned theatrical release in English Canada was canceled. Knelman felt that, although it was "not one of Arcand's greatest films," it was "quite interesting" and likely to attract "Arcand fans who live in Toronto," where part of the film takes is set. Indeed, it was surprising that English Canadian audiences were not given the chance to see Arcand's latest film on the big screen, especially since he is the only Canadian director to have won the Academy Award for Best Foreign Language Film. However, as Knelman's article makes clear, it is far from the only film to have fallen through the cracks in the contemporary state of film distribution, and the director's next film would suffer a similar and even more dispiriting fate.

When *La chute de l'empire américain* was released in Quebec in the summer of 2018, it enjoyed what can only be called a mixed reception, but one critic (Yakabuski 2018) thought it was "Mr. Arcand's best film" or at least "his most boisterously urgent one." This is only a slight exaggeration as an assessment of a film that offers a typically complex weaving together of different genres and tones to challenge the spectator. However, its prospects were immediately damaged by the workings of the globalized film market: the U.S. rights had been bought by Sony, which stipulated that it could not be released simultaneously in an English subtitled version (as is normal practice in Quebec) in order to prevent video piracy before its U.S. release date, then scheduled for the fall (Kelly 2018b). Although the film was screened at the Toronto International Film Festival in September, it could not be released immediately in the rest of Canada because Sony had not yet confirmed the exact date for the U.S. release. As it turned out, the film did not go on (limited) release in North America until June 2019, one year after its premiere in Quebec, and then with minimal publicity.

After the director's efforts to differentiate *Le règne* from his earlier films, the title of his new film was calculated to remind audiences of his past achievements, and at least one reviewer described it as the completion of a trilogy, after *Le déclin* and *Les invasions* (Ehrlich 2018). Yet it was also a return to the crime genre that he had not revisited since his first fiction films in the 1970s. In this case, he turned to the heist film, a subgenre of the crime film, and the working title, until quite close to its release date in Quebec, was *Le triomphe de l'argent* (The triumph of money).[8] This title would have made it seem more like a companion piece to *Le règne*, and Arcand was duly charged with "opportunism" (Lanlo 2018) for making a last-minute change in order to cash in on his previous success. Since there is only a token reference to the American Empire, this seems like a plausible criticism, but as we shall see, the film's depiction of contemporary society does make it into an even more urgent sequel to *Le déclin*.

Arcand claimed that the title had been changed because, while he was working on the film, he came to realize that the original title did not "give a clear impression of the film" (quoted in Marin 2018); the heist plot sets the narrative going, but the crime film premise provides the impetus for a broader reflection on the state of modern society. This does not mean that it is an antigenre film (see chapter 3), since many heist films also raise awkward questions about prevalent attitudes to money and social class, and while the formula usually consists of the planning, execution, and aftermath of a robbery, a structure that Arcand had ironically borrowed in *Le confort et l'indifférence* (see chapter 2), the balance between these elements can vary considerably. *La chute* omits the planning stage and only touches on the execution because Pierre-Paul (Alexandre Landry) comes into possession of the loot by accident; the main focus is on the aftermath, in which the inadvertent criminal has to find a way, legal or illegal, of hanging on to the money.[9]

In *Le déclin*, Dominique argues that the American Empire is in decline because of the obsessive pursuit of individual pleasure; thirty years later, this diagnosis may still be relevant, but the new film's concern extends to how this way of life has given birth to a society dedicated to the accumulation of individual wealth at the expense of those who lack it—in other words, the ever-widening gap between the rich and the poor. Although Arcand explained that the initial idea for the film was "inspired by a 2010 shooting in a Montreal clothing store owned by a gangster," he also said that it was "guided by offshore tax havens . . . and the difficult lives of the homeless" (quoted in Marin 2018). The heist film allowed him to develop a plot that draws parallels between the activities of criminals who resort to violence in the pursuit of money and those of respectable businessmen and lawyers who use subtler methods with the same goal and with equally disastrous results.

The precredits sequence takes place in a restaurant where Pierre-Paul is telling his girlfriend, Linda (Florence Longpré), that he believes he is too intelligent to be successful, and he reels off the names of successful writers, philosophers, and politicians who were, he claims, quite stupid, ending his list with a sneering reference to Donald Trump. He has a PhD but is working as a delivery driver because it pays more than teaching, and he tells her he feels that intelligence is a "handicap." When Linda, a bank teller and single mother, reminds him of how many people voted for Trump, he tells her, "Imbeciles worship cretins," and she accuses him of having contempt for ordinary people. Yet Pierre-Paul has a strong sense of social justice: he volunteers in a shelter for homeless people and always gives money to beggars when he passes them in the street. Despite his erudition, he is shy and diffident, modestly referring to himself as "a man without qualities." Like Jean-Marc in *L'âge des ténèbres*, he seems an unlikely hero, but with typical Arcandian irony, he becomes a more sympathetic character after he commits an illegal act that initially makes him seem like the crass materialists the film denounces.

Linda walks out, and a phone-in radio show heard in the background during their conversation, discussing the salaries of professional athletes, ends by concluding that "the market decides" what they are worth. The credits then begin with a jarring cut to loud rap music as two black youths steal a car and hold the staff at a clothing store (called Hollywood) at gunpoint, ordering them to fill two large bags with money from the safe. The heist goes wrong when a white gangster enters the store, and a gun battle breaks out. While this is going on, Pierre-Paul arrives on the scene in his delivery van and watches in shock as the robbers run out of the store. One of them is shot dead, and the other runs off wounded, leaving two bags stuffed with money, and Pierre-Paul stares at the bags, long enough to allow the viewers to think about what they would do in this situation, until he suddenly goes into action and carries them into his van. His motives remain unclear, and as we watch him hide the loot in his book-filled apartment, the film draws on the ambivalence that is central to the heist film: between respect for the law and dislike for banks and other financial institutions. While he later justifies his actions by the idea that he can use the money to do good, in order to do so, he must evade both the police and the gangsters who are trying to recover the loot, and he must also launder the "dirty" money.

To this end, he assembles a "motley crew of criminal masterminds" (Ehrlich 2018), rather like Daniel recruiting his disciples in *Jésus de Montréal*. Sylvain "the Brain" Bigras (Rémy Girard) is a former motorcycle gang member, just released from prison, where he has been working on a business degree, and we first see him in a classroom where the lecturer is describing financial rules governing offshore accounts and how people get around them. Camille Lafontaine (Maripier Morin) is a high-class prostitute to whom Pierre-Paul is attracted because she quotes Racine on her website and because she has adopted the name Aspasie, a courtesan in ancient Greece who, he delightedly explains, was a friend of Socrates.[10] Wilbrod Taschereau (Pierre Curzi) is technically not a criminal but a lawyer who is an expert in finding ways for his wealthy clients not to pay taxes. The "gang" will eventually be expanded to include Camille's Chinese chauffeur; Linda, who insists she feels no loyalty to a bank whose CEO earns one hundred times her salary; and the wounded robber, who has been tortured by the gangsters from whom the money was stolen, for which Pierre-Paul feels responsible. As in most heist films, the film invites us to identify with them and want them to succeed, but Arcand uses this sense of complicity to develop an even more explicit critique of a society in which money seems to have become the only thing of value.

Like many of Arcand's films, *La chute* becomes generically unstable. The title encourages us to view it as what Allan Hunter calls "a sardonic, solidly entertaining fusion of crime caper and state of the nation rumination" (2018). Yet the lightness of tone that the word "caper" implies is contradicted by its depiction of gang warfare, which evokes recent Hollywood gangster films (much as the ending of *Gina* draws on the iconography of the action thriller; see chapter 3). It turns out that the black owner of the store, a former gang member, organized the heist, and the money belonged to a rival gang. The shootings during the heist, the torture sequence, and the execution of the store owner when he is unable to repay the money are all depicted graphically. There are many abrupt shifts in tone, particularly in the first half of the film, as the action proceeds in short sequences between Pierre-Paul's attempts to hide the money, his gradual romantic involvement with Camille, the police investigation, the wounded man's search for help, the gang's activities, and discussions of the unjust workings of the social system. As a result, there are numerous montage effects, typical of the "mosaic" structures that the director has always favored, contrasting and comparing the different threads of the plot.

As in *Le règne*, all the main characters are white; in keeping with its urban setting, the film acknowledges the racial diversity of contemporary Quebec but in ways that are often calculatedly provocative. The violence is associated with two gangs, one run by blacks and the other by Irish and Jewish thugs. Inevitably, there were accusations of stereotyping, but Arcand is again using clichés to disturb and provoke. In one sequence, Taschereau, who has earlier inveighed against "the reign of political correctness," lectures the two police officers assigned to the case about how his global financial operations require him to respect the different moral systems of the countries he deals with. He offers the analogy that if a man wants to beat his wife, this would be forbidden in Canada, but if he moved to Pakistan, Islamic law would allow him to do so with impunity. He then turns around and accuses the officers of racism. Arcand's straightforward presentation of the lawyer's argument leaves the viewers to make any judgments, but as we shall see, Taschereau will be the only member of the gang who is brought to justice, even if his financial transactions are quite legal.

The main target of the satire is the world of high finance and the legal and political systems that support it. Taschereau uses digital technology to make contacts that will enable Pierre-Paul and his gang to send the stolen money on a circuitous journey around the globe to the safety of a Swiss bank, much as the robbers earlier used smartphones and the internet to get a key for the vehicle they steal before the heist. If the underworld and the overworld are part of the same system, using different methods to become rich, Pierre-Paul and his gang use the methods of the establishment against it. Their behavior is contradictory, but Arcand has never been shy of contradiction, especially if it disrupts the smooth functioning of the dominant ideology.

As so often happens in Arcand's films, the ending unsettles audience expectations. In this case, the apparently happy ending, in which the criminals get to keep the money and Pierre-Paul and Camille fall in love, left at least one critic wondering if "the filmmaker is being ironic or dreadfully romantic" (Bouchard 2018, 51), and others questioned the sincerity of his apparent conversion from pessimism to optimism, implying that he was motivated only by commercial considerations. However, such criticisms miss—or ignore—the rich vein of irony that runs through the film: this "fairy-tale" outcome has been prepared for by the comedy that stems from the couple's naivety or, as Arcand would put it, their lack of realism. Once he has taken the money, Pierre-Paul has no idea what to do with it, and he is saved only by the actions of Bigras, the seasoned criminal; Camille is obviously more experienced and more familiar with avoiding the law, but she reacts in surprise when he tells her about the street people she simply has not seen in her pampered life. They both know little, like many spectators, about the intricacies of high finance to which Taschereau introduces them; the film offers many facts and figures that illustrate how the rich accumulate wealth in the present social system and draws attention to the euphemisms and jargon that enable it to keep functioning.

The film may be "realistic" in its depiction of violence and in its treatment of the more sophisticated workings of high finance, but the romantic plot and Pierre-Paul's activities after the heist are overtly unrealistic. When Pierre-Paul logs into the Aspasie website, the music on the soundtrack is an instrumental version of the aria sung by Rufus Wainwright at the beginning of *L'âge des ténèbres*, and this music becomes a leitmotif for their relationship. The effect is to suggest that she is as much an illusion as the woman in Jean-Marc's fantasy, even if Camille eventually emerges as more down-to-earth than the persona she has created. At one point, Pierre-Paul quotes Aristotle to the effect that "happiness is directly linked to luck," and he is lucky that nobody sees him when he takes the money or when he carries it into his apartment, that Bigras removes the bags from the self-storage unit where Pierre-Paul has stored them before the police arrive, that a student demonstration delays the police when they receive a tip-off about the money laundering, and that the two cops assigned to the case do not see through the flimsy alibis he offers them. From another perspective, his luck may be seen as the workings of "providence," as suggested by a friend who also volunteers at the shelter and tells him, "The Lord rewards the just."

The ending oscillates between the film's playful elements and its serious themes. After the money is safely laundered, Pierre-Paul invites the cops who are still following him to help feed the homeless in the shelter, where he accuses one of them of "defending the indefensible" and suggests that there may be a revolution. But Arcand typically provokes the radicals in the audience when the cop assures him that his job will be safe because the first thing that is wanted after a revolution is "an efficient police force." This same cop has earlier expressed hatred for Taschereau because a similarly devious lawyer ruined his father, a piece of bad luck that prevented him from getting a PhD; he gets his revenge in a sting operation that allows the police to arrest Taschereau for soliciting a minor.[11] He is thus the only one of Pierre-Paul's gang to be arrested—and not for his involvement in dealing with the stolen money. The film ends with the young couple walking away together, followed by a cut to the "sobering coda" (Ehrlich 2018), a documentary montage of close-ups of some of the Inuit who live on the streets of Montreal, leaving us to contemplate the distance between the "fairy tale" and the reality. In a press conference after the release of the film, Pierre Curzi nicely captured the impact of this ending, which, he suggested, "says: look, this money is dirty, and all of a sudden at the end, is it going to be clean? Is it going to solve all the problems?" (quoted in Marin 2018).

According to the director, the film deals with the way in which "Québécois (Judeo-Christian) values have been progressively replaced by American values" (quoted in Lanlo 2018), and it thus paints a pessimistic or, to use Arcand's own word (quoted in Kelly 2018a, C1), "dystopian," view of the state of Quebec in the twenty-first century. However, as we have come to expect, the director's dark view of history is complemented by his commitment to making the most of the present. As he puts it, money is "ambivalent," and it can be used to "do either good or bad" (quoted in DeMara 2018, L6). The problem is that in the current state of affairs, it is most often used to enrich the already rich, while those who do not have enough only get poorer. Whether Pierre-Paul's project of using the loot for good purposes will ever come to pass is uncertain, but the intention powers a film "with one foot stuck in reality and the other in a socialist fairy tale where everyone is happy to share the wealth and solve each other's problems" (Ehrlich 2018).

Although its title proclaims continuity, the only characters from Arcand's earlier films who make (brief) appearances are Joseph (Benoît Brière) and Marcel (Gaston Lepage), the street people from *Joyeux calvaire*.[12] Arcand himself saw it as a "throwback to my first films" (quoted in DeMara 2018, L6), and its crime plot certainly links it to *La maudite galette,* in which people who did not commit the crime also get away with the loot, but it is even closer to the seriocomic exposure of a completely corrupt system in *Réjeanne Padovani,* in which businessmen, police, and gangsters work comfortably together. Apart from the return to the crime film, the representation of Montreal evokes the depiction of the city in *Les Montréalistes* as a commercial center that had strayed far from its missionary origins. In *La chute,* shots of the city looking down from above resemble those in *Jésus de Montréal,* although here the beauty of these images is undercut by an awareness of the contrast between the wealth represented by all the high-rise buildings and the poverty of the street people down below. Pierre-Paul is a more troubled successor to Daniel, while the ethical dilemma provoked by his theft extends Arcand's ambivalence about the tension between material and spiritual values.

As Konrad Yakabuski recognized, the film is a testimony to Arcand's ability to "transpose universal themes onto a local canvas" and to bring together "high-brow and low-brow Quebec culture" (2018). The director's critics have accused him of thus betraying the specificity of the Québécois identity and the integrity of art cinema, but one of the hallmarks of his films is not to settle for one thing over the other. He explores the contradictions of the human condition as they have manifested themselves in Quebec since the Quiet Revolution. The projected fall of the American Empire may confirm Dominique's thesis in *Le déclin,* in accord with Arcand's own historical analysis, but in *La chute,* as in his other works, he tries to balance his dystopian worldview with Louise's belief that "the best we can do is to try to be happy." Which, of course, is much easier if we have enough money.

Although Arcand had benefited enormously from the sale of the international rights to his three great successes, the treatment accorded *La chute de l'empire américain* is a symptom of the vulnerability of Quebec cinema (and other small film industries) in the contemporary global media-marketplace. It is also an ironic confirmation of the film's central concern with the impact on Quebec of a culture in which market forces have taken precedence over all other considerations. If the Quiet Revolution opened Quebec up to the outside world, the outside is now also very much inside, and the economic power of Sony, a Japanese-based multinational corporation, brought short-term economic benefits but harmed the film's long-term prospects because of the delayed release of an English subtitled version of the film. It is uncertain that the film would have been another major success with a more timely release, but it would certainly have made much more of an impact.

If this film turns out to be Arcand's last, it is, despite the way it has been treated, a worthy ending to a long career that began when Quebec cinema, outside the

NFB, was an artisanal affair. As we have seen, he became an often-controversial commentator on the momentous social and political changes that have occurred in Quebec during his lifetime, and he was a key figure in the growth of the domestic film industry, which has flourished in the last twenty years but is now once again endangered. It remains to be seen whether Arcand has been right in his pessimistic view of the future of Quebec as a distinct francophone culture, but his films offer a rich testimony to the complex and contradictory factors that have shaped the present situation and that need to be addressed in order to move forward.

ACKNOWLEDGMENTS

I would like to thank Homer Pettey and R. Barton Palmer for inviting me to write what has turned out to be the first book of this series. I hope it represents an auspicious beginning. I would also like to thank Nicole Solano and Maggie Tibbits at Rutgers University Press for their encouragement and patience. Thanks are also due to Rob MacMorine at Brock University for his help with the photos.

FILMOGRAPHY

This filmography includes only the works discussed in this book. Details of Arcand's other short films and television commercials can be found in La Rochelle (2005).

1962 *Seul ou avec d'autres* (*Alone or with Others*)
Screenplay: Denys Arcand and Stéphane Venne
Directors: Denys Arcand, Denis Héroux, and Stéphane Venne
Cinematographer: Michel Brault
Editor: Gilles Groulx
Music: Stéphane Venne
Sound: Marcel Carrière
Producer: Denis Héroux
Production: Association générale des étudiants de l'Université de Montréal
Cast: Nicole Braün, Pierre Létourneau, Michelle Boulizon, Marie-José Raymond, Guy Rocher, Marc Laurendeau, and Marcel Saint-Germain
(16 mm, black and white, 64 minutes)

1964 *Champlain*
Script: Denys Arcand
Director: Denys Arcand
Cinematographer: Bernard Gosselin
Editors: Werner Nold and Bernard Gosselin
Illustrations: Frédéric Back
Music: The Montreal Brass Quintet and Kenneth Gilbert
Commentators: Gisèle Trépanier and Georges Dufaux
Production: National Film Board of Canada
(16 mm, color, 28 minutes)

1965 *Les Montréalistes* (*Ville-Marie*)
Script: Andrée Thibault
Director: Denys Arcand
Cinematographer: Bernard Gosselin
Editor: Monique Fortier
Music: The Renaissance Singers of Montreal, Pierre Henry, and Pierre Schaeffer

Commentators: Gisèle Trépanier and Gilles Marsolais
Producer: André Belleau
Production: National Film Board of Canada
(16 mm, color, 27 minutes)

1965 *La route de l'Ouest* (*The Westward Road*)
Script: Denys Arcand
Director: Denys Arcand
Cinematographer: Bernard Gosselin
Editor: Werner Nold
Music: Kenneth Gilbert, Sorcha ni Ghuairim, and La societé de musique d'autrefois
Commentator: Christian Delmas
Producer: André Belleau
Production: National Film Board of Canada
(16 mm, color, 28 minutes)

1965 *Montréal, un jour d'été* (*Montreal on a Summer's Day*)
Director: Denys Arcand
Cinematographer: Bernard Gosselin
Editor: Denys Arcand
Music: Stéphane Venne
Producer: Raymond-Marie Léger
Production: Office du film du Québec
(35 mm, color, 12 minutes)

1966 *Volleyball*
Director: Denys Arcand
Cinematographers: Jean-Claude Labrecque, Gilles Gascon, Jean Roy, and Thomas Vamos
Editor: Denys Arcand
Sound: Bill Graziadei, Jacques Drouin, Ron Alexander, and Roger Lamoureux
Producer: Jacques Bobet
Production: National Film Board of Canada
(35 mm, black and white, 13 minutes)

1967 *Parcs atlantiques* (*Atlantic Parks*)
Director: Denys Arcand
Cinematographer: Gilles Gascon
Editor: Denys Arcand
Music: François Cousineau
Producers: Jacques Bobet and André Belleau
Production: National Film Board of Canada
(35 mm, color, 17 minutes)

1971 *On est au coton* (We're fed up)
Director: Denys Arcand
Cinematographers: Alain Dostie and Pierre Mignot
Editor: Pierre Bernier
Research: Gérald Godin
Producers: Marc Beaudet and Pierre Maheu
Production: National Film Board of Canada
(16 mm, black and white, 173 minutes, original release version 159 minutes)

1971 *La maudite galette* (*Dirty Money*)
Screenplay: Jacques Benoît
Director: Denys Arcand
Cinematographer: Alain Dostie
Editor: Marguerite Duparc
Music: Michel Hinton, Gabriel Arcand, and Lionel Thériault
Producer: Marguerite Duparc
Production: Cinak, Les Films Carle-Lamy, and France Film
Cast: Marcel Sabourin (Ernest), Luce Guilbeault (Berthe), René Caron (Roland), J. Léo Gagnon (Arthur), Jean-Pierre Saulnier (Rosaire), and Gabriel Arcand (Ti-Bi)
(35 mm, color, 100 minutes)

1972 *Québec: Duplessis et après . . .* (*Quebec: Duplessis and After*)
Director: Denys Arcand
Cinematographers: Alain Dostie, Réo Gregoire, Pierre Letarte, and Pierre Mignot
Editors: Denys Arcand and Pierre Bernier
Sound: Serge Beauchemin and Jacques Drouin
Research: Gérald Godin
Producer: Jacques Larose
Production: National Film Board of Canada
Actors: Gisèle Trépanier and Robin Spry
(16 mm, black and white, 115 minutes)

1973 *Réjeanne Padovani*
Screenplay: Denys Arcand and Jacques Benoît
Director: Denys Arcand
Cinematographer: Alain Dostie
Editors: Marguerite Duparc and Denys Arcand
Music: Willibald Gluck and Walter Boudreau
Art direction: Robert Scheen and Louis Ménard
Producer: Marguerite Duparc
Production: Cinak

Cast: Luce Guilbeault (Réjeanne), Jean Lajeunesse (Vincent), Pierre Thériault (Dominique), Frédérique Collin (Hélène), Hélène Loiselle (Jeannine), Roger Lebel (Desaulniers), Jean Pierre Lefebvre (Jean-Pierre), René Caron (Biron), J. Léo Gagnon (Bouchard), Margot MacKinnon (Stella), Gabriel Arcand (Carlo), Jean-Pierre Saulnier, Céline Lomez (Manon), and Guylène Lefort (Micheline)
(35 mm, color, 94 minutes)

1975 *Gina*
Screenplay: Denys Arcand and Jacques Benoît
Director: Denys Arcand
Cinematographer: Alain Dostie
Editor: Denys Arcand
Music: Michel Pagliaro and Barbara Benny
Art direction: Michel Proulx
Producer: Pierre Lamy
Production: Les Productions Carle-Lamy
Cast: Céline Lomez (Gina), Claude Blanchard (Bob), Frédérique Collin (Dolorès), Gabriel Arcand (the director), Serge Thériault (the assistant cameraman), André Gagnot (the cameraman), Jocelyn Bérubé (Titel), Paule Baillargeon (Rita), Roger Lebel (the manager), Louise Cuerrier (Carole), Gilles Marsolais (the producer), Donald Lautrec (Gina's boss), and Donald Pilon, Denise Filiatrault, and Marcel Sabourin (themselves)
(35 mm / 16 mm, color / black and white, 94 minutes)

1977 *Duplessis*
Screenplay: Denys Arcand
Director: Mark Blandford
Production: Société Radio-Canada
Cast: Jean Lapointe (Duplessis), Gabriel Arcand (Ti-Bi), Pierre Curzi (a reporter), and Patricia Nolin (Auréa Cloutier)
(16 mm, black and white, seven 50-minute episodes)

1981 *Le confort et l'indifférence* (*Comfort and Indifference*)
Director: Denys Arcand
Cinematographer: Alain Dostie
Editor: Pierre Bernier
Sound: Serge Beauchemin
Producer: Roger Frappier
Production: National Film Board of Canada
Cast: Jean-Pierre Ronfard (Machiavelli)
(16 mm, color, 109 minutes)

1983 *Empire, Inc.*
Screenplay: Douglas Bowie (with Jacques Benoît on episode 2)
Directors: Douglas Jackson (episodes 1, 3, 4) and Denys Arcand (episodes 2, 5, 6)
Cinematographer: Alain Dostie
Producer: Mark Blandford
Production: Canadian Broadcasting Corporation
Cast: Kenneth Welsh (James Munroe), Martha Henry (Catherine), Jennifer Dale (Cleo), and Gabriel Arcand (Gene)
(16 mm, color, six 50-minute episodes)

1984 *Le crime d'Ovide Plouffe* (*The Crime of Ovide Plouffe*)
Screenplay: Roger Lemelin
Director: Denys Arcand
Cinematographer: François Protat
Editor: Monique Fortier
Music: Olivier Dassault
Art direction: Jocelyn Joly
Producers: Gabriel Boustani and Justine Héroux
Production: International Cinema Corporation, Société Radio-Canada, National Film Board of Canada, Filmax, and Film A2
Cast: Gabriel Arcand (Ovide), Anne Létourneau (Rita), Donald Pilon (Stan), and Pierre Curzi (Napoléon)
(35 mm, color, 107 minutes)

1986 *Le déclin de l'empire américain* (*The Decline of the American Empire*)
Screenplay: Denys Arcand
Director: Denys Arcand
Cinematographer: Guy Dufaux
Editor: Monique Fortier
Music: François Dompierre
Art direction: Gaudeline Sauriol and Denis Sperdouklis
Producers: Roger Frappier and René Malo
Production: Corporation Image M & M and National Film Board of Canada
Cast: Rémy Girard (Rémy), Dominique Michel (Dominique), Dorothée Berryman (Louise) Louise Portal (Diane), Pierre Curzi (Pierre), Yves Jacques (Claude), Geneviève Rioux (Danielle), Daniel Brière (Alain), and Gabriel Arcand (Mario)
(35 mm, color, 102 minutes)

1989 *Jésus de Montréal* (*Jesus of Montreal*)
Screenplay: Denys Arcand
Director: Denys Arcand

Cinematographer: Guy Dufaux
Editor: Isabelle Dedieu
Music: Yves Laferrière, François Dompierre, and Jean-Marie Benoît
Art direction: François Séguin
Producers: Roger Frappier, Pierre Gendron, Doris Girard, Gérard Mital, and Jacques-Éric Strauss
Production: Max Films and Gérard Mital Productions
Cast: Lothaire Bluteau (Daniel), Johanne-Marie Tremblay (Constance), Rémy Girard (Martin), Robert Lepage (René), Catherine Wilkening (Mireille), Gilles Pelletier (Father Leclerc), and Yves Jacques (Richard Cardinal)
(35 mm, color, 119 minutes)

1991 "Vue d'ailleurs" (Seen from afar)
Episode in *Montréal vu par . . .* (*Montreal Sextet*)
Screenplay: Paule Baillargeon
Director: Denys Arcand
Cinematographer: Paul Sarossy
Editor: Alain Baril
Music: Yves Laferrière
Producer: Denise Robert
Production: Atlantis Films and Cinémaginaire
Cast: Rémy Girard (consul), Paule Baillargeon (consul's wife), Domini Blythe (old lady), Guylaine Saint-Onge (young woman), and Raoul Trujillo (lover)
(35 mm, color, 20 minutes)

1993 *Love and Human Remains*
Screenplay: Brad Fraser
Director: Denys Arcand
Cinematographer: Paul Sarossy
Editor: Alain Baril
Music: John McCarthy
Producers: Roger Frappier and Peter Sussman
Production: Max Films and Atlantis Films
Cast: Thomas Gibson (David), Ruth Marshall (Candy), Mia Kirshner (Benita), Cameron Bancroft (Bernie), Joanne Vannicola (Jerri) Matthew Ferguson (Kane), and Rick Roberts (Robert)
(35 mm, color, 98 minutes)

1996 *Joyeux calvaire* (*Poverty and Other Delights*)
Screenplay: Claire Richard
Director: Denys Arcand
Cinematographer: Guy Dufaux

Editor: André Daigneault
Music: Yves Laferrière
Producer: Denise Robert
Production: Cinémaginaire, with Radio-Canada
Cast: Gaston Lepage (Marcel), Benoît Brière (Joseph), and Lorne Brass (Stanley)
(35 mm, color, 90 minutes)

2000 *Stardom*
Screenplay: Denys Arcand and Jacob Potashnik
Director: Denys Arcand
Cinematographer: Guy Dufaux
Editor: Isabelle Dedieu
Music: François Dompierre
Art direction: Zoe Sakellaropoulo
Producers: Denise Robert, Robert Lantos, and Philippe Carcassonne
Production: Alliance Atlantis, Serendipity Point, Cinémaginaire, and Cine B Productions
Cast: Jessica Paré (Tina), Charles Berling (Philippe Gascon), Dan Ackroyd (Barry Levine), Robert Lepage (Bruce Taylor), Frank Langella (Blaine de Castillon), and Camilla Rutherford (Toni)
(35 mm, color/black and white, 100 minutes)

2003 *Les invasions barbares* (*The Barbarian Invasions*)
Screenplay: Denys Arcand
Director: Denys Arcand
Cinematographer: Guy Dufaux
Editor: Isabelle Dedieu
Music: Pierre Aviat
Art direction: François Séguin
Producers: Denise Robert, Daniel Louis, and Fabienne Vonier
Production: Cinémaginaire and Pyramid Productions
Cast: Rémy Girard (Rémy), Stéphane Rousseau (Sébastien), Marie-Josée Croze (Nathalie), Isabelle Blais (Sylvaine), Marina Hands (Gaëlle), Dorothée Berryman (Louise), Pierre Curzi (Pierre), Yves Jacques (Claude), Louise Portal (Diane), Dominique Michel (Dominique), Toni Cecchinato (Alessandro), Johanne-Marie Tremblay (Constance), Gilles Pelletier (Father Leclerc), Gaston Lepage (Security Guard), Daniel Brière (Alain), and Roy Dupuis (Gilles)
(35 mm, color, 112 minutes, international release 98 minutes)

2007 *L'âge des ténèbres* (*Days of Darkness*)
Screenplay: Denys Arcand
Director: Denys Arcand

Cinematographer: Guy Dufaux
Editor: Isabelle Dedieu
Music: Philippe Miller
Art direction: François Séguin
Producers: Denise Robert, Daniel Louis, Philippe Carcassonne, and Dominique Besnehard
Production: Cinémaginaire and Mon Voisin Productions
Cast: Marc Labrèche (Jean-Marc), Sylvie Léonard (Sylvie), Diane Kruger (Star), Emma de Caunes (Journalist) Macha Grenon (Béatrice), Caroline Néron (Carole), Didier Lucien (William), Rufus Wainwright (singer), Pierre Curzi (Pierre), Johanne-Marie Tremblay (Constance), and Gilles Pelletier (Father Leclerc)
(35 mm, color, 104 minutes)

2014 *Le règne de la beauté* (*An Eye for Beauty*)
Screenplay: Denys Arcand
Director: Denys Arcand
Cinematographer: Nathalie Moliavko-Visotzky
Editor: Isabelle Dedieu
Music: Pierre-Philipee Côté
Art direction: Patrice Bengle
Producers: Denise Robert and Andrea Puig
Production: Cinémaginaire
Cast: Éric Bruneau (Luc), Mélanie Thierry (Stéphanie), Melanie Merkosky (Lindsay), Marie-Josée Croze (Isabelle), Michel Forget (Roger), Johanne-Marie Tremblay (Manon), and Juana Acosta (Juana)
(35 mm, color, 102 minutes)

2018 *La chute de l'empire américain* (*The Fall of the American Empire*)
Screenplay: Denys Arcand
Director: Denys Arcand
Cinematographer: Van Royko
Editor: Arthur Tarnowski
Art direction: Patrice Bengle
Producer: Denise Robert
Production: Cinémaginaire
Cast: Alexandre Landry (Pierre-Paul), Maripier Morin (Aspasie), Rémy (Sylvain "The Brain" Bigras), Pierre Curzi (Taschereau), Florence Longpré (Linda), Gaston Lepage (Marcel), and Benoît Brière (Joseph)
(35 mm, color, 129 minutes)

NOTES

INTRODUCTION DENYS OF QUEBEC

1. *Un homme et son péché* (*Séraphin: Heart of Stone*; Charles Binamé, 2002) was the most popular film of the year in Quebec, beating several Hollywood blockbusters; *Aurore* (Luc Dionne, 2005), based on the actual events that inspired the original film, was less successful.
2. The definitions of these terms overlap confusingly. Quebec filmmakers tended to call their films "direct," in that they promoted an engagement between the filmmakers and their subjects unlike the cinéma vérité practiced by English Canadian (and U.S.) filmmakers, who supposedly favored a "fly-on-the-wall" observational approach. However, the French filmmaker Jean Rouch, whose work had an enormous influence in Quebec, preferred to call his films "cinéma vérité" on the grounds that they produce a "truth" that is specific to cinema.
3. Other magazines have provided an engaged view of Quebec cinema in the past—notably, *Objectif* (1960–1967), *Cinéma Québec* (1971–1978), and *Copie zéro* (1979–1988).
4. There are also academic journals in both official languages—*Canadian Journal of Film Studies* and *Cinéma(s)*—that frequently publish articles on Canadian films.
5. The brutal treatment of those arrested is powerfully captured in Michel Brault's *Les ordres* (*Orders*; 1974).
6. In fact, this controversial bill was an extension of the Official Languages Act, enacted in 1974 by the previous Liberal provincial government led by Robert Bourassa.
7. Arcand has recently used the term *dystopian* to describe his vision (quoted in Kelly 2018a, C1).
8. It should be noted that, while objectivity was the official policy of the NFB at this time, many direct cinema filmmakers were interested in calling the ideology into question. However, Arcand was never fully integrated into the direct cinema movement and did not adopt its techniques in his fiction films in any straightforward way (see chapter 1).
9. Arcand refers to his "ensemble" films in the production notes for *Love and Human Remains* (1993; see chapter 5).
10. In praising Buñuel's *La charme discrète de la bourgeoisie* (*The Discreet Charm of the Bourgeoisie*; 1972), Arcand explains that the film is "very 'badly' shot—which I absolutely love" (quoted in Johnston 2004).

CHAPTER 1 ALONE OR WITH OTHERS

1. The English title given here, a literal translation from the French, is the one used by the NFB at the 1963 Cannes Film Festival, but the film was first released in English in a truncated version called *Moontrap*, with an added commentary. A full subtitled version was finally released in 2000 under the title *Of Whales, the Moon and Men*, and in the 2007 DVD release of the trilogy that Perrault made about the people of the Île-aux-Coudres, it became *For the Ones to Come*.
2. Venne, however, played down the role of improvisation in the film, claiming that the dialogue, "as far as the content is concerned," was "constructed in advance," and the actors were

free only to improvise in the way it was spoken. The filmmakers were not, he said, "slaves to improvisation" (quoted in Lever 1991, 406).

3. Les Cyniques would go on to present many enormously popular stage shows and make a series of hit records.

4. For a discussion of *À tout prendre* and its reception, see my chapter in *Claude Jutra Filmmaker* (Leach 1999, 67–95). In an article called "Cinéma et sexualité," originally published in *Parti pris* in 1964, Arcand argued that the break with the past in Jutra's film was superficial and its treatment of sexuality hardly an advance on films like *La petite Aurore* (La Rochelle 2005, 313–314). For more on this article, see chapter 3.

5. This phrase plays on the formula *folie à deux*, a psychological term for a shared psychosis. The implication is that the devotion of the founders of Ville-Marie was psychotic.

6. There appears to be some confusion about the order in which Arcand made the last two films of the trilogy, since some sources suggest *La route de l'ouest* came before *Les Montréalistes*. The production schedules must have overlapped significantly.

CHAPTER 2 SUBJECTIVE DOCUMENTARIES

1. The essay film has a long history, but in its recent manifestations, it is most often associated with the work of the French filmmaker Chris Marker, whose first major contribution, *Lettre de Sibérie* (*Letter from Siberia*), appeared in 1958. Marker's approach is similar to Arcand's in his refusal of certainties and prevailing dogmas, but unlike the Quebec filmmaker, he relies heavily on voice-over commentary.

2. Claude Jutra had used a similar situation to undercut the idea of documentary authenticity in *Félix Leclerc troubadour* (1959), in which, after the writer/singer greets the film crew, he informs us that this is "the first lie" because the shooting had already been going on for several days (see Leach 1999, 49–51).

3. As Arcand explained, "Noise is a recurring theme in the film," and he wished he had "modern THX technology to convey just how unbearable it really is" (quoted in La Rochelle 1995, 34).

4. Arcand later claimed that he had an agreement with King that "if he did not like the film I would personally cut out his scenes" rather than "violate his trust" (quoted in Morisette 2005).

5. As with several other DVD sets devoted to the work of its francophone filmmakers, the NFB did not feel it necessary to provide this set with English subtitles.

6. Arcand had already experienced the imposition of a commentary onto one of his films, albeit in rather less urgent circumstances. *Volleyball* was supposed to encourage young Canadians to take up the sport. In what the DVD collection of Arcand's documentaries calls "the original French version," there is not a word of French but simply a lyrical depiction of matches between the men's and women's teams from the United States and the Soviet Union. As Arcand explains on the DVD, the government department that commissioned the film thought the players were so good that it would discourage young people from taking up the sport, so a facetious commentary was added to the English version designed to show how easy it was to play the game.

7. The other films, all released in 1971, include two fairly conventional biographical documentaries—*Je chante à cheval avec Willie Lamothe* (*I Sing on Horseback with Willie Lamothe*; Lucien Ménard and Jacques Leduc) and *Peut-être Maurice Richard* (*Maurice Richard Perhaps*; Gilles Gascon)—and *On est loin du soleil* (*We Are Far from the Sun*; Jacques Leduc), a

fiction film in which the situations of members of a modern working-class family in Montreal evoke various stages in the life of Brother André, who was canonized as a miracle worker after his death in 1937.

8. Gilles Vigneault's song "Mon Pays," one of the anthems of modern Quebec, begins with the line, "Mon pays, ce n'est pas un pays, c'est l'hiver" (My country is not a country, it's winter).

9. The allusion seems to be to the Hammer horror film *Dracula Has Risen from the Grave* (Freddie Francis, 1969).

10. Laporte was later found dead in the trunk of a car. His kidnapping and death are depicted in Pierre Falardeau's *Octobre* (see the introduction).

11. This narrative structure resembles that of a heist film, built around the planning, execution, and consequences of an armed robbery (see Sloniowski and Leach 2017, 2).

12. The term *cultural dope* derives from Stuart Hall's critique of the Frankfurt school's attitude to mass culture (1981, 232), although later writers often changed the phrase to *cultural dupe*.

CHAPTER 3 DIRTY MONEY

1. A more literal translation of the title would be *The Damned Loot*.

2. Just before Arcand made *La maudite galette*, Lefebvre had finished one of his greatest films, *Les maudits sauvages* (*Those Damned Savages*), whose subtitle describes it as "an almost historical film" because its timeline moves fluidly and unpredictably between 1670 and 1970. Arcand would go on to play an important role in Lefebvre's own crime film, *On n'engraisse pas les cochons à l'eau claire* (*Pigs Are Seldom Clean*; 1973), about which Peter Harcourt comments, "It is the only film by Lefebvre that I could imagine having been made by someone else—by Denys Arcand, for example" (1981, 64). The gang rape in this film anticipates the one in *Gina*.

3. I am quoting here from Niogret's review of *La maudite galette*, originally published in *Positif*, the French film journal that had been *Cahiers*' major rival but whose political outlook had much in common with *Cahiers*' new direction.

4. Edgar G. Ulmer's *Detour* (1945) is perhaps the most apposite comparison with Arcand's film.

5. We do not see the television screen, but the soundtrack we hear is from *Les maudites sauvages*.

6. Benoît's script had specified a Tino Rossi love song, but Arcand replaced it with a "country-folk" melody cowritten by his brother Gabriel (La Rochelle 2005, 129).

7. However, Arcand has also said that he and Benoit wrote the scenario "in two months": "Without reflecting on it for a second, without asking questions. I corrected it once, that's all" (quoted in Coulombe 1993, 37).

8. In addition, Lefebvre, who took the role of the minister's secretary, had more than a passing resemblance to Bourassa.

9. Martin Knelman suggested that the film "doesn't mention Trudeau or the Laporte kidnapping or the War Measures Act, but all these things are lurking about" (1977, 76).

10. Ironically, the minister's secretary persuades the newspaper editor to kill the story of the assault by giving him details about construction costs and how much the project has run over budget, as if a story of economic mismanagement will be less harmful publicity than one about a violent attack on a reporter.

11. Louis Hémon's *Maria Chapdelaine* (1913) depicts the hardships of pioneer life in Quebec and celebrates its heroine, who, after her fiancé dies in a blizzard, marries a man she does not love for the sake of her family and the future of French Canada. Arcand would later write a screenplay for a projected adaptation (see chapter 4).
12. For a fuller discussion of the implications of Carle's film style, see Leach 1984.
13. Apparently, the phrase "déshabiller la Québécoise" (undress the Quebec girl), attributed to Héroux when he made *Valérie,* was actually a (mis)quotation of Arcand's words in this article (Belzile 1995, 9).
14. Since the filmmakers are not named in the film, I will refer to them by their functions on the crew. The actor Gilles Marsolais should not be confused with the critic of the same name.
15. The screenplay indicates that she is called Brigitte, like the stripper Arcand and his crew met in Coaticook, but her name is not mentioned in the film.
16. The word *infernal* is used to describe both sources of noise in the screenplay included in the dossier on the film edited by Pierre Latour.
17. The sound man's silent presence made such a small impact that there seems to be no record of the actor's name.
18. Sabourin had, of course, starred in *La maudite galette.* The distance between Arcand's crime films and Hollywood films like *The French Connection* is alluded to playfully when, after the take, he wanders across to the crew and asks the soundman if the microphone was in shot, a common complaint against cheaply made Canadian films at the time. When he is assured that it was not, Sabourin comments, "It must be the first time."

CHAPTER 4 FALL AND RISE

1. It is unlikely that Arcand ever met his notorious uncle. His parents never mentioned him because "the family was ashamed of him" (La Rochelle 2005, 76).
2. Up to this point, the series had remained silent on Duplessis's private life other than showing him repeatedly ignoring the devotion of Auréa Cloutier (Patricia Nolin), his longtime secretary, who is clearly but silently in love with him.
3. The simultaneous production of film and television versions became quite common at this time, and several subsequent adaptations of classic Quebec novels adopted this strategy in the coming years, including Carle's *Maria Chapdelaine.*
4. The bombing of the plane was based on an actual event. That Ovide's love interest is French, as is the actual bomber, was due to the fact that the film (like *Les Plouffe*) was a Canada-France coproduction.
5. Two other films that emerged from this initiative, both in 1986, were Léa Pool's *Anne Trister,* a well-received art film, and Yves Simoneau's heist film, *Pouvoir intime* (*Blind Trust*).
6. Vandelac had worked for Arcand when he was doing research for the film, but she dissociated herself from the finished product (Godard 1988, 133–134).
7. The setting is Lake Memphrémagog, as the screenplay makes clear, but it is not named in the film. The lake is situated south of Montreal and separates Quebec from Vermont.
8. Jean Larose argued that "the film rests throughout on a reductive conflation of thought and 'fucking'" (1987, 11), an objection that is perversely similar to Mario's in the film. The only character who stands outside the heterosexual assumptions of the other characters is Claude, who is gay and, according to Barbara Godard, "shares with the women the limited power of the victim." She nevertheless finds him "the most openly misogynist" of the four men (1988, 136).

9. Much has been made of an apparent misprint on the cover of the book that Arcand had created to make it look more attractive, which omits the word *le* and thus suggests the past is still present. If this has any significance, it should be seen as a Freudian slip.
10. According to Bart Testa, Roger Frappier filmed these shots after the main filming was over (2002, 179).
11. The review was by the magazine's regular film reviewer Robert Fulford, normally an art critic, who adopted the pseudonym Marshall Delaney for his film reviews.
12. Another difference between the two texts is that the play does very specifically refer to Quebec's history and the impact of separatism, but this is mainly confined to a long oration by one of the characters. The film, directed by Robert Martin, opens the text out by including several sequences set outside the suburban home that is the only set in the play, but in doing so, it loses much of the play's claustrophobic power.
13. In fact, these characters are Ivan Karamazov and Pavel Smerdyakov, and the play is an adaptation of Dostoevsky's *The Brothers Karamazov*. Since they are not named in the film, I have left them anonymous.
14. Lepage is an internationally known creator of collective theatrical pieces (who would himself become a film director), and as an inside joke, his René is at first resistant to acting in a collectively authored play. Wilkening, a French actress, was cast partly because the film was a Canada-France coproduction, but Arcand justified the choice by explaining that he wanted the character to be "a foreigner from the beginning, someone with an accent . . . to reflect the milieu of advertising, which is filled with foreigners" (quoted in Marsolais and Racine 1989, 8).

CHAPTER 5 OF BEAUTY AND DEATH IN THE DIGITAL EPOCH

1. Arcand also appears as himself in Patricia Rozema's segment in which a clumsy anglophone visitor in search of romance (played by Sheila McCarthy as essentially the same character she played in Rozema's *I've Heard the Mermaids Singing* [1987]) enters a fantasy world inspired by the character's viewing of *Le déclin*.
2. These comments by Arcand are quoted from production notes included in the Arrow Films PAL DVD of the film. All subsequent quotations about the film taken from this source are designated in the text as (DVD).
3. Postproduction took place in Toronto (Loiselle and McIlroy 1995, 8).
4. Mia Kershner also followed her performance in Arcand's film with a role as a "schoolgirl" stripper in Egoyan's *Erotica* (1994), released a few months later.
5. Réal La Rochelle has suggested that the reception of *Love and Human Remains* in Quebec was partly due to the poor quality of the French-dubbed version (2005, 218).
6. Ducharme had written the screenplay for *Les bons débarras* (*Good Riddance*; Francis Mankiewicz, 1980), a film that depicts characters who are as isolated from mainstream society as those in *Joyeux calvaire*, although they live in a remote rural setting rather than the city.
7. An especially amusing/depressing montage effect in the CBC broadcast occurred when a commercial for an expensive brand of running shoes was followed immediately by a shot of Joseph soaking his aching feet in a bowl of water. In view of the English title, it was as if "poverty" was confined to the movie and the "other delights" to the world of publicity.
8. The final budget was between $11 million and $12 million (sources differ).
9. The working title for the film was *15 Moments*, an allusion to Andy Warhol's famous claim that in the future everyone will enjoy 15 minutes of fame.

10. See chapter 2 for Arcand's description of *Québec: Duplessis et après . . .* as a "mosaic of images."
11. The security guard from whom Sébastien vainly seeks help is played by the same actor (Gaston Lepage) as the guard at Saint Joseph's Oratory in *Jésus de Montréal* and may well be the same character.
12. As a minor example of this phenomenon, I once found copies of *Les invasions barbares* in the "action" section of a video store.
13. Several critics have objected that Claude's survival undercuts the seriousness of the implication in the earlier film that he had contracted AIDS, but Arcand explained that he had "a kidney problem that was later corrected" and is now "in a very stable relationship. He's the most stable of all the men" (quoted in Howell 2003a, C4).
14. The screenplay makes clear that Diane is now teaching part time at a college outside Montreal.
15. Unusually, the film was remade in English Canada as *The Grand Seduction* (Don McKellar, 2013), with virtually the same plot but set in Newfoundland. Not surprisingly, in view of the general lack of interest in English Canadian cinema, it proved much less popular than the original.
16. *Les invasions barbares* is also dedicated to Ming Xia, the Chinese girl adopted by Arcand and his partner and producer, Denise Robert.

CHAPTER 6 LIVING IN THE SHADOWS

1. The blonde woman is named as Veronica Star in the screenplay, and the reporter is Karine Tendance, but neither is named in the film.
2. Arcand had been present at a similar event that took place annually near Shawinigan, and this contact paid dividends since all the extras in the film brought their own costumes (Coulombe 2007).
3. What I have called a "commune" is described in the screenplay as an old people's home, housed in a building that was "possibly a former convent" (Arcand 2007, 170–171). However, this is not specified in the film, and apart from Constance, we see only one resident, who is wearing "colored and embroidered clothes, like in the 1960s" (171).
4. The distributors tried to moderate this effort to differentiate the film with a poster that depicted the cast of young, mainly unknown actors above a line that read, "After *Le déclin de l'empire américain* and *Les invasions barbares . . .*"
5. The actors who do return (Marie-Josée Croze, Yves Jacques, Johanne-Marie Tremblay) have roles clearly differentiated from those of the earlier films.
6. The film's working title was *Deux nuits* (Two nights), which would have made the affair with Lindsay more central than it is in the final version, although these two nights do have an almost catastrophic effect.
7. La Rochelle is quoting from the unpublished screenplay, but the film does not make clear how much time has passed.
8. Arcand's use of the crime film in the 1970s to reflect on social tensions in Quebec had been followed up in two earlier heist films: *Pouvoir intime* (*Blind Trust*; Yves Simoneau, 1986) and *Le dernier tunnel* (*The Last Tunnel*; Érik Canuel, 2004).
9. Pierre-Paul's name is another of Arcand's wry allusions to Christian tradition. Apart from the allusion to Saint Peter and Saint Paul, the name also evokes the saying, "Robbing Peter to pay Paul."

10. Aspasie (or Aspasia) was the powerful mistress of Pericles in Athens in the fifth century BCE. Morin was well known as a television host, and many reviewers expressed surprise at her strong performance in her first film role.
11. Taschereau is thus brought down not by his financial manipulations but by his love of beauty, as seen in his past affair with Camille and the valuable painting in his office. He tells the police, "It takes money to appreciate beauty," as demonstrated in Arcand's previous film.
12. Rémy Girard and Pierre Curzi, the two actors most associated with Arcand's later films, do reappear, but their characters are clearly different from those in the earlier films.

REFERENCES

Aird, Robert. 2013. "Présentation: Les Cyniques et leur époque." In *Les Cyniques: Le rire de la révolution tranquille*, edited by Robert Aird and Lucie Joubert, 11–38. Montreal: Triptyque.

Alemany-Galway, Mary. 2002. *A Postmodern Cinema: The Voice of the Other in Canadian Film*. Lanham, Md.: Scarecrow.

Alioff, Maurie. 1989. "Denys Arcand's *Jésus de Montréal*." *Cinema Canada* 164 (June–July): 16–17.

———. 2000. "Media Mania and the Beauty of Beauty: Denys Arcand's *Stardom*." *Take One* 9, no. 29 (Fall): 8–12.

Arcand, Denys. 1972. "*La maudite galette*." *Cinéma Québec* 2, no. 1 (September): 11.

———. 1975. "Une réflexion sur l'état actuel de la civilisation." In *Réjeanne Padovani*, edited by Robert Lévesque, 10–11. Montreal: Les Éditions de l'Aurore.

———. 1976. "Le vide et le plein." In *Gina*, edited by Pierre Latour, 17–18. Montreal: L'Aurore.

———. 1986. *Le déclin de l'empire Américain*. Montreal: Boréal.

———. 1989. *Jésus de Montréal*. Montreal: Boréal.

———. 2003. *Les invasions barbares: Scénario*. Montreal: Boréal.

———. 2005. *Hors champ: Écrits divers 1961–2005*. Montreal: Boréal.

———. 2007. *L'âge des ténèbres: Scénario*. Montreal: Boréal.

Arcand, Denys, and Gerald Godin. 1971. "Un film didactique." *Cinéma Québec* 1, no. 2 (June–July): 33–4.

Augé, Marc. 1995. *Non-places: Introduction to an Anthropology of Supermodernity*. Translated by John Howe. London: Verso.

Bachand, Denis. 2006. "Denys Arcand, réalisateur et scénariste: Les voies croisées du documentaire et de la fiction." In *Le cinéma au Québec: Tradition et modernité*, edited by Stéphane-Albert Boulais, 91–112. Montreal: Éditions Fides.

Barker, Adam. 1990a. "Actors, Magicians and the Little Apocalypse." *Monthly Film Bulletin* 57, no. 672 (January): 4.

———. 1990b. "*Jésus de Montréal*." *Monthly Film Bulletin* 57, no. 672 (January): 3–4.

Barrette, Pierre. 2003. "La fin des bacchanales." *24 Images* 115 (Summer): 4–5.

———. 2007. "La détresse et le désenchantement ou l'âge du mépris." *24 Images* 136 (March–April): 4–5.

Beauchemin, Jacques. 2002. *L'histoire en trop: La mauvaise conscience des souverainistes québécois*. Montreal: VLB Éditeur.

Beaulieu, Janick. 1997. "Décrocheurs de chez nous." *Séquences* 188 (January–February): 48–49.

Bédard, Éric. 2006. "Présences de Maurice Séguin dans le cinéma québécois." *Globe: Revue internationale d'études québécoises* 9, no. 2, 163–180.

Belzile, Ginette. 1995. "Deux ou trois choses que l'on sait d'elle." *Ciné-bulles* 14, no. 2 (Summer): 7–10.

Bergeron, Carl. 2012. *Un cynique chez les lyriques: Denys Arcand et le Québec*. Montreal: Boréal.

Bersianik, Louky. 1988. "The Empire of the Status Quo: On *The Decline of the American Empire*." Translated by Erika Grundmann. *Tessera* 4 (Summer): 48–53.

Bewes, Timothy. 1997. *Cynicism and Postmodernity*. London: Verso.
Bilodeau, François. 1986. "Au sujet du *Déclin de l'empire américain* de Denys Arcand: Bourrasque glaciale." *Liberté* 285:68–73.
Bissonnette, Lise. 1982. "Denys Arcand and 'Le confort et l'indifférence.'" *Ciné-tracts* 16 (Winter): 74–76.
Bonitzer, Pascal. 1974. "L'espace politique." *Cahiers du cinéma* 249 (February–March): 39–42.
Bonneville, Léo. 1965. "Le cinéma québécois à l'heure de la révolution tranquille." *Séquences* 40 (February): 12–19.
———. 1972. "Entretien avec Michel Brault." *Séquences* 68 (February): 4–14.
———. 1973. "Entretien avec Denys [*sic*] Héroux." *Séquences* 71 (January): 4–10.
———. 1979. *Le cinéma québécois par ceux qui le font*. Montreal: Éditions Paulines.
———. 1982. "*Le confort et l'indifférence*." *Séquences* 108 (April): 18–20.
———. 1984. "*Le crime d'Ovide Plouffe*." *Séquences* 118 (October): 34–36.
———. 1989. "Denys Arcand." *Séquences* 140 (June): 12–19.
Borghini, Andrea. 2017. "On Being Cynical." Accessed 31 December 2017. https://www.thoughtco.com/on-being-cynical-2670600.
Bouchard, Frédéric. 2018. "Avoir le coeur à l'argent." *Ciné-bulles* 36, no. 3 (Summer): 51.
Bourdeau, Roger. 1987–1988. "Le Québec, Machiavel et Arcand . . ." *Copie zéro* 34–35 (December–March): 29–31.
Boury, Jean-Louis. 1975. "Messieurs, tueurs et putes." In *Réjeanne Padovani*, edited by Robert Lévesque, 107–108. Montreal: Les Éditions de l'Aurore.
Carrière, Louise. 1997. "Une 'comédie': *Le déclin de l'empire américain*." *Ciné-bulles* 16, no. 2 (Summer): 38–41.
Castiel, Élie. 1994. "*De l'amour et des restes humains*." *Séquences* 171 (April): 38–39.
———. 2007. "*L'âge des ténèbres*: La vie rêvée." *Séquences* 251 (November–December): 35–36.
Charbonneau, Alain. 1994. "Entretien avec Denys Arcand." *24 Images* 72 (Spring): 6–11.
Chevrier, Henri-Paul. 1987–1988. "La lucidité et le désespoir." *Copie zéro* 34–35 (December–March): 34–36.
Christiano, Kevin J. 2007. "The Trajectory of Catholicism in Twentieth-Century Quebec." In *The Church Confronts Modernity: Catholicism since 1950 in the United States, Ireland, and Quebec*, edited by Leslie Woodcock Tentler, 21–61. Washington, D.C.: Catholic University of America Press.
Cinéma Québec. 1971. "*On est au coton* et la lutte des classes." *Cinéma Québec* 1, no. 2 (June–July): 31.
Cornellier, Dominique. 2014. "*Le règne de la beauté* ou la dictature du vide." *Le Devoir*, 24 May. Accessed 29 October 2018. https://www.ledevoir.com/non-classe/409086/le-dernier-arcand-le-regne-de-la-beaute-ou-la-dictature-du-vide-absolu.
Coulombe, Michel. 1993. *La vraie nature du cinéaste*. Montreal: Boréal.
———. 2000. "Entretien avec Denys Arcand." *Ciné-bulles* 19, no. 1 (Fall): 4–9.
———. 2001. "Entretien avec Bernard Émond." *Ciné-bulles* 19, no. 2 (Winter): 4–9.
———. 2007. "Qu'est-ce qui cloche avec Denys Arcand?" *L'Actualité*, 8 November. Accessed 8 July 2018. https://lactualite.com/culture/2007/11/08/quest-ce-qui-cloche-avec-denys-arcand/.
Craig, Gerald M. 1963. *Lord Durham's Report*. Toronto: McClelland & Stewart.
Daigneault, Claude. 1975. "Constat de l'époque actuelle." In *Réjeanne Padovani*, edited by Robert Lévesque, 101–102. Montreal: Les Éditions de l'Aurore.
———. 1976. "Gina: Le Québec de la démission." In *Gina*, edited by Pierre Latour, 112–113. Montreal: Les Éditions de l'Aurore.

Dassas, Véronique. 1987–1988. "La critique féministe et *Le déclin de l'empire américain.*" *Copie zéro* 34–35 (December–March): 56–57.

Daudelin, Robert. 1980. "The Encounter between Fiction and the Direct Cinema." In *Self Portrait: Essays on the Canadian and Quebec Cinemas,* edited by Pierre Véronneau and Piers Handling, 94–106. Ottawa: Canadian Film Institute.

DeGryse, Marc. 1987–1988. "Arcand ou la vie d'artiste." *Copie zéro* 34–35 (December–March): 42–44.

De Koninck, Marie-Charlotte. 1995. "Quand les médias ont transformé la culture." In *Jamais plus comme! Le Québec de 1945 à 1960,* edited by De Koninck, 141–169. Montreal: Fides.

DeMara, Bruce. 2018. "Denys Arcand's Love/Hate Thing for Montreal." *Toronto Star,* 11 September, L6.

Demers, Maxime. 2018. "Denys Arcand revient à ses premiers amours." *Le Journal de Montréal,* 15 June. Accessed 29 October 2018. https://www.journaldemontreal.com/2018/06/15/denys-arcand-revienta-ses-premiers-amours.

Dorland, Michael. 1982a. "*Le confort et l'indifférence.*" *Cinema Canada* 82 (March): 32–33.

———. 1982b. "Telling an Anglo Tale." *Cinema Canada* 83 (April 1982): 46.

———. 1983. "Denis Héroux: La coproduction, c'est moi." *Cinema Canada* 100 (October): 14.

———. 1984. "Denys Arcand's *Le crime d'Ovide Plouffe.*" *Cinema Canada* 112 (November): 24–25.

———. 1986. "Renaissance Man." *Cinema Canada* 134 (October): 15–19, 21.

Dumont, Fernand. 1997. *Raisons communes.* Montreal: Boréal.

Dyer, Richard. 1993. *The Matter of Images: Essays on Representations.* London: Routledge.

Ehrlich, David. 2018. "'The Fall of the American Empire Review': Denys Arcand's Heist Comedy Is a Socialist Fairy Tale." *IndieWire,* 6 September. Accessed 19 November 2018. https://www.indiewire.com/2018/09/the-fall-of-the-american-empire-review-denys-arcand-tiff-2018-1202001248/.

Élia, Maurice. 1998. "*Réjeanne Padovani* de Denys Arcand." *Séquences* 194 (January–February): 15.

Evans, Gary. 1991. *In the National Interest: A Chronicle of the National Film Board of Canada from 1949 to 1989.* Toronto: University of Toronto Press.

Fléouter, Claude. 1975. "César Borgia à Montréal." In *Réjeanne Padovani,* edited by Robert Lévesque, 102. Montreal: Les Éditions de l'Aurore.

Fradet, Pierre-Alexandre. 2014. "Craindre le ridicule or exprimer sa joie? Snobisme et méta-snobisme." *Séquences* 291 (July–August): 59.

Fraser, Brad. 1996. *Love and Human Remains: The Screenplay.* Edmonton: NeWest Press.

Frye, Northrop. 1971. *The Bush Garden: Essays on the Canadian Imagination.* Toronto: Anansi.

Galiero, Simon, and Bernard Émond. 2009. *La perte et le lien: Entretiens sur le cinéma, la culture et la société.* Montreal: Médiaspaul.

Gay, Richard. 1972. "*La maudite galette*: Notre condition interrogée." *Cinéma Québec* 2, no. 3 (November): 25–27.

———. 1975. "Notre condition de violés." *Cinéma Québec* 4, no. 2 (April): 11–14.

Godard, Barbara. 1971. "*Québec: Duplessis et après* and *Peut-être Maurice Richard.*" *Take One* 3, no. 7 (September–October): 32–33.

———. 1988. "'The Empire of the Status Quo': To the Second Degree or a Reply to Louky Bersianik." *Tessera* 5 (September): 129–143.

Godin, Pierre. 1991. *La difficile recherche de l'égalité: La révolution tranquille.* Vol. 2. Montreal: Boréal.

Gravel, Jean-Philippe. 2003. "Denys Arcand, d'un '*déclin*' à l'autre." *Ciné-bulles* 21, no. 3 (Summer): 22–29.

Guilbeault, Luce. 1987–1988. "I Lost It at *La maudite galette*." *Copie zéro* 34–35 (December–March): 46.

Gural, Anna, and Benoît Patar. 1982. "Denys Arcand: Silence, on tourne." *24 Images* 13–14 (July–August): 47–56.

Habib, André. 2004. "*Les invasions barbares* ou le triomphe d'un malentendu." *Hors champ*, 22 March. Accessed 31 March 2018. https://www.horschamp.qc.ca/spip.php?article133.

Hall, Stuart. 1981. "Notes on Deconstructing the Popular." In *People's History and Socialist Theory*, edited by Raphael Samuel, 227–240. London: Routledge & Kegan Paul.

Hamblet, Edwin C. 1970. *Marcel Dubé and French-Canadian Drama*. New York: Exposition Press.

Haque, Eve. 2012. *Multiculturalism within a Bilingual Framework: Language, Race and Belonging in Canada*. Toronto: University of Toronto Press.

Harcourt, Peter. 1981. *Jean Pierre Lefebvre*. Ottawa: Canadian Film Institute.

———. 2003. "Wotcha Lookin' at, Anyway? An Examination of Point-of-View in Denys Arcand's *Stardom*." *CineAction* 61:2–9.

———. 2006. "*Le déclin de l'empire américain/The Decline of the American*." In *The Cinema of Canada*, edited by Jerry White, 145–152. London: Wallflower.

Harkness, John. 1989. "The Improbable Rise of Denys Arcand." *Sight and Sound* 58, no. 4 (Autumn): 234–238.

Hofsess, John. 1975. *Inner Views: Ten Canadian Film-Makers*. Toronto: McGraw-Hill Ryerson.

Holden, Stephen. 2016. "Sigh . . . Even Rich People Can Suffer." *New York Times*, 15 April. Accessed 29 October 2018. https://www.nytimes.com/2016/04/15/movies/an-eye-for-beauty-review.html.

Houle, Michel, Jacques Leduc, and Lucien Hamelin. 1971. "Entretien." In *Cinéastes du Québec 8: Denis Arcand*, 12–31. Montreal: Conseil Québécois pour la Diffusion du Cinéma.

Howell, Peter. 2003a. "Arcand Is Back." *Toronto Star*, 21 November, C1, C4.

———. 2003b. "A Director in His Prime: Denys Arcand's *Les invasions barbares*." *Take One* 43 (September–December): 28–31.

———. 2007. "Darkness Descends on Cannes." *Toronto Star*, 26 May, H10.

Hunter, Allan. 1990. "Passion Play." *Films and Filming* (January): 10–12.

———. 2018. "*The Fall of the American Empire*: Toronto Review." *Screen Daily*, 6 September. Accessed 19 November 2018. https://www.screendaily.com/reviews/the-fall-of-the-american-empire-toronto-review/5132370.article.

Ibranyi-Kiss, A. 1974. "How to Have Your Cake and Eat It Too . . . à la Denys Arcand." *Cinema Canada* 13 (April–May): 56–58.

Irving, Joan. 1977. "Looking Back at Duplessis." *Montreal Star*, 3 December, D16.

Jean, Marcel. 1987–1988. "L'histoire chez Denys Arcand: La marque du passé sur les temps présents." *Copie zéro* 34–35 (December–March): 27–28.

———. 1989a. "Dossier: Denys Arcand." *24 Images* 44–45 (Fall): 39.

———. 1989b. "Entretien avec Denys Arcand." *24 Images* 44–45 (Fall): 46–53.

———. 1989c. "L'éternel retour." *24 Images* 44–45 (Fall): 62–63.

———. 2014. *Dictionnaire des films québécoises*. Montreal: Éditions Somme Toute.

Johnston, Sheila. 2004. "Film-Makers on Film: Denys Arcand." *Daily Telegraph*, 31 January. Accessed 5 July 2018. https://www.telegraph.co.uk/culture/film/3611242/Film-makers-on-film-Denys-Arcand.html.

Jutras, Pierre, Réal La Rochelle, and Pierre Véronneau. 1987–1988. "Conversation autour d'un plaisir solitaire." *Copie zéro* 34–35 (December–March): 4–12.

Kelly, Brendan. 2018a. "Laughing as We Fall." *Montreal Gazette*, 29 June, C1.

———. 2018b. "Quebecers Have to Wait for English Version of New Arcand Film." *Montreal Gazette*, 20 June. Accessed 21 November 2018. https://montrealgazette.com/news/local-news/denys-arcands-fall-of-the-american-empire-is-coming-in-french-only.

Kemp, Philip. 2004. "The Last Laugh." *Sight and Sound* 14, no. 3 (March): 36–37.

Knelman, Martin. 1977. *This Is Where We Came In: The Career and Character of Canadian Film*. Toronto: McClelland & Stewart.

———. 2015. "Three Movies That Fell through the Cracks." *Toronto Star*, 27 March. Accessed 25 June 2019. https://www.thestar.com/entertainment/movies/2015/03/27/canadian-movies-that-fell-through-the-cracks.html.

Lafortune, Jean-Marie. 2013. "Le cynisme élevé à la puissance IXE-13." In *Les Cyniques: Le rire de la révolution tranquille*, edited by Robert Aird and Lucie Joubert, 413–439. Montreal: Triptyque.

Lanlo, Jean-Marie. 2018. "*La chute de l'empire américain*." *Cinéflic*, 25 June. Accessed 21 November 2018. http://www.cinefilic.com/2018/06/la-chute-de-lempire-americain.html.

Lapalme, Michel. 1977. "Maurice Séguin: The New Canon Groulx." In *Society and Conquest: The Debate on the Bourgeoisie and Social Change in French Canada, 1700–1850*, edited by Dale Miquelon, 64–67. Toronto: Copp Clark.

La Presse. 1971. "Dossier *On est au coton*." 17 July, D9.

La Rochelle, Réal. 1971. "Presentation." In *Cinéastes du Québec 8: Denis Arcand*, 2–9. Montreal: Conseil Québécois pour la Diffusion du Cinéma.

———. 1987–1988. "Denys Arcand: La tentation du lyrisme." *Copie zéro* 34–35 (December–March): 13–17.

———. 1995a. "Descente aux enfers." *Ciné-bulles* 14, no. 1 (Winter–Spring): 19–21.

———. 1995b. "Sound Design and Music as *Tragédie en musique*: The Documentary Practice of Denys Arcand." In *Auteur/Provocateur: The Films of Denys Arcand*, edited by André Loiselle and Brian McIlroy, 32–51. Westport, Conn.: Praeger.

———. 2005. *Denys Arcand: A Life in Film*. Translated by Alison Strayer. Toronto: McArthur.

———. 2014. *Denys Arcand: Mille plateaux*. Quebec: Les Presses de l'Université Laval.

Larose, Jean. 1987. *La petite noirceur: Essais*. Montreal: Boréal.

Latour, Pierre. 1976. "Un tournage normal." In *Gina*, edited by Pierre Latour, 13–17. Montreal: L'Aurore.

———. 1979. "Notes sur *La maudite galette*." In *La maudite galette*, edited by Pierre Latour, 13–15. Montreal: VLB Éditeur.

Laurendeau, Francine. 2007. "Denys Arcand." *Séquences* 251 (November–December): 38–39.

Lavoie, André. 1994. "*Love and Human Remains*." *Ciné-bulles* 13, no. 1 (Winter): 46–47.

———. 1997. "Entre Buffalo et Beyrouth." *Ciné-bulles* 15, no. 4 (Winter): 43.

———. 2003. "Sous les pavés du bavardage, un plage de non-dits." *Ciné-bulles* 21, no. 3 (Summer): 18–21.

Leach, Jim. 1984. "The Sins of Gilles Carle." In *Take Two: A Tribute to Film in Canada*, edited by Seth Feldman, 160–168. Toronto: Irwin.

———. 1999. *Claude Jutra Filmmaker*. Montreal: McGill-Queen's University Press.

———. 2003. "Dark Satanic Mills: Denys Arcand's *On est au coton*." In *Candid Eyes: Essays on Canadian Documentaries*, edited by Jim Leach and Jeannette Sloniowski, 87–102. Toronto: University of Toronto Press.

———. 2011. *Film in Canada*. 2nd ed. Toronto: Oxford University Press.

Lemieux, Olivier. 2016. "Denys Arcand et l'"alie-nation' québécoise: Une lecture séguiniste de *Réjeanne Padovani*." *Nouvelles vues* 18 (Fall). Accessed 23 January 2019. http://www.nouvellesvues.ulaval.ca/en/no-18-automne-2017-cinema-roman-espace-dirige-par-d-belanger-et-t-carrier-lafleur/notes-de-recherche/denys-arcand-et-l-alie-nation-quebecoise-une-lecture-seguiniste-de-rejeanne-padovani-par-olivier-lemieux/.

Lever, Yves. 1991. *Le cinéma de la révolution tranquille: De panoramique à Valérie.* Montreal: Yves Lever.

Lévesque, René. 1968. *An Option for Québec.* Toronto: McLelland & Stewart.

Lévesque, Robert. 1975a. "Padovani le jongleur." In *Réjeanne Padovani,* edited by Robert Lévesque, 9–10. Montreal: Les Éditions de l'Aurore.

———. 1975b. "Un film pour la capagne électorale." In *Réjeanne Padovani,* edited by Robert Lévesque, 100. Montreal: Les Éditions de l'Aurore.

———. 1979a. "Comme un révelateur." In *La maudite galette,* edited by Pierre Latour, 94–95. Montreal: VLB Éditeur.

———. 1979b. "Une étape importante dans le cinéma québécois." In *La maudite galette,* edited by Pierre Latour, 96–97. Montreal: VLB Éditeur.

Lockerbie, Ian. 1996. "The Ethnic Other in Quebec Cinema." In *Difference and Community: Canadian and European Cultural Perspectives,* edited by Peter Easingwood, Konrad Gross, and Lynette Hunter, 119–130. Amsterdam: Rodopi.

Loiselle, André. 1995. "'I Only Know Where I Come From, Not Where I Am Going': A Conversation with Denys Arcand." In *Auteur/Provocateur: The Films of Denys Arcand,* edited by André Loiselle and Brian McIlroy, 136–161. Westport, Conn.: Praeger.

———. 2007. *Cinema as History: Michel Brault and Modern Quebec.* Toronto: Toronto International Film Festival.

———. 2008. *Denys Arcand's* Le déclin de l'empire américain *and* Les invasions barbares. Toronto: University of Toronto Press.

Loiselle, André, and Brian McIlroy. 1995. "Introduction." In *Auteur/Provocateur: The Films of Denys Arcand,* edited by André Loiselle and Brian McIlroy, 1–9. Westport, Conn.: Praeger.

Lopate, Phillip. 2017. "In Search of the Centaur: The Essay-Film." In *Essays on the Essay Film,* edited by Nora M. Alter and Timothy Corrigan, 109–133. New York: Columbia University Press.

Lyotard, Jean-François. 1984. *The Postmodern Condition: A Report on Knowledge.* Translated by Geoff Bennington and Brian Massumi. Minneapolis: University of Minnesota Press.

MacKenzie, Scott. 2004. *Screening Québec: Québécois Moving Images, National Identity, and the Public Sphere.* Manchester: Manchester University Press.

Maclure, Jocelyn. 2003. *Quebec Identity: The Challenge of Pluralism.* Translated by Peter Feldstein. Montreal: McGill-Queen's University Press.

Mandolini, Carlo. 2000. "Papier glacé, média froid et cinéma muet." *Séquences* 210 (November–December): 50–52.

Marcorelles, Louis. 1979. "Le constat de l'American Way of Life." In *La maudite galette,* edited by Pierre Latour, 99. Montreal: VLB Éditeur.

Marcuse, Herbert. 1991. *One-Dimensional Man: Studies in the Ideology of Advanced Industrial Societies.* Boston: Beacon.

Marin, Stéphanie. 2018. "'Le pouvoir de l'argent' est au coeur du dernier film de Denys Arcand." *L'Actualité,* 19 June. Accessed 21 November 2018. https://lactualite.com/actualites/2018/06/19/le-pouvoir-de-largent-est-au-coeur-du-dernier-film-de-denys-arcand/.

Marshall, Bill. 2001. *Quebec National Cinema.* Montreal: McGill-Queen's University Press.

Marsolais, Gilles. 1968. *Le cinéma canadien.* Montreal: Éditions du Jour.

———. 1989. "Du Spirituel dans l'art: Critique de *Jésus de Montréal*." *24 Images* 44–45 (Fall): 40–43.

———. 1992. "*On est au coton* de Denys Arcand." *24 Images* 59 (Winter): 58–59.

———. 2011. *Cinéma québécois: De l'artisanat à l'industrie.* Montreal: Triptyque.

Marsolais, Gilles, and Claude Racine. 1989. "Entretien avec Denys Arcand à propos de *Jésus de Montréal*." *24 Images* 43 (Summer): 4–9.

Martineau, Richard. 2018. "Revoir *Le règne de la beauté*." *Le Journal de Montréal,* 19 June. Accessed 29 October 2018. https://www.journaldemontreal.com/2018/06/19/revoir-le-regne-de-la-beaute.

Mauriac, Claude. 1979. "Là ou le meurtre paraît naturel." In *La maudite galette,* edited by Pierre Latour, 99–100. Montreal: VLB Éditeur.

Mazella, David. 2007. *The Making of Modern Cynicism.* Charlottesville: University of Virginia Press.

Mietkiewicz, Henry. 1991. "Denys Arcand's Horizons Extend Far beyond Quebec." *Toronto Star,* 9 November, F8.

Morisette, Isabelle. 2005. "The Documentary Worlds of Denys Arcand." *Offscreen* 9, no. 5 (May). Accessed 3 November 2018. https://offscreen.com/view/denys_arcand.

Morris, Peter. 1984. *The Film Companion.* Toronto: Irwin.

Moyes, Craig. 2006. "*On est au coton / Cotton Mill, Treadmill*." In *The Cinema of Canada,* edited by Jerry White, 91–100. London: Wallflower.

Nelson, Joyce. 1990. "*Jesus of Montreal*: Culling the Living Flower." *This Magazine* 23, no. 6 (January–February): 25–27.

Niogret, Hubert. 1979. "Une subversion complète . . ." In *La maudite galette,* edited by Pierre Latour, 100. Montreal: VLB Éditeur.

O'Brien, Tom. 1990. "*Jesus of Montreal*." *Film Quarterly* 44, no. 1 (Fall): 47–50.

Ouellet, Fernand. 1977. "French-Canadian Nationalism: From Its Origins to the Insurrection of 1837." In *Society and Conquest: The Debate on the Bourgeoisie and Social Change in French Canada, 1700–1850,* edited by Dale Miquelon, 171–186. Toronto: Copp Clark.

Patenaude, Michel. 1963. "*À tout prendre*." *Objectif* 23–24 (October): 41–43.

Patry, Mario. 2011a. "Denys Arcand: Première Partie." *Séquences* 271 (March–April): 12–15.

———. 2011b. "Jouvences sur Denys Arcand: Deuxième partie." *Séquences* 272 (May–June): 10–13.

Perreault, Luc. 1971. "La violence d'un jeune cinéma (jusqu'ici) doux." *La Presse,* 29 May, D9.

———. 1972a. "De père en fils." *La Presse,* 24 June, C9.

———. 1972b "Duplessis n'est pas encore mort." *La Presse,* 24 June, C9.

———. 1972c. "Né pour un petite pain." *La Presse,* 9 September, C9.

———. 1973. "Un cinéaste que prend des risques." *La Presse,* 29 September.

———. 1974. "*Gina* et Pierre Lamy: C'est le film qui devient la vedette." *La Presse,* 25 May, E13.

———. 1975. "Denys Arcand veut pêcher son marsouin." *La Presse,* 25 January, D13.

———. 1976a. "Gina au jour le jour—journal de tournage (extraits)." In *Gina,* edited by Pierre Latour, 115–121. Montreal: L'Aurore.

———. 1976b. "*On est au coton* refait surface." *La Presse,* 24 January, D9.

Perron, Éric. 2003. "Le cinéma québécois va-t-il vraiment bien?" *Ciné-bulles* 21, no. 3 (Summer): 2–3.

Pérusse, Denise. 1987–1988. "*Le déclin*: Une stratégie filmique oscillant entre le cliché et l'ironie." *Copie zéro* 34–35 (December–March): 49–51.

———. 1995. "Gender Relations in *The Decline of the American Empire*." In *Auteur/Provocateur: The Films of Denys Arcand*, edited by André Loiselle and Brian McIlroy, 69–89. Westport, Conn.: Praeger.

Pessoa, Fernando. 1991. *The Book of Disquiet*. Translated by Margaret Jull Costa. London: Serpent's Tail.

Pevere, Geoff. 2002. "Fishy." In *North of Everything: English-Canadian Cinema since 1980*, edited by William Beard and Jerry White, 100–104. Edmonton: University of Alberta Press.

Pike, David L. 2012. *Canadian Cinema since the 1980s: At the Heart of the World*. Toronto: University of Toronto Press.

Pohl, Frederik, and Frederik Pohl IV. 1981. *Science Fiction Studies in Film*. New York: Ace Books.

Poirier, Christian, and Mélissa Thériault. 2012. "Cinéma, éthique et politique: La societé québécoise au prisme de *Réjeanne Padovani*." *Nouvelles Vues* 13 (Winter–Spring). Accessed 23 January 2019. http://www.nouvellesvues.ulaval.ca/no-13-hiver-printemps-2012-le-cinema-quebecois-et-les-autres-arts-dirige-par-elspeth-tulloch/article-hors-dossier/cinema-ethique-et-politique-la-societe-quebecoise-au-prisme-de-rejeanne-padovani-par-christian-poirier-et-melissa-theriault/.

Pontaut, Alain. 1969. "Notes préliminaires." In *Les Beaux Dimanches*, by Marcel Dubé, 5–17. Ottawa: Leméac.

Porter, Anna. 2013. "*Amour*: No Gentle End." *Queen's Quarterly* 120, no. 2 (Summer): 275–279.

Posner, Michael. 1993. *Canadian Dreams: The Making and Marketing of Independent Films*. Vancouver: Douglas & McIntyre.

Ramirez, Bruno. 2014. *Inside the Historical Film*. Montreal: McGill-Queen's University Press.

Rascaroli, Laura. 2009. *The Personal Camera: Subjective Camera and the Essay Film*. London: Wallflower.

Renaud, Nicolas. 2002. "Le secret honteux du *Déclin de l'empire americain*." *Hors Champ*, December. Accessed 31 July 2004. http://www.horschamp.qc.ca.php3?idarticle=74.

Ricard, François. 1994. *La génération lyrique: Essai sur la vie et l'oeuvre des premiers-nés du baby-boom*. Montreal: Boréal.

Rioux, Marcel. 1969. *La question du Québec*. Paris: Éditions Seghers.

Roy, André. 1989. "Jésus des médias: Critique de *Jésus de Montréal*." *24 Images* 44–45 (Fall): 44–45.

———. 2000. "Le déclin de Denys Arcand." *24 Images* 103–104 (Fall): 87.

Rudin, Ronald. 1997. *Making History in Twentieth-Century Quebec*. Toronto: University of Toronto Press.

Schwartzwald, Robert. 1991. "Fear of Federasty: Quebec's Inverted Fictions." In *Comparative American Identities: Race, Sex, and Nationality in the Modern Text*, edited by Hortense J. Spillers, 175–195. New York: Routledge.

Scully, Robert Guy. 1972a. "Denys Arcand 'au milieu de la bébelle.'" *Le Devoir*, 9 September.

———. 1972b. "La 'galette' à D. Arcand." *Le Devoir*, 20 May.

———. 1972c. "Maurice Duplessis de retour (au cinéma)." *Le Devoir*, 23 June, 15.

———. 1973. "Denys Arcand réalisateur: De la justesse au cinéma au désespoir en politique." *Le Devoir*, 6 October, 21.

———. 1975. "Un film politique qui communique." *Le Devoir*, 25 January, 13.

Séguin, Maurice. 1977. "The Conquest and French-Canadian Economic Life." *Society and Conquest: The Debate on the Bourgeoisie and Social Change in French Canada, 1700–1850*, edited by Dale Miquelon, 67–80. Toronto: Copp Clark.

Sénécal, Henri-Paul. 1964. "Court métrages de l'ONF." *Séquences* 38 (October): 41–42.

———. 1966. "Court métrages de l'ONF." *Séquences* 46 (October): 51–52.

Shuster, Nat. 1974. "*Réjeanne Padovani*: Rancid Scent of Corruption." *Motion* (May–June): 45.

Simons, Tony. 2004. "Denys Arcand: *Jésus de Montréal*." In *Where Are the Voices Coming From? Canadian Culture and the Legacies of History*, edited by Coral Ann Howells, 151–165. Amsterdam: Rodopi.

Sklar, Robert. 1986a. "*Decline of the American Empire*." *Cineaste* 15, no. 2, 46–47.

———. 1986b. "Decline of the American Empire: An Interview with Denys Arcand." *Cineaste* 15, no. 2, 48–50.

———. 1990. "Of Warm and Sunny Tragedies: An Interview with Denys Arcand." *Cineaste* 18, no. 1, 14–16.

Sloniowski, Jeannette, and Jim Leach. 2017. "Introduction: . . . Of Heists and Men." In *The Best Laid Plans: Interrogating the Heist Film*, edited by Jeannette Sloniowski and Jim Leach, 1–8. Detroit: Wayne State University Press.

Tadros, Jean-Pierre. 1972a. "Disséquer l'homme politique québécois." *Cinéma Québec* 2, no. 1 (September): 18–22.

———. 1972b. "*La maudite galette*." *Cinéma Québec* 1, no. 9 (May–June): 26–29.

———. 1973. "*Réjeanne Padovani*: Un film dramatique pour provoquer une série de sentiments." *Cinéma Québec* 3, no. 1 (September): 17–23.

Testa, Bart. 1987. "Denys Arcand's Sarcasm: A Reading of *Gina*." In *Dialogue: Canadian and Quebec Cinema*, edited by Pierre Véronneau, Michael Dorland, and Seth Feldman, 203–222. Montreal: Mediatexte.

———. 1995. "Arcand's Double-Twist Allegory: *Jesus of Montreal*." In *Auteur/Provocateur: The Films of Denys Arcand*, edited by André Loiselle and Brian McIlroy, 90–112. Westport, Conn.: Praeger.

———. 2002. "The Decline of Frivolity and Denys Arcand's American Empire." In *Canada's Best Features*, edited by Gene Walz, 174–206. Amsterdam: Rodopi.

Thérien, Gilles. 1990. "L'empire et les barbares." *Cinémas* 1–2 (Fall): 9–19.

Townend, Paul. 2001. "*Stardom*." *Take One* 9, no. 30 (Winter): 41–42.

Tremblay-Daviault, Christiane. 1981. *Un cinéma orphelin: Structures mentales et sociales du cinéma québécois*. Montreal: Québec/Amérique.

Trudeau, Pierre Elliott. 1998. *The Essential Trudeau*. Edited by Ron Graham. Toronto: McClelland & Stewart.

Vallières, Pierre. 1971. *White Niggers of America*. Translated by Joan Pinkham. Toronto: McClelland & Stewart.

———. 1973. "Le refus de l'imposture." *Cinéma Québec* 3, no. 3 (November–December): 8–9.

Véronneau, Pierre. 1987–1988. "De l'incertitude au paradoxe: De l'histoire, ou la singularité originelle d'Arcand." *Copie zéro* 34–35 (December–March): 24–26.

———. 1995. "Alone and with Others: Denys Arcand's Destiny within the Quebec Cinematic and Cultural Context." In *Auteur/Provocateur: The Films of Denys Arcand*, edited by André Loiselle and Brian McIlroy, 10–31. Westport, Conn.: Praeger.

Wade, Mason. 1968. *The French Canadians 1760–1967*. Rev. ed. Toronto: Macmillan.

Walsh, Richard. 2003. *Reading the Gospels in the Dark: Portrayals of Jesus in Film*. Harrisburg, Pa.: Trinity.

Weinmann, Heinz. 1987. *Du Canada au Québec: Généalogie d'une histoire*. Montreal: L'Hexagone.

———. 1990. *Cinéma de l'imaginaire québécois: De la petite Aurore à Jésus de Montréal*. Montreal: L'Hexagone.

Wilkins, Peter. 1995. "No Big Picture: Arcand and His U.S. Critics." *Auteur/Provocateur: The Films of Denys Arcand*, edited by André Loiselle and Brian McIlroy, 113–135. Westport, Conn.: Praeger.

Wood, Robin. 1989. "Towards a Canadian (Inter)national Cinema." *CineAction* 16 (Spring): 59–63.

Wright, Judy, and Debbie Magidson. 1974. "'Making Films for Your Own People': An Interview with Denys Arcand." *This Magazine* 8, no. 4 (November–December): 21–27.

Yacowar, Maurice. 2004. "Corporate Invasions/Barbarian Invasions." *Queen's Quarterly* 111, no. 1 (Spring): 86–95.

Yakabuski, Konrad. 2018. "Denys Arcand's Morality Tale a Gut Check for Quebec, and Us All." *Globe and Mail*, 7 July. Accessed 19 November 2018. https://www.theglobeandmail.com/opinion/article-denys-arcands-morality-tale-a-gut-check-for-quebec-and-us-all/.

Žižek, Slavoj. 2015. *Trouble in Paradise: From the End of History to the End of Capitalism*. London: Penguin.

INDEX

ABOUT THE AUTHOR

JIM LEACH is professor emeritus in the Department of Communication, Popular Culture, and Film at Brock University, St. Catharines, Ontario. He is the author of books on filmmakers Alain Tanner and Claude Jutra, as well as *British Film* and *Film in Canada*. He has also published a monograph on *Doctor Who*, coedited a volume on Canadian documentary films, and developed a Canadian edition of an introductory film studies textbook.